WILLIAM LINDESAY

THE GREAT WALL IN 50 OBJECTS

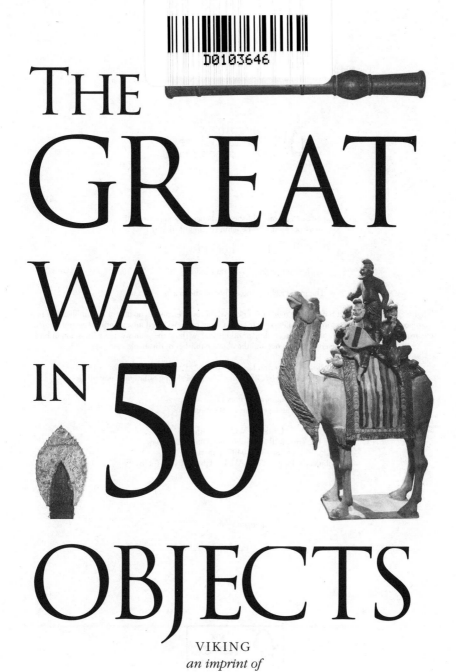

VIKING
an imprint of
PENGUIN BOOKS

PENGUIN BOOKS

UK | USA | Canada | Ireland | Australia
India | New Zealand | South Africa | China

Penguin Books is part of the Penguin Random House group of companies
whose addresses can be found at global.penguinrandomhouse.com.

Penguin
Random House
PENGUIN BOOKS CHINA

This paperback edition published by Penguin Group (Australia)
in association with Penguin (Beijing) Ltd, 2015

1 3 5 7 9 10 8 6 4 2

Text copyright © William Lindesay, 2015

The moral right of the author has been asserted.

Cover and text design by Steffan Leyshon-Jones © Penguin Group (Australia)
Printed and bound in China by RR Donnelley Asia Printing Solutions Limited

National Library of Australia
Cataloguing-in-Publication data:

Lindesay, William, author.
The great wall in 50 objects /William Lindesay.
9780734310484 (paperback)
Art objects, Chinese, Great Wall of China (China)--History.

951

penguin.com.cn

MIX
Paper from
responsible sources
FSC
www.fsc.org
FSC™ C101537

To Qi

Also by William Lindesay

The Great Wall Explained
The Great Wall Revisited:
From the Jade Gate to Old Dragon's Head
Images of Asia: The Great Wall
Alone on the Great Wall

CONTENTS

THE GREAT WALL IN 50 OBJECTS

FOREWORD

Franz Kafka once wrote about the Great Wall of China, upon which he had never set foot: construction of the reportedly 5000-kilometre wall is carried out in one-kilometre sections by small groups of workers, leaving thousands of gaps along the line, in the hope they will be filled in slowly and gradually. But no one knows when, if ever, the gaps will be filled in. In fact, no one knows what the complete Great Wall is like. The workers certainly don't, nor does the 'authority', or the nomads.

This great myth of the Wall, fabricated and ruminated by Kafka, sounds oddly true today. Every year more than 20 million visitors go to see the unprecedented man-made construction, yet so little is known about it. How was the Wall built, anyway? (That was Kafka's question.) How did it work as a defence system? What has happened to it during the past 2000 years? Ancient Chinese historians have a reputation for meticulously recording almost everything, but not in the case of the Wall – perhaps due to the imperial scholars' avoidance of rough work on the wild frontiers, or simply because the Wall's vastness in space and time went way beyond their grasp. Possibly for very similar reasons, modern accounts of the Great Wall are equally scarce, if not more so.

In modern times, the unknown becomes scarcer every day. Unknowns attract curious people, but it takes someone seriously curious to grapple with such an unknown as the Wall. Fortunately for William Lindesay – and the rest of us – he meets the requirements. As a geographer, he is curious enough to have spent the best part of his adult life trying to know the Wall (twenty-eight years so far). Better still, as an endurance athlete whose marathon personal best is two hours and thirty-nine minutes (he says he should have done better), he was sturdy enough to have covered the length of the Wall on foot. In my opinion, he is the right man to talk to if you want to know anything about the Wall.

William is no stranger to Chinese outdoor enthusiasts and Great Wall aficionados. Everyone is familiar with the signposts he set up on trails leading up to the Great Wall: 'Take Nothing but Photographs, Leave Nothing but Footprints.' Many joined William in picking up litter on the Wall, and he's been arranging such activities since 1998. His knowledge of the Wall and his passion for it make him many people's hero. Mine too.

I met William in person in the summer of 2011 when he proposed a story for the Chinese edition of *National Geographic* magazine, where I was editor. He was planning an expedition in Mongolia to search for a 'missing' section of the Wall, and the magazine eventually published an exclusive account of his exciting discoveries. The next year, *Nat Geo* in Beijing helped fund his second expedition in Mongolia, looking for other little known Great Wall segments. This was serious fieldwork, among the first that had been done on that part of the Wall.

The theme of this book originated in an idea William had during his Mongolian expeditions: a new story of the Great Wall, put together using objects he had seen, collected or studied over the years – a story told through Wall-related artefacts. I liked the idea immediately, and in time the magazine rolled it out as a 'virtual exhibition on paper'.

William's new approach to the Wall somehow reminds me of

Kafka's story: a colossal construction made up of small segments, a Wall that one could not know as a whole but only as discrete parts. And I see William's effort as a response to the Kafka myth. Every story tells you something about the Wall, and what matters is not its total but how the parts look when you put them together.

Ye Nan
Editor, National Geographic
(Chinese-language edition), 2009–2013
Beijing, Summer 2014

INTRODUCTION

One rarely finds a perfect story of the distant past, complete and in one place, and certainly not for such a complex series of land-marking structures known simply as the Great Wall of China. Rather, one must embark on a journey, gather the parts of the story and slowly piece them together.

My quest for the 'Wall' – which is actually a discontinuous series of fortifications surviving from numerous dynastic ages, in diverse shapes, forms and conditions – has led me since 1986 to trace their remains across deserts, steppeland and mountains. The walls themselves were always my main pathways, direct routes – until now.

In 2012, I decided to come down from the Wall, so to speak, to investigate stories that were in the periphery – running beneath, beside, inside and out – and, sometimes, took place very far away from the Wall itself. This foraging took me into farmyards, mu-seums, libraries, galleries, universities, workshops and collectors' homes. I was looking for things which, one way or another, were inextricably linked to the story of the Wall, yet physically were no longer part of it, or perhaps had never been.

This book chronicles my efforts in following leads, hunting objects down, gathering them up, piecing them together and making connections between them – all in order to elucidate unknown, overlooked or misunderstood episodes of the Great

Wall story. Though a scattered and disparate lot, the items investigated shared a common quality: all were storytelling objects. I became increasingly attracted to them, these solid sources, confident they'd help me further penetrate the Wall's mysteries, and discover more of its elusive personality.

Through these objects, I wanted to tell a comprehensive Wall story, from its reasons to its ruins. For a year or two, I realised, I would have to curtail my time at the Wall itself and travel more widely – I would need to go to places where there might be just a single object to see, one person to meet, a sole point to learn.

I began to draft a list of those historical figures I wanted to visit. Builders who had recorded their construction productivity on stone tablets. Weapons masters who had buried landmines. Bowyers who had made composite bows by laminating together ibex horn, birch wood and deer sinew. A cartographer who had arranged the Wall's global debut by including it on his map of the world. An author whose work takes us to the Wall's farthest reaches.

From initiation to completion, this work was carried out over twenty-five months – for good reason, as will be explained below. A process with a production time averaging two weeks per object soon established itself. Selecting objects and contacting curators or owners came first. Next came my visit, or revisit, to meet, view, handle and photograph the object. On returning home, there was discussion, research, writing, rewriting and translating to be done.

Completing a factual book in two years may seem fast, but the idea behind it had a much longer gestation. I had been tilted towards this imaginative approach by four distinct realisations, which occurred at different times and places during my Wall researches.

The first came in the form of questions that arose during my solo traverse of the Ming Great Wall on foot in 1987. I felt the structure's majesty, but its remoteness and eerie silence made me wonder about various 'hows'. How long did it take to complete certain sections? How were rocks cut? How could enough wolf dung be collected to be placed at the ready to make the so-called 'wolf smoke' that warned of an enemy's approach? What weapons did defenders use? How about the attackers? What bits of the Wall had been chipped off or picked up? What chunks had been gouged out? As my field knowledge grew, I saw more clearly what had gone missing, and where I might find the answers to my questions.

Some were, as expected, in Wall-side museums, and it was in these that I experienced a second realisation. The placement of an artefact behind glass deprived it of personality. Most objects were gagged, displayed and labelled with a name, a date and a brief matter-of-fact description, and were unable to divulge their stories. Some were even kept in storerooms, away from the public. They needed interviewing and representing. I felt impelled to give these relics from the past the ability to speak to the people of the present, and vice versa: people have the right to see for themselves, or digitally access, things from the past.

My third eye-opening moment: it was in Mongolia that I realised the importance of studying the Great Wall from two sides, rather than just one. Landscapes of desert and steppe, climatic events of drought and *tzud* winters, hunters and the hunted, horses and riders, bows and stirrups – all were startling, less well-known parts of the Great Wall story. Objects from these cultures, needed to be given a voice.

My fourth realisation occurred randomly, in diverse places and at different times. In a gallery in London's West End, where I laid hands on the world's first internationally published atlas which contained a map of China. In the British Library, where I thumbed through files recording Aurel Stein's 1907 investigations of the Han Dynasty Wall, built 2100 years ago. In leafy, well-to-do Bucks County, Pennsylvania, where I walked up the driveway of a mansion, home of the writer of the first book published on the Great Wall. I understood that the Wall now exists beyond China and Mongolia.

I had four groups of possible objects: items that were missing, artefacts that needed jailbreaking, things from the 'other' side, and aspects that had become international. They were like four threads, I realised, whose full beauty could only be seen once they were woven together. Collating them – effectively curating an exhibition – would have been the traditional way of doing this, but herding cats came to mind. I knew that the chances of such an exhibition happening were slim, but I treasured it as a worthwhile study, a journey that I should make when an opportunity materialised. That came earlier than expected, in the summer of 2012, when I was invited to create what became known as a 'virtual exhibition'.

The previous year I had organised my first expedition in Mongolia, focusing on a new area of Great Wall exploration and research. I was looking at long sections of walls there, labelled on the country's own maps as 'The Wall of Genghis Khan'. My findings were published in the Chinese-language edition of *National Geographic*. In China there was great interest in my conclusion that these structures were what I termed 'The Great Wall Outside China'. On the back of several successful print features, and an online report which became the most popular on the magazine's English-language website, Ye Nan asked me for further Great Wall story ideas.

This was my opportunity to entwine my four threads as a serialised 'Virtual Exhibition of the Great Wall', which would run as monthly features. It was both a stimulating and intimidating challenge to regularly deliver so many Great Wall stories for readers of the magazine in China. I needed to decide how many objects to include, and how we would roll the stories out each month.

How many objects? Surely a structure as long as the Great Wall merited a telling with a good number. The construction history of the Great Wall, actually a series of border-defence systems, spans approximately 2000 years from around the third century BC to the mid-seventeenth century, during which time umpteen different great walls – perhaps sixteen – built by different dynasties appeared in the northern territories of their domains. Of these, it is the Ming Dynasty Great Wall which is the face of the great walls as the world knows it today. As it's 'only' 500 years old on average, and therefore the best preserved of all the great walls, there is a plethora of antiquities that show and tell its history. That dynastic period alone could generate fifty objects worthy of study. But the Great Wall's story goes well beyond the Ming Wall's story; at least equal coverage of the pre-Ming era seemed reasonable.

Was there any need to choose a round number, other than for neatness' sake? One hundred objects, I decided, would be too many for the magazine to commit to, and for readers to absorb. I'd conceived my project, after all, as an exhibition which would showcase only the most enlightening, significant stories. This was not an academic project, a storage room; I wanted the exhibition to be succinct, accessible and personal.

The first major international exhibition I ever saw was back in 1972, when the British Museum marked the fiftieth anniversary of the discovery of the tomb of Tutankhamun by Howard Carter; it had displayed just fifty antiquities from the treasure-crammed tomb. That had been enough to ignite my interest in Egypt, and ancient history, forever. Thus, I decided on fifty.

That worked out at one object every forty-five years or so throughout the 2300-year lifetime of the Great Wall. While setting them in context and highlighting each epoch's major political movements and cultural currents, I would choose the bulk of my objects to stand at every twist and turn of the Great Wall's story, and a few to explain some absences and to account for the major nomadic intrusions. This was the broader Great Wall story, played out between the north and south across a wide frontier that may be described as the Great Wall theatre of war.

My initial draft list, the editor remarked concernedly, was composed of only thirty-five objects. I was not perturbed by the shortfall; it was by design. As with all journeys, I expected to meet various strangers along the way, so I earmarked some space to accommodate them.

Faithfully, the editor supported this approach, commissioned the series and named it 'Great Wall 50'; two pieces would run each month for twenty-five consecutive issues. By signing on the dotted line, I committed to delivering on deadline every month for over two years. I readied myself to go out to dozens of locations, with the aim each time of becoming intimately acquainted (or sometimes reacquainted) with an object. If things went to plan, the trips would combine to allow a procession of personages to tell their object's place in the famous structure's story.

Four months before 'Great Wall 50' was to begin, my wife, Wu Qi, and I had a brainstorming walk on paths winding up to the Wall from our farmhouse. We discussed all aspects of the project: whether to call them 'objects', 'antiquities' or even 'people'? Exactly how would I do the work – or, rather, how would *we* do it, because Qi would be working closely with me, as translator and researcher?

While most things on my wish list were antiquities or cultural relics, there were some anomalies. And while many were related closely to a nameable individual, some were anonymous. Besides, how had I come to know these people? In most cases it was via the object they created, not vice versa. If I used the term 'antiquity', how might I justifiably include something as fascinating as wolf smoke, which was intangible and momentary? The all-encompassing term 'object' seemed to be the safest option, because anything and everything is an object.

From midsummer 2012, our lives began to revolve around the Great Wall 50 project. As translator, Qi's work – a blend of rewriting, rearranging and cross-cultural crafting – required regular discussions of each object's qualities and significance from both our perspectives. A history major, she was also an admirably thorough researcher; Qi is a stickler for accuracy and consistency, so her work also functioned as an invaluable cross-check.

Each month we admitted two relatively unknown objects – sometimes complete strangers – into the study of our home in Beijing. Four weeks later they would become familiar, things we knew well, by which time we were ready to pass what we had written about them to our good friend and historical advisor Wang Xuenong, emeritus curator of the Shanhaiguan Great Wall Museum. After going back and forth on historical points with him, we would submit the two works to Evelyn Rao at *National Geographic*, for her editorial touches prior to publication.

The series launched in the magazine's September 2012 issue, telling the very contrasting stories of how foreigners and Chinese commonly first learned about the existence of a 'Great Wall'. This pairing formed part of a longer introduction, to be followed by objects arranged chronologically, according to the stories they told, although not always strictly based on their dates of production, up to the modern era. The approach produced the five collections of objects you will meet in the five parts of this book.

Of all my Great Wall travels, the journey I took in visiting my fifty objects for this virtual exhibition was the longest, and the most unusual. These objects touch upon every episode of the Wall's history, and reach into every important era of China's past and present. They reveal how the Great Wall was built, operated, attacked, abandoned, regarded, mythologised, misunderstood, explored, mapped, photographed and politicised – and how it became a worldwide story. Although I didn't realise it at the outset, by the journey's end I had compiled not just my own personal history of the Great Wall, but also a Great Wall personnel history.

Here it is, then, the book that is the result of the leap I took, the detours I made, the objects I saw and the people I met: *The Great Wall in 50 Objects.*

William Lindesay
March 2015

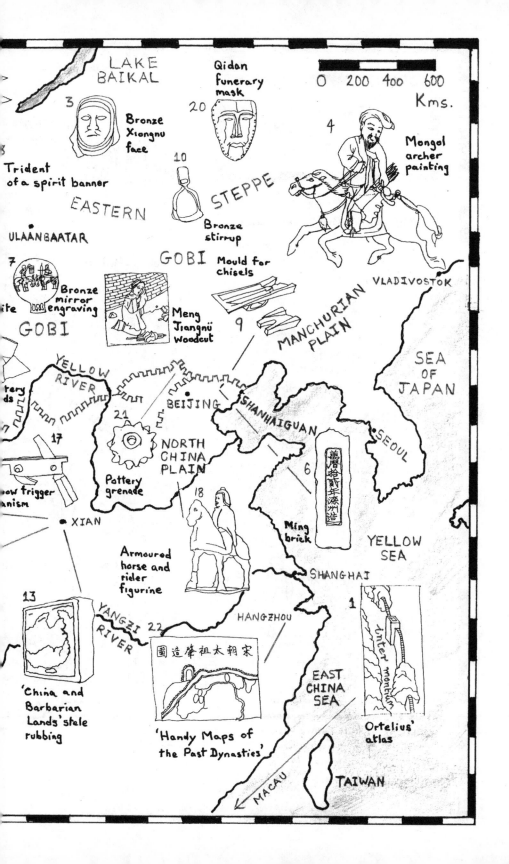

LAKE BAIKAL

3 Bronze Xiongnu face

Qidan funerary mask 20

4 Mongol archer painting

Trident of a spirit banner

EASTERN

10

STEPPE

Bronze stirrup

ULAANBAATAR

GOBI Mould for chisels

7

Bronze mirror engraving

ite

GOBI

Meng Jiangnü Woodcut

9

MANCHURIAN PLAIN

VLADIVOSTOK

SEA OF JAPAN

YELLOW RIVER

tery ds

BEIJING

SHANHAIGUAN

SEOUL

21

NORTH CHINA PLAIN

6

17

Pottery grenade

Ming brick

YELLOW SEA

ow trigger anism

XIAN

18

Armoured horse and rider figurine

SHANGHAI

13

YANGZI RIVER

22

HANGZHOU

1

inter montium

'China and Barbarian Lands' stele rubbing

宋朝太祖肇造圖

'Handy Maps of the Past Dynasties'

EAST CHINA SEA

Ortelius' atlas

MACAU

TAIWAN

0   200   400   600
                    Kms.

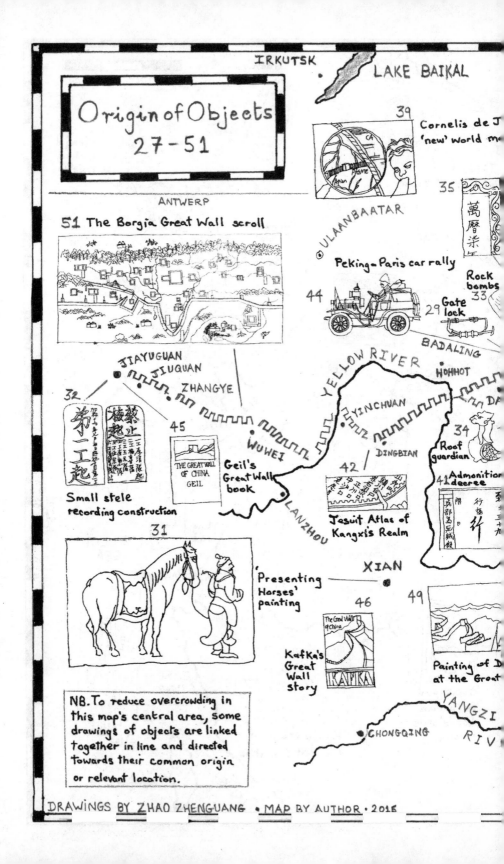

IRKUTSK

LAKE BAIKAL

Origin of Objects
27 - 51

39

Cornelis de J
'new' world m

35

ANTWERP

51 The Borgia Great Wall scroll

萬曆卅

ULAANBAATAR

Peking-Paris car rally

Rock
bombs
33

44

Gate
lock
29

BADALING

YELLOW RIVER

HOHHOT

JIAYUGUAN

JIUQUAN

ZHANGYE

YINCHUAN

DA

32

45

WUWEI

DINGBIAN

34

THE GREAT WALL
OF CHINA
GEIL

Geil's
Great Wall
book

42

Roof
guardian

41 Admonition
decree

行

Small stele
recording construction

Jesuit Atlas of
Kangxi's Realm

31

LANZHOU

XIAN

'Presenting
Horses'
painting

46

49

The Great Wall
of China

KAFKA

Kafka's
Great
Wall
story

Painting of D
at the Great

YANGZI

NB. To reduce overcrowding in
this map's central area, some
drawings of objects are linked
together in line and directed
towards their common origin
or relevant location.

CHONGQING

RIV

DRAWINGS BY ZHAO ZHENGUANG ⚫ MAP BY AUTHOR ⚫ 2015

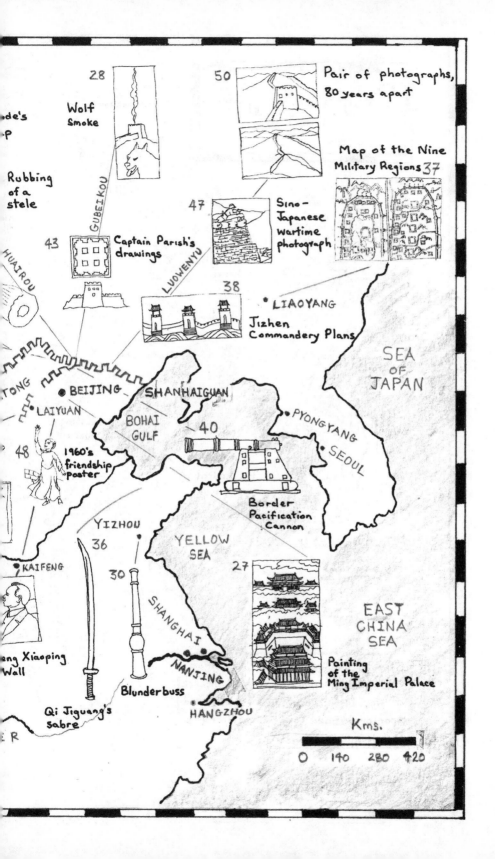

28
Wolf Smoke

50
Pair of photographs, 80 years apart

de's
P

Rubbing of a stele

Map of the Nine Military Regions 37

GUBEIKOU

43
Captain Parish's drawings

47
Sino-Japanese wartime photograph

HUAIROU

LUOWENYU

38
Jizhen Commandery Plans

• LIAOYANG

SEA OF JAPAN

TONG

• BEIJING
SHANHAIGUAN

• LAIYUAN
BOHAI GULF

40

• PYONGYANG

• SEOUL

48
1960's friendship poster

Border Pacification Cannon

YIZHOU

36
• KAIFENG

30

YELLOW SEA

27

SHANGHAI

ng Xiaoping
Wall

NANJING

EAST CHINA SEA

Painting of the Ming Imperial Palace

Qi Jiguang's sabre

Blunderbuss

HANGZHOU

R

Kms.

0   140   280   420

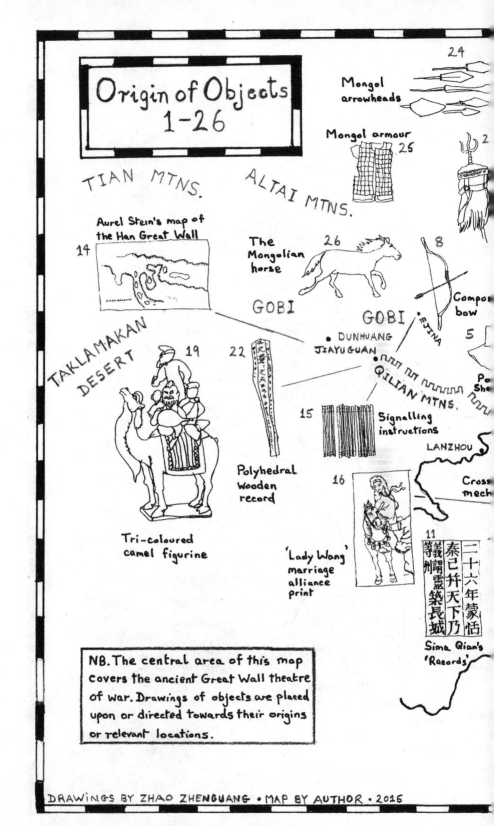

Origin of Objects
1-26

24
Mongol arrowheads

Mongol armour
25

2

TIAN MTNS.

ALTAI MTNS.

Aurel Stein's map of the Han Great Wall
14

The Mongolian horse
26

8

Compo[?] bow

GOBI

GOBI

5

• DUNHUANG

• EJINA

JIAYUGUAN

TAKLAMAKAN DESERT

19

22

QILIAN MTNS.

Po[?] She[?]

15

Signalling instructions

LANZHOU

Polyhedral wooden record

16

Cross mech[?]

Tri-coloured camel figurine

'Lady Wang' marriage alliance print

11

二十六年蒙恬
秦已幷天下乃
義惆霊築長城
等

Sima Qian's 'Records'

NB. The central area of this map covers the ancient Great Wall theatre of war. Drawings of objects are placed upon or directed towards their origins or relevant locations.

DRAWINGS BY ZHAO ZHENGUANG • MAP BY AUTHOR • 2015

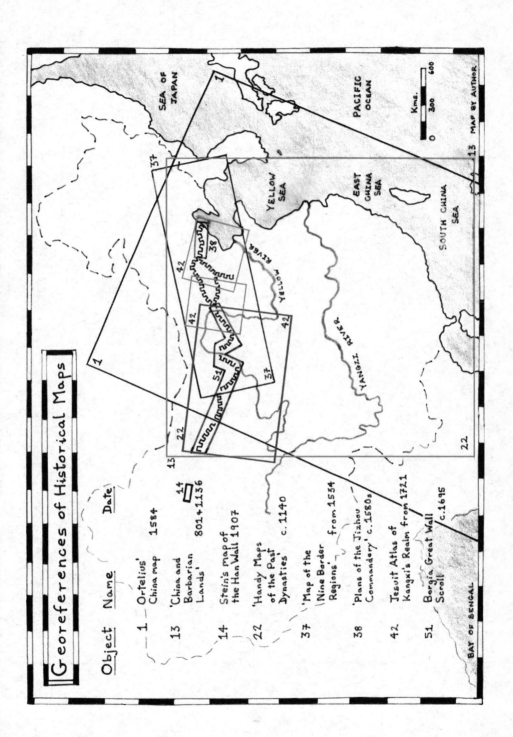

Georeferences of Historical Maps

Object	Name	Date
1	'Ortelius' China map	1584
13	'China and Barbarian Lands'	801 + 1136
14	Stein's map of the Han Wall	1907
22	'Handy Maps of the Past Dynasties'	c. 1140
37	'Map of the Nine Border Regions'	from 1534
38	'Plans of the Jizhou Commandery'	c. 1580s
42	Jesuit Atlas of Kangxi's Realm	from 1721
51	Borgia Great Wall Scroll	c. 1695

SEA OF JAPAN

PACIFIC OCEAN

Kms.

0   300   600

MAP BY AUTHOR.

YELLOW SEA

EAST CHINA SEA

SOUTH CHINA SEA

YELLOW RIVER

YANGZI RIVER

BAY OF BENGAL

Part One

SURVEY: EIGHT KEYS

Objects from various dates

When I hike with 'first footers' up to a section of Wild Wall, as opposed to those parts of it tamed for tourists and rebuilt with steps, I'm often asked during the final stage of our approach: 'How are we actually going to get *up* onto it?' Indeed, you can't just ascend such an edifice anywhere. You need to know where, for example, a collapse might provide a place you can clamber up, or where there are safe footholds.

As we start our journey, even though it is 'off-Wall', the question 'Where should we begin?' is equally valid. It's just as important to find an accessible entry point to the story of the Great Wall, to ensure we successfully find our way onto the right path.

For this reason, I'm not starting off with the *oldest* objects relating to the Wall. Rather, I've selected eight key objects – of various ages, and not in any order – that will help to answer our most important questions as we set out: How did we hear about the Wall? Who was it built for? What was it built with?

Understanding these objects will prepare us for the journey ahead. We'll make a more or less chronological traverse of the Wall's 2000-year-long operational history. For now, though, and for once, time isn't important.

1.

ON REACHING EUROPE

Abraham Ortelius' Theatre of the World *atlas*

Imagine, four centuries ago, someone setting off on a long journey. What might they have taken to help them to communicate, and make a statement about themselves, their country, their society, and their place in the world? The English navigator Sir Francis Drake spent three years sailing around the world, from 1577 to 1580. In his cabin we would have found a copy of the world's first atlas.

The first edition of *Theatrum Orbis Terrarum* had been published in 1570 in Antwerp, today's Belgium, by Abraham Ortelius. It was a geographical revelation, depicting the world in a shape and form that would be recognisable by someone today. This book not only helped Drake voyage around the world, it also showed those with whom he shared it what the rest of the world was like and where he came from. It demonstrated that people of all regions were part of the same world.

Two decades after Drake's expeditions, in 1601, the Italian Jesuit missionary Father Matteo Ricci (1552–1610) arrived in Beijing. In order to honour the reigning Wanli Emperor (who ruled from 1572 to 1620), as well as to promote European knowledge and convince his imperial majesty that a superior understanding

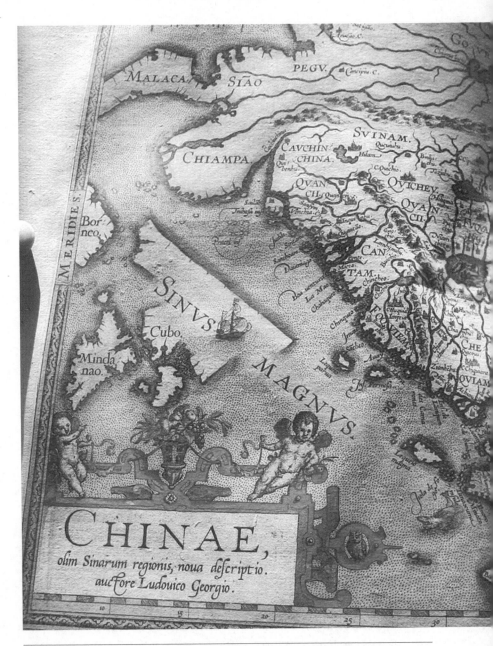

DESCRIPTION:	*Theatrum Orbis Terrarum*, or *Theatre of the World*, an atlas published by Abraham Ortelius (1527–98)
SIGNIFICANCE:	Considered the first world atlas; contains the first internationally published map of China and image of the Great Wall

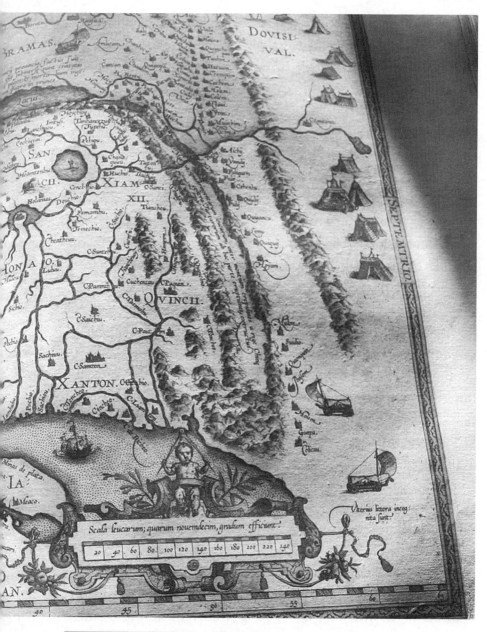

ORIGIN:	Antwerp, Belgium, 1584
LOCATION:	Private collection of Maarten Buitelaar, Beijing

of the world was granted by God to his followers, Ricci had prepared some gifts. Included was a copy of the Ortelius atlas.

Why did this giant of books attract such intellectually elite customers?

Never before had anybody put maps of so many different nations together within two boards. Placing countries side by side opened up a new era: people could discover a new world, beyond what they could see with their own eyes. Other countries existed. Ortelius' atlas was a showcase of contemporary knowledge, paving the way to the future.

Ortelius' success relied on him having a network of informants capable of collecting the latest geographical observations from around the world. Mariners, merchants and missionaries were propelled, respectively, by a curiosity to explore, by the need for new raw materials, and by Rome's desire to convert the benighted to Christianity, adventures which defined the 1500s as the core century of the Age of Discovery. People with very different goals, but all of them travellers, returned with (or sent back) observations, hearsay, reports and knowledge that had been collected by Ortelius' team.

In the early 1580s, a Spanish Benedictine monk named Arius Montanus, an Orientalist, visited Ortelius' atelier in Antwerp carrying a manuscript map of China. The scroll thus completed the final stage of its long journey, over several years and through many careful hands.

The Spaniard had been entrusted with the precious scroll by Luiz Jorge de Barbuda, a Portuguese geographer who had summarised what was known of Ming China by Jesuit brothers who had lived in Macao since 1557. With embellishments and supplementary information, including extracts from a Spanish booklet on China, published in Seville in 1570 by the Jesuit Bernadino Escalante, Ortelius drew up his first China map.

He premiered it in the 1584 edition of *Theatrum Orbis Terrarum*.

Four hundred and twenty five years later, I feel privileged to examine a copy of the 'Theatre', which covers half of my large desktop. It's almost an arm in length and two hands in width, and it's a clenched fist in thickness. It's heavy. It is bound in thick, dark-brown, leather-covered boards. In turning its pages, I'm travelling during the most exciting time in history for any geographer. As I do, I wonder what the first owner of this atlas thought when he saw certain maps. Iceland, for example, shows a volcano, Hekla, blowing its top, spouting red lava, and the seas around this glaciated hell are inhabited by all kinds of monsters. How did one distinguish between the map's fact and fiction?

'Arriving' in China might have prompted similar concern: there, a wall arced across the north of an empire, and beneath it was a sentence in Latin which translates as: 'A wall of 400 leagues [1800 kilometres] between the banks of the hills, built by the King of China against the attacks of barbarians.' Would viewers of this map really have believed that a wall, a structure normally built around cities, had been constructed in such an extraordinary manner?

The annotation in Latin explained its basic function, and symbols showed that it was replete with towers or guard stations. And the segmented line of the structure – wall, mountain range, wall – showed that its strategists had 'borrowed the mountains' and incorporated natural features such as cliffs into their defence plan.

True or false, partly or wholly, this China map was a milestone, even then. It was the first map of China ever published in the West, and contained the first internationally published and widely seen image of the Great Wall. Chinese woodblock-printed maps had shown the structure during the Southern Song Dynasty in the twelfth century (see Object 21) but they had only limited domestic circulation. In contrast, 'Theatres' containing China maps sold an estimated 5425 copies in six languages across Western Europe over twenty-eight years.

In 2002, as I became increasingly concerned at the destruction of the landscape quality of the Great Wall to the north of Beijing by the encroachment of development, I nominated the 'Wallscape' of the Beijing Municipality to be recognised as an endangered site by the World Monuments Fund. Needing to promote the notion that the Wall was as much a part of China's geography as of its history, I submitted this map as early published evidence of the Great Wall as a landscape feature.

The Ortelius atlas is a monumental book that gave the world beyond China and neighbouring lands its first tantalising, and amazing, view of the Wall. In Europe's mapmaking centres, as the decades passed, it was upgraded in cartographic stature, from a curious, semi-mythical feature to an established geographical detail; by the early eighteenth century it was a scientifically mapped landmark (see Object 42).

In keeping with this emergence, it underwent name changes too, initially receiving a proper name – the Chinese Wall – and then, in recognition of its known scale, becoming the Great Wall. For succinctness, I often prefer to use a variation of Ortelius' original term, converting his 'wall' into 'the Wall'. The article and the capital combine well to express the structure's uniqueness: it's in a class of its own.

2.

A Place of No Return

Meng Jiangnü's Endless Search for her Husband *woodblock print*

I've asked hundreds of Chinese people how they first heard about the Great Wall, and most tell me it's from the legend of Meng Jiangnü. The heartbreak of the woman whose husband was conscripted to build the Great Wall has had millions of retellings – and undergone scores of alterations – over more than 1200 years. It has engaged the attention of the masses over these centuries as a teahouse tale, as a drum song chanted in villages, as poems recited in rural 'culture stations', and as operas sung and acted on stage. Nowadays you can even watch videos of the story on your mobile. I recently heard a less familiar rendition that is relevant to the preservation of the Wall today. It could be used to help save the monument from one of its most relentless modern attacks.

Professor Wilt Idema, a Chinese literature scholar at Harvard University, recently authored a book on the diversiform legend: *Meng Jiangnü Brings Down the Great Wall: Ten Versions of a Chinese Legend*. He summarises: 'The legend of Meng Jiangnü, the tale of the virtuous wife of Qi Liang, achieved its canonical version in Liu Xiang's 'Biographies of Exemplary Women' (*Lienü Zhuan*). Qi Liang's wife would only acquire the surname Meng during the

Tang Dynasty, when the setting of the story was moved forward to the reign of the first emperor of Qin.'

One aspect is common to all versions, as Professor Idema points out. 'The legend is a classic tale of a tyrant's folly, and variations mostly detail the moral turpitude of the First Emperor.'

I will discuss two versions. The first is a *Jiangnan* or 'Southern' edition, as illustrated by our object: a coloured woodblock print. The second rendering, new to my ears and even to Professor Idema's, I heard in Beijing's suburbs. It gives the legend an eerie, present-day relevance.

Printed and coloured by woodblocks cut and inked by Sun Wenya, a Shanghainese in the late Qing, circa 1890, as a Lunar New Year's illustration, the ten-panel captioned print is designed to be viewed like a strip cartoon, column by column, from right to left.

In (1) soldiers with an arrest warrant for Wan Xiliang (yes, a different name) arrive in Suzhou with orders to take him to the capital. A 'wanted' poster announces that a reward of 1000 *liang* of silver will be paid for his arrest. Apparently, the Emperor wants to exploit Wan's labours in building the Great Wall, believing that his surname, which is a homonym of 'ten thousand', indicates that he'll somehow magically provide the work of the same number of men. (Interestingly, Emperor Qin Shihuang was believed to have also executed all unfortunate subjects in his empire surnamed 'Hu' – which is a homonym for the generic term 'barbarian' – after a soothsayer predicted that 'the Hu will topple the Qin'.)

In (2) Wan Xiliang bids farewell to his parents and heads for Songjiang, becoming a fugitive, and (3) he takes refuge in a garden, where he chances on a view of Lady Meng bathing in her back yard. (4) The encounter is considered intimate because 'a naked woman cannot be seen by two men', and Lady Meng is faced with two choices – marriage or suicide. Fortunately, the couple love one another. (5) They marry, but soon after Xiliang's luck runs out and he's arrested, put in chains and marched off as a conscript to build the Great Wall.

(6) Lady Meng prepares some winter clothes to take to him. (7) One night, the lonely wife has a nightmare that convinces her that Xiliang has died at the Great Wall. (8) Chinese 'Valentine's Day', the seventh day of the seventh lunar month, comes around, and Lady Meng is overcome with melancholy. (9) Bidding farewell to her parents, she heads north to search for her husband. (10) Lady Meng asks here, there and everywhere for her husband.

What happens next? There's only one sheet of the woodblock print in the British Library's collection, leaving us on the edge of our seats. For the rest of the story we can refer to some well-known oral versions.

When Lady Meng arrives at the Wall she's told that Xiliang has died and been buried in the fill of the Wall. Her wails and tears cause the fortification to collapse, revealing his bones, which she gathers up. She's arrested, taken to the imperial capital and sent before the Emperor, who decides not to execute her when he sees her beauty. She seduces the Emperor, persuading him to arrange a state funeral and erect memorial arches and temples in her husband's name. With this achieved, she escapes, jumps in a river and is reunited with her beloved in heaven.

It is from this legend that the majority of Chinese people, past and present, have heard of the Great Wall – not from the name of the emperor who built it, but from the name of a woman whose heart was broken by it. The story's popularity created a belief that if a man was conscripted to work on the Wall, he would never return to his home town or to his wife. Consequently, the name of the Great Wall in Chinese, *Wanli Changcheng*, became a byword for a death sentence. This might explain why, in later dynasties, especially the Ming, the defences were simply called *biancheng*, or border defences, thus avoiding the original term's connotations.

DESCRIPTION:	A coloured woodblock print entitled *Meng Jiangnü's Endless Search for Her Husband*, by artist Sun Wenya
SIGNIFICANCE:	Illustrates part of the most enduring legend of the Great Wall, by which most Chinese first learn about the monumental structure

ORIGIN:	Shanghai, China, circa 1890s
LOCATION:	British Library, London (OR 5896)

And now a second version, which I heard in around 2002. After walking a section of Wall in Yanqing District, to the west of Badaling, I found a driver to take me back to Beijing. Inevitably, our talk turned to where I'd been, whereupon he asked: 'Do you know the legend of Meng Jiangnü?'

'Why don't you tell me your version?' I said.

His long story washed over me like an overly familiar pop song, becoming background music to my deeper thoughts of getting home and enjoying my wife's home comforts. Then my ears pricked up at something the driver was saying. '. . . Lady Meng examined the names of the dead workers inscribed on the Wall's bricks, and, there it was: Wan Xiliang.'

At that moment, the reconstructed Great Wall at Badaling came into sight. Sardonically, I remarked that on virtually every brick of its ramparts, trodden by 8 million people each year, was etched the name of a tourist.

'That's not a wise thing to do,' snarled the driver. 'Those foolish tourists don't understand the Great Wall's history: writing one's name on one of its bricks is a death knell.'

As China has become wealthier, and more people can travel to see the Wall for themselves, large numbers have thoughtlessly carved or penned their names on its bricks. At Badaling it's difficult to find a single brick without graffiti. By early 2014 the amount of graffiti on the Wall's bricks had become such a problem that the authorities managing one of the other main tourist Wall sections close to Beijing, Mutianyu, decided on a controversial attempt to contain it. Graffiti is allowed within one of the interiors of a battle platform. Its inside walls are draped with changeable covers; once filled up, they are replaced.

In our attempt to deal with this vandalism, and preserve the Wall, I think the driver's version of Meng Jiangnü's legend is the one we should promote, if only for its potential as a haunting deterrent.

3.

THE ENEMY AT FIRST SIGHT

Bronze face of a Xiongnu warrior

In my eyes, the historical value of an object lies in its ability to initiate an inter-generational conversation, and this object, a face in bronze, certainly does. It's a unique piece among hundreds of bronze artefacts in the collection of the late Mr Purevjav Erdenechuluun, collected between 1996 and 2011 from all over Mongolia, and only recently put on display in a vault under the largest equestrian statue in the world, of Genghis Khan, outside Ulaanbaatar.

To me, it was a face that stood out from a crowd. In the museum's exhibition hall stands a map depicting where various artefacts were excavated or collected. An array of thumbnail photos shows arrowheads, totems, lance motifs, swords, daggers, knives, belt buckles and animal decorations. It was from this map that the Xiongnu warrior gazed out at me. As I looked into his eyes, I pondered whether I was meeting a representative, generic face or some particular individual. When we stare into the face of a Qin terracotta warrior, it is thought we are seeing an actual person; perhaps I was engaging in a similar historical dialogue when I looked into the eyes of this Xiongnu warrior.

It may be the tiniest object of the entire fifty, but its date – from the second century BC – means it is around twenty centuries old. If we assume that generations occur every twenty-one years or so, or five times per century, then this object allows us to connect with a person from around 100 generations ago. It was a time when two large and powerful empires were in conflict. The bronze was found, and is assumed to have been made, in Dundgovi Aimag, or 'Middle Gobi', Province, a landscape where the steppeland deteriorates in quality towards the south, becoming desert.

At about the time this object was created, circa 145 BC, the Chinese chronicler Sima Qian, author of *Shiji*, or *Records of the Grand Historian* (see Object 11), was born in present-day Hancheng, Shaanxi Province. Our knowledge of the Xiongnu, or Huns, comes entirely from Chinese sources, and that means Sima Qian; the Xiongnu themselves were illiterate and without a script of their own. Even the *History of the Later Han* (*Hou Han Shu*), written five centuries after Sima Qian, used *Shiji* as its main source.

Sima Qian described the Xiongnu as the earliest nomadic enemy of ancient China, and the reason for the building of the first *Wanli Changcheng*, or Great Wall. This small bronze, probably a belt decoration, is a very rare self-depiction of a Xiongnu, or a Hunnu, as they called themselves, which means 'People of the Sky'.

The Chinese, however, had a different view of the Xiongnu, whose lands occupied a vast swathe along China's northern edge. In accordance with China's *Tianxia* political and philosophical scheme of geographical hierarchy ('All Under Heaven' – or, more directly, China at the centre of the world), the Xiongnu were demonised as foreigners at the edge who refused to acknowledge Chinese superiority. Indeed, the Hunnu militarily challenged Chinese domination, eventually inflicting major defeats on the Western Han, and forcing its early emperors into humiliating appeasement policies (see Object 15).

The Xiongnu were said to have used knives to scarify their own faces in order to appear more bellicose. A plausible explanation of the evolution of the character *xiong* – 匈 – is that the central cross component represents those facial scars, beneath a helmet. The Xiongnu were commonly described as marauders who produced nothing but the meat and milk they consumed, and who owned nothing of value except the goods they stole or extorted from their productive Chinese neighbours.

Recent archaeological finds throughout Mongolia (examples of which abound in the same private collection of which this bronze Xiongnu face forms a part) evidence a different side to the Xiongnu story: that they produced large quantities of exquisite goods themselves. The majority of artefacts, some utilitarian, others clearly for decorative or ritual use, show their people's close relationship with nature. Common motifs such as the deer, gazelle, ibex, argali and camel highlight the Xiongnu reliance on hunting wild beasts for food and clothing, and on domesticating some for transport. Among the latter, the horse held pride of place in the nomadic society, becoming the most revered and prized of the 'six snouts' (the others were the sheep, goat, cow, yak and camel). If man is in the picture at all, he is usually shown anonymously, impersonally.

This object is different. This man has a roundish face, large eyes, a broad nose and a moustache above quite thick lips. His head is wrapped in a scarf. The Xiongnu were the first truly federated nomadic people; they created a state in 209 BC that was ruled by a *shanyu* (equivalent in stature to a khan). It stretched from Korea in the east to the Tianshan or Heavenly Mountains in the west, from Lake Baikal in the north to the Ordos Desert in the south. The steppe confederacy's timely establishment made it an effective counterweight to the might of the newly unified dynastic Qin empire, which defended itself with the *Wanli*

DESCRIPTION:	Bronze ornament of a Xiongnu face; measures 3 centimetres by 3 centimetres; second century BC
SIGNIFICANCE:	Image of the first powerful steppe people: the Xiongnu, or 'Huns'
ORIGIN:	Undurshil Soum, Dundgovi Aimag, Mongolia
LOCATION:	Museum of the Great Hunnu Empire, Erdene, Ulaanbaatar; private collection of the late Mr Purevjav Erdenechuluun

Changcheng. Some researchers believe the unification of China under the Qin actually catalysed unity across the steppe as a means of building an effective military response to the larger, more powerful entity of imperial China.

The precise reason for the object's crafting and its journey down 100 or more generations is open to debate. It has a ring-like opening on its reverse, thick enough for threading onto a sash or leather thong, so it seems most likely it functioned as a belt decoration. Belts were important adornments of the nomads, symbolic of the wearer's valour and status. They functioned as hangers for everyday tools and weapons, ranging from awls to knives and swords. According to *Mongoliin Nuuts Tovchoo*, or 'The Secret History of the Mongols', the first historical account of steppe life from the early thirteenth century, the exchange of belts was seen as an oath of allegiance between friends.

To us, this tiny belt decoration shows the true face of a people who were the prime reason behind the first Great Wall's construction – people who made objects of beauty themselves, who did not have scarred faces, and who called themselves the Hunnu.

4.

Observing a Ceasefire

Painting of a Mongol archer

It was in 2003 that I first saw the Mongol archer on horseback, in the most unexpected of places: cantering within a dimly lit cabinet in the gallery of Chinese art in London's Victoria and Albert Museum. I was immediately entranced by my chance meeting with him, so far from his homeland. Neither the museums at either end of the Great Wall, at Shanhaiguan and Jiayuguan, nor those which showcased national collections in the capital, Beijing, had such a clear illustration of the nemesis of China's northern frontier between the thirteenth and the seventeenth centuries. Produced by a Chinese artist in the *gongbi* style (of realistic portrayal), this was the first image I had seen of a Mongol, the nomads whose invasions took all of China from Han majority rule, and whose threatening posture, after their ousting, led to the construction of China's greatest Wall, that of the Ming Dynasty.

Gazing at the image, I saw a true likeness. With a recent visit to Mongolia fresh in my mind, I noticed that this man rode the stocky Mongolian breed still used on the steppe today (see Object 25). His bow, too, was of the recurved composite design (see Object 8), a fragmented example of which I'd seen in an Ulaanbaatar museum. His boot looked exactly the same as an armour-plated pair in the same museum (see Object 26). And he wore the flowing 'dell' robe still worn by the steppeland herders of today. The painting was described as having been produced in China.

I wondered under what circumstances a Ming artist might have made a painting of a Mongol. They were commonly perceived as the arch-enemy. Could it have been for familiarisation?

That notion had contemporary significance. The war in Iraq was raging, and American troops had been issued a pack of playing cards depicting the fifty-two most wanted members of Saddam Hussein's regime. The US Defense Department had explained the logic: it was a method of making known their arch-enemies, the most wanted men in Iraq, to US troops. It gave them targets with high price tags.

Yet this Mongol was not clad in armour, ready for war, but was dressed in a traditional dell cloak. Its blue was a significant colour, being favoured for festival occasions. He is shown wearing a serene expression, carrying his bow and quiver full of arrows. He has certainly not been humiliated or demonised by the artist for propaganda purposes.

The subject belongs to a category that barely seems to exist in Chinese art. Can't we say that most art is produced for appreciation? Traditionally, in China, that had meant a stock of unchanging genres: peaceful images of birds, insects, fish, flowers and idyllic landscapes, complemented by the highest form of art, not brushstrokes but calligraphy. This painting has none of that: it's a maverick subject, without a calligraphic character. I don't think it was painted for appreciation.

I asked Freda Murck, an American who has studied Chinese painting for thirty years, for her opinion. She happened to be in London and went along to the V&A, where the curator of Chinese paintings, Zhang Hongxing, showed her the mounted scroll.

'The quality is low and it has serious authenticity problems, which is funny to say as it has no attribution,' commented Murck. 'The brushwork is wobbly and undistinguished.' She also noted that it had a number of collector's seals, recording its ownership and appreciation; one of the Qianlong Emperor had clearly been faked in an attempt to enhance the object's value.

Wang Ning, a former Sotheby's Chinese art expert, pointed me towards works by esteemed horse painters, notably Zhao Mengfu, the Yuan Dynasty artist. Looking at his works, I saw art for art's sake. I felt the peace, timelessness and emotion of grazing one's own horse, training one's own steed, all captured by Zhao Mengfu's magnificent brushstrokes. He painted from inspiration, and for others' appreciation. When I returned to my archer, the question of the reason for its production loomed even larger: art for what sake?

I asked a number of other experts – not of art, but of Ming history and steppe history – to comment, but they shied away from the challenge. The painting is an anomaly. It doesn't conform. It doesn't belong to any genre or school. So that invites us to think outside the square.

If it wasn't produced for familiarisation, demonisation or appreciation, then for the purposes of the Ming Great Wall's story I would categorise it as a product of what I might call 'accommodation'. Following the restoration of Han rule after almost five centuries' domination of North China by people of northern nomadic origins, various policies were pursued by Ming emperors to prevent a repetition of that history: another invasion and period of rule by the Mongols.

While border defence construction was the cornerstone of the dynasty's defence policy, its rulers employed other approaches too, including what was termed 'checking barbarians with barbarians' and 'fighting barbarians with barbarians'. Both policies included

DESCRIPTION:	*Gongbi*-style painting of a Mongol archer
SIGNIFICANCE:	A rare image of a nomadic warrior
ORIGIN:	China, anonymous artist, mid to late Ming (sixteenth to seventeenth century)
LOCATION:	Victoria and Albert Museum, London

the cross-border exchange of goods, which ranged from occasional to regular in frequency. Some became known as horse-tea markets, and at such venues nomads came to trade with merchants. I wonder, therefore, whether this painting might have been painted on such an occasion, indicating such an interaction. Here, the Mongol is depicted realistically, not as a foe. He is in traditional garb, not battle dress.

Regardless of its artistic quality in the eyes of experts, this painting for us is a revelation. It gives insight into a little-known moment, a ceasefire of sorts, within an otherwise long and violent history. This mounted archer sat briefly and peacefully to be painted; those before him rode in waves, charging as cavalry, fighting battles.

5.

Just Add Water

Pottery sherds from the desert floor

When I visited my first museums as a child, I ignored the typical welcome that most curators have in store for visitors: an avenue of cabinets containing broken bits of pots. I always breezed past these dull artefacts, hurrying toward the exciting, glistening antiquities of gold.

No matter what country you are in, the first exhibits to greet you in most museums are the pots. Broken pots. Many of the pots we use today have not changed much since our distant cousins used them, hundreds or even thousands of years ago — another reason they fail to capture the imagination of most people. But, as any archaeologist will confirm, we've learned much more about our past from the pots our ancestors made, used and dropped than from their more artistic antiquities. The latter are the gushing socialites who give good first impressions; the former, the pots, are the quiet, unassuming friends whose qualities are slower to emerge.

I can tell you that you feel much more enthusiastic about broken old pots when you've found the pieces yourself. When you pick up a potsherd and examine it, the excitement that wells up inside you is not because the broken pottery is so many hundreds of years' old. It arises when you think about what the pot might have contained, who might have used it, when and why.

So, let's discover some together. We are walking along a section of the Great Wall. The age, location and morphology of the rampart are not vital; the Wall is six to eight metres high and made of mud (and it's among the best-preserved Great Wall of its type that I've ever seen). This part of the Wall is in Ningxia, running along the edge of dry foothills that rise in height westwards, growing into the Helan Mountains. It's a desert region pocked with patches of drought-resistant shrubs. Unsurprisingly, there's no permanent human presence here. But there used to be. Evidence abounds in the remains of the Great Wall, which records man's one and only major intrusion into this hostile landscape.

The evidence rises before us in a spectacular way: a towering high and immensely long rampart, clearly a sizeable human effort made under testing environmental conditions. It was both a survival challenge for the men who operated this defensive structure and a logistics challenge for its builders – the planners and strategists who organised the army families to do the labour.

Walking beside the Wall, we're attracted by the pieces of pot strewn across the desert floor. It seems that every ten steps, a piece of pottery glistens on the surface of the earth. We start to collect the sherds. The largest are about the size of a small hand, the smaller ones the size of business cards. Most are glazed, and slightly curved. The broken edges reveal that they are very coarse sand pots, with thick, vitreous glazes of different colours: dark brown, lighter brown, bluish-purple, greyish-green. A mosaic builds up. I take a photograph.

What were they used for, and why do they remain in such quantity? I sent the photograph to Wang Ning, a ceramics expert formerly of Sotheby's. 'The photo is very interesting, although it's extremely difficult, if not impossible, to figure out the age of the

DESCRIPTION:	Glazed pottery sherds
SIGNIFICANCE:	An indication of the large amount of water used in certain sections of the Wall
ORIGIN:	Found beside rammed sections of Ming Great Wall in the Ningxia Hui Autonomous Region, China
LOCATION:	Author's collection, Beijing

sherds,' he writes. 'The vessels would seem to have been utilitarian – the glaze indicating they were probably used for water retention; unglazed pots are porous. Judging by the lipped rims on some of them, the earliest possible date for them would be Ming, but they could also be much later, even as late as the twentieth century, because water storage jars never changed much from Ming times.'

So we know the jars were used for water storage, and that they do almost certainly date from the Ming, when people either built the Wall here or were garrisoned upon it. But why were the pots so large, I wondered. From their curvatures I estimated they were about an arm's length in diameter, and more than waist-high.

I found what I believed to be the missing link within an hour; like the potsherds themselves, it was right beside the Wall. A piece of stone, worked, not natural in shape, that had a hollowed centre into which a pole-like handle could be inserted. It was the rock head of a broken ramming tool used by the Wall builders, who tamped down the damp earth within a wooden frame as they built up, layer by layer, the seven-metre height of the Wall.

Another memorable Great Wall experience provided the background details. As a geologist, I had learned to appreciate the guiding principle of uniformitarianism: the idea that present processes show us how past environments were created. In China, I knew, occasionally it was possible to see how things were done in the past from how they are still being done today. In Gansu I had stumbled across a team of villagers building a rammed-earth wall. They used versions of the tool I had found, and did their ramming work to the collective chant of a folk song about Meng Jiangnü's tears bringing down the Wall (see Object 2). Strangely, they were working on a day when summer thunderstorms rumbled all around, and it was raining. I asked why.

'Just after the rain is the perfect time,' they told me. 'It saves us bringing in the water – that would be very troublesome, as our water source is so far away.'

And that, I'm sure, is our answer. These large containers were originally used for storing water 'imported' as an essential material for building the rammed-earth Wall, which required wet earth. We may never know how far the water was carted – maybe a few hundred metres or a few kilometres from a well, or perhaps as far as 30 kilometres away, from the Yellow River. It's almost certain too, that once building of this section of Wall had been completed, the containers continued to be used for water storage by the soldiers garrisoned at the Wall. I found some potsherds on the tops of watchtowers, also made of rammed earth, suggesting just such an 'after use' by soldiers.

There they have lain since, broken by nature or smashed to prevent others from using them, until now. For, whether in a museum or the field, to most who see them, they are simply boring old potsherds to be walked past.

6.

PREFABRICATION

An inscribed brick from the Ming Wall

In my search for a single object that would convey most vividly the immense human effort that went into the construction of the Great Wall, I was on the lookout for the tools used to cut its rocks. Standing at the foot of a sheer face of the Ming Wall's megalithic foundation blocks, I saw hundreds of chisel marks. As I ran my finger down one of these striations, I felt in contact with the quarryman who had cut the stone. I could almost hear the cacophony of chisels clashing with rock crystals.

At the zenith of Wall building, in the 1570s, perhaps tens of thousands of stonemasons were at work. They've long since gone but their work still stands. And it bears hundreds of thousands of indelible signatures: their chisel marks. But where have all the chisels gone? There must have been thousands in use.

I found one exhibited in Shanhaiguan's Great Wall Museum, but the curator, Mr Pan Yue, expressed reservations about its provenance and age. That's because chisels, being indestructible, would never have been retired from duty – they were just used and used. It was possible that the museum's chisel had been used decades earlier; while it may have been used to cut rocks for the Great Wall nearby, nothing had been proved. Amazingly, these objects have, since their duties' end, been inherited and reused, not put aside, collected and treasured as antiquities. Their absence from collections of relics is conspicuous, and that itself is a point to be learned.

What, then, is my object representing labour and materials? It's something almost as vivid as a chisel: a brick from the Wall. It is not a standard brick, which were produced by the million, but a much rarer example known as a 'stamped brick'. Like a chisel, it carries a chain of individuals' fingerprints, from kiln worker to porter to bricklayer. This object was made. Somebody stamped its moist clay with a relief-carved wooden chop bearing Chinese characters, and then put it into a kiln. After firing, it was removed, stacked and then transported – probably several kilometres at least, but maybe much more – to its place of use, the building site of a section of the Great Wall. There, it was placed in the battlement by a bricklayer, who used a trowel to ladle on mortar. Finally, he 'pointed' the mortar – spread it flatly and neatly – between the bricks. And there it stood for several centuries, until it was gouged out and gathered as a museum piece because it had an inscription.

As a Great Wall building material, brick ranks as a latecomer. Bricks were only used on the Ming Great Wall, and not in any pre-Ming structures. (I am excluding adobe bricks, which are sunbaked, not kiln-fired.) Bricks allowed architects to incorporate design features to make the ramparts more 'user-friendly' for the guards posted along them. The standard size and weight of bricks made construction easier, too. Formatted sections of Wall became the norm, with loopholes and embrasures spaced out along the battlements in an organised way.

The use of bricks increased from the 1570s. As more were produced, at a higher cost, efforts were made to ensure their quality, which could vary greatly depending on the materials and methods used. Many existing sections of the Wall were widened or heightened around the 1570s, with the makeover materials being bricks. This period could be called the 'brick renovation' of the Great Wall.

Bricks can be found with a number of different types of inscription. This particular example weighs the standard 12.5 kilograms; bricks can weigh a few hundred grams less because of weathering or chips along their surfaces. That's heavy – about the weight of a small bag of grocery shopping. The inscription on our brick is deep, and the eight characters, enclosed within an oblong cartouche, read: *Wanli shiernian Luanzhou zuo*. This translates as 'Made in the twelfth year of the Wanli Emperor's reign at Luanzhou [in Hebei]' – that is, in 1584. Other stamped bricks recorded the army division that was building the section, or simply the kiln from which bricks were sourced. Some bear a chop reading *cha shou jian*, pronouncing them as having been inspected and approved for use.

According to *Tiangong Kaiwu*, or 'The Exploitation of the Works of Nature', an early seventeenth-century manual of Chinese technological processes compiled by Song Yingxing, the best earth for bricks should be 'sticky' and dug from beneath cropland. It then underwent cold processing, exposing it to sun and rain for some days, to rid it of impurities through decomposition. Mounds would be dug over by workers, watered and left to dry, then churned by the treading of oxen, a process repeated for two to three weeks. Next, workers packed the damp, sticky earth into wooden brick moulds. The bricks were then dried (but not sun-dried) for between one and two months before being fired.

The largest extant 'brickworks' at the Great Wall was discovered at Banchangyu, Funing County, Hebei Province, in 1999. There, some sixty-six kilns are estimated to have produced around 300 000 bricks per month – truly industrial-scale production. Hand in hand with such voluminous and higher-cost production

DESCRIPTION:	A brick bearing a stamped inscription from the Ming Dynasty Great Wall, made in AD 1584
SIGNIFICANCE:	The most widely used 'prefabricated' building material in the Ming Great Wall
ORIGIN:	Luanzhou, near Tangshan, Hebei Province
LOCATION:	Shanhaiguan Great Wall Museum

came efforts to ensure the bricks' quality, and to prevent profiteering and use of sub-standard materials.

Firing was the most important stage of all. The temperature inside the kiln was maintained between 800 and 1000 degrees Celsius. The top of a kiln would be closed to reduce the amount of oxygen inside the firing chamber; through the chemical process that took place, brown dried bricks would become 'baked' bluish-grey. Each firing took several days. Bricks were then ready to begin their journey up to the Wall, along the Wall, and down through the ages.

The use of bricks on the Ming Wall marks the structure's modernisation by the use of standardised materials. Production-line manufacturing at an unprecedented scale was required. Quality checks and stamping, recording when the bricks were made, where, for whom and by whom, were carried out. These procedures signify the instigation of a system that ensured the Wall would stand fast against China's enemies over many centuries. When we look at this brick, and at the millions of others like it, we can see that they have stood the test of time.

7.

ACCELERATED WARFARE

Bronze mirror showing cavalry

If you asked someone from each continent to name their most loyal ally in war over the centuries, even millennia, the deepest thinkers would likely give the same unexpected answer: the horse.

Dogs may be man's best friend, but in conflict the horse has been pre-eminent for around 5000 years. Rameses II (or 'the Great') fought the Hittites at the Battle of Kadesh with his chariots in 1274 BC. The Duke of Wellington defeated Napoleon at the Battle of Waterloo in 1815, with his cavalry prominent. A century or so ago the British used an estimated 6 million horses in World War I. It was this cataclysmic clash, however, that spurred new battle innovations, and the tank was invented to break the deadlock of trench warfare.

It's an understatement to say that the horse has a major role in the Great Wall's story. In brief, a Great Wall exists to stop horses. Without horses, the nomadic people of the north lacked any means of attacking the sedentary societies of the south. Later we'll explore the horse's transportation advantages, but at this point we will focus on an object that warns of a new style of warfare on China's northern perimeter: archers on horseback. Their appearance forced the Chinese to change the way they fought and invent

DESCRIPTION:	Bronze mirror with engravings of mounted horsemen
SIGNIFICANCE:	An early depiction of nomadic cavalry
ORIGIN:	Khuld Soum, Dungovi Province, Mongolia, between the ninth and eighth centuries BC
LOCATION:	Museum of the Great Hunnu Empire, Erdene, Ulaanbaatar; private collection of the late Mr Purevjav Erdenechuluun (access courtesy of Mrs Nemkhehbayer)

border defence walls. This violent cultural conflict precipitates the Great Wall story.

Within the splendid bronze collection of the late Mr Purevjav Erdenechuluun in Ulaanbaatar there are many artefacts depicting horses. Our object, a bronze mirror, is the first to show the strong alliance between man and horse in warfare on the Mongolian Steppe. Its front was smooth and highly polished, creating a reflective surface, while a naive decorative scene showing two riders in collision was etched on its rougher reverse. One rider carries a bow and arrow, drawn and at the ready, while the other prepares to fend off the attack with his shield. It is one of the earliest known depictions of cavalry conflict not only in the region but worldwide.

Man's special relationship with the horse on the Mongolian steppe began in around 3000 BC. Wild horses were captured. As herders managed other domesticated animals, the horse assumed its upper-class role, becoming the most prized among the 'six snouts'. Horses provided swift, personal transport, which allowed riders to overcome survival challenges and advantage themselves in the hunt for wild animals that were fleet of foot and, in time, against stationary and cumbersome human opponents. But that was still a few centuries away.

In 2012 I watched a six-year-old boy riding a horse around his family's *ger*, or felt tent, on Mongolia's Eastern Steppe. Each child of every nomadic family learns to ride within a few years of learning to walk, and throughout their lives riding is an extension of their own mobility: vital to their very existence. Traditionally, a man's wealth was measured in the number of horses he owned, and to go on foot signified poverty.

Herding always involved a quest for greener pastures over the horizon, leading herders to new seek ground and hunting opportunities. This helped hone their archery skills. Hunting on horseback advantaged man against wild animals, in both speed and endurance. Expeditions frequently resulted in interactions with adjacent clans, and violent conflict often arose over access to the most desirable pastures, rivers, lakes and wells. Travel on horseback, hunting and fighting thus became commonplace, and the people of the steppe became good at it.

At this time riders rode without the aid of stirrups, which would only be invented during the third century AD (see Object 10). Controversy therefore exists over how effectively 'pre-stirrup' nomadic cavalrymen could fight. As riders lacked stability on their mounts, it may have been that horses functioned primarily as transportation rather than as true 'war horses': men may have had to halt, or even dismount, in order to fire their bows. Whatever methods were used, the sedentary crop-growing people of China first encountered hostile nomadic cavalry in around the fifth century BC.

Among the earliest recorded events were those occurring circa 300 BC, by which time, based on our object's approximate date, the nomadic peoples of the steppe had already accrued several centuries' cavalry experience. Archery from horseback had become a traditional and highly valued military skill. In the Great Wall theatre of war that was to be, these swift, manoeuvrable warriors notched up decisive victories against their opponents, who at the time were either on foot or in chariots. Infantry fighters were slow and low, while chariots were limited to flat ground.

The use of cavalry created a new type of military engagement. An army could now strike by surprise, and was not restricted to flat, open ground. Horsemen could retreat as quickly as they attacked. Their Chinese opponents couldn't beat them, so they tried at first to copy them. King Wuling of the Zhao State, circa 300 BC, trained his infantry in horse-riding and archery; he even advocated the redesign of warriors' robes to make arrow handling, nocking (loading) and drawing the bow easier. Still, it remained amateurs against professionals. Months or years of practice was no match for a lifetime's, and the nomads' cavalry maintained their dominance. The challenge of excelling at both horsemanship and archery proved immensely difficult.

We have reason to believe that the steppe nomads were perhaps the earliest and most excellent archers of all. Our bronze mirror's engravings show both an attacker and a defender riding and fighting, whereas archaeological evidence from elsewhere, although almost the same time – Assyrian bas-reliefs dating from the ninth century BC – show the Arabian horse (which is much larger) carrying two riders, one for controlling the horse and the second in pillion for archery. The apprenticeship of life on the steppe appears to have given people there the skills to perform both tasks simultaneously.

King Wuling (circa 325–299 BC) of the Zhao State was among the first Chinese monarchs ruling territory that fringed nomadic lands to adapt the time-honoured tactic of enclosing towns and cities in walls. For millennia walls had been signature defence structures across China, but Wuling adapted them to his own local needs, changing their shape, scale and location. He built high defences that ran across the countryside for an extraordinary length. Thus, the *chang cheng*, or 'long wall', appeared as a new-style defence in the increasingly regular conflicts between peoples of the north and the south.

8.

DECISIVE ADVANTAGE

A nomadic composite bow

As a child, I soon progressed from throwing stones and using a pole as a cudgel, spear or sword to making a bow. With sticks abounding in the woods, I searched for ones that were long, straight and of even thickness. Most importantly, they had to be flexible and springy. After making a notch at either end, I would knot a length of garden string in one. To complete the stringing, I would flex the stick to a concave form and then attach the string to the other end. My bowstring would 'twang' promisingly, like a harp, giving a hint of its potential. Short garden canes were readymade arrows: straight and light. All I needed to do was cut a notch at one end and sharpen the other.

For me, the thrill of using a bow and arrow for the first time was a milestone of childhood, like learning to ride a bike or swim. Archery extends your capability: instead of being limited by the strength of your arm, you can suddenly reach much further, and faster. My arrows – especially the first clusters – flew with impressive speed, covering quite a distance. But there was a limit: my bows never lasted too long. They seemed to be 'pre-loaded' with a set number of shots, or several days' use, and then they'd virtually self-destruct. When drawn, there would be a heart-wrenching snapping noise – technically known as an 'exploding' bow. The outside edge of the bow always tore apart from repeated use.

This simple childhood experience linked me with the history of weapons development. As a Briton, naturally I came to know first of Robin Hood's exploits, and of the showers of arrows discharged from the English longbow archers at Agincourt in 1415. But it was universally accepted that the world's greatest archers were in fact the Mongols, who rode out of the steppe in the thirteenth century and conquered half the world with their bows.

A specimen of what they used is displayed at the Museum of the Great Hunnu Empire, outside Ulaanbaatar. It's a fragment of its former self. Rather like the chisels we've already met (see Object 6), these bows were once ubiquitous, but precious few remain. That's because their four organic components are preserved only under fairly long-shot circumstances, both social and environmental. Compounding the problem is the fact that Mongol bows were laminated, and things joined together tend to fall apart along the joins.

How, therefore, might we appreciate what the notoriously lethal Mongol bow and archer was actually capable of? In the National Museum of Mongolian History in Ulaanbaatar is a replica of the 'Genghis Khan Stele', a piece of granite about 1.5 metres "in height; the original is in the State Hermitage Museum in St. Petersburg, Russia. The five-line inscription in Uighur-Mongol script lets us appreciate what the bow, in a marksman's hands, was capable of achieving. It reads: 'After his conquest of Sartaul [the Khwarazm Empire, centred around today's Uzbekistan], Genghis Khan convened an assembly of Mongolian dignitaries, at which Esungge hit a target from 335 *alds* [536 metres].' The assembly, circa AD 1225, seems to have included a *naddam*, or celebration of the three manly sports, one of which was archery. Esungge's ultra-distance crack shot was well worth commemoration – it was an incredibly long and accurate shot.

The historian's dream is, of course, to go back in time and see how things were actually done. I'm always on the lookout for what I call living continuities: examples of the same process or activities continuing unchanged, to this day. The *naddam* remains as an annual display of Mongolia's martial and equestrian culture. Archery is a top sport. Archers don't use modern carbon fibre bows, the kinds you see during an Olympic archery competition; they still use their culture's traditional composite bows. Surely someone, somewhere in Mongolia, must still craft them, I speculated, and I set out to find them.

After making enquiries, I visit an apartment cum workshop in a tenement block in Ulaanbaatar's suburbs. Dozens of half-made bow frames hang on the walls. In a corner of the room is a pile of ibex horns. Bunches of deer sinews are hung up to dry. Perched on a bench rests a vulture's wing, waiting to be plucked by a fletcher. Using a wheezing blowlamp, a young lad puts finishing touches to an arrowhead. I've found the closest thing to a medieval bowyer in today's Mongolia: the bow and arrow workshop of Batmunkh and son.

Batmunkh hands me one of his 'unstrung' bows. It's about 1.5 metres long. One side is pale birch bark, naively decorated with black motifs, which cover the bow's birch spine. The belly is marbled horn, with evenly spaced bands of fibrous strands – ten in total – covered by some kind of resin. Overall, the bow has a wavy form with two straight ends.

I feel the weapon's power as I'm taught to 'string' the bow. I'm sat down, knees apart, my palms facing upwards and at arm's length. I'm instructed to grip both ends of the bow at the interfaces between its curvy limbs and straight ends, and pull it forcefully against my knees, which are positioned on either side of the bow's leather handle.

I pull, then I pull harder. The bow hardly flexes and my knees feel the force. I pull much, much harder, actually concerned that the bow might fracture; I'm using a great amount of strength now, and I'm uncertain whether the wood, let alone the horn, is capable of withstanding such stress.

'Agh, you need to pull much harder!' the Batmunkhs chorus.

With my knees and abdomen braced for the big pull, I unleash my greatest effort, finally flexing the bow just enough to allow Batmunkh to seat the loops at either end of the bowstring in their notches. The shape of the bow has been completely transformed: it is now 'recurved'. Holding it in my left hand, I see how its flat ends are angled away from me. I strum the bowstring – it's extremely taut. The bow is now alive.

Outside, in open space, I use my three middle fingers to draw the string. Batmunkh has told me this bow has a twenty-seven kilogram draw weight. That means drawing it is like lifting your check-in and carry-on bags together – with just three fingers. The recurve 'unwinds' and the bow appears to change from having two parts to just one. Its limbs lengthen, and the mechanical advantage of its unique construction begins to manifest itself. The stress in the bow's limbs – the tension along its outside face, and the compression along its inside belly – will be transferred to the string at the moment of release.

When I shoot, the arrow flies fast, high and far. Much faster, higher and further than my homemade bows ever fired. At 300 kilometres per hour the arrow arcs towards a target some sixty metres away.

What I find amazing about this method of bow manufacture is the fact that laminating different materials together produces a weapon that is actually strengthened – to such an extent that it afforded the Mongols massive advantages over their enemies. According to Dr Gongor Lhagvasuren, deputy director of the

Mongolian National Institute of Physical Education: 'The stele of Genghis Khan explains in part the excellence of the Mongolian military and the reasons for their successful thirteenth-century campaigns.'

I see the Mongolian composite bow as a product of necessity and environment, a masterpiece of materials and mechanics. Necessity drives invention, and the harsh steppe life was initially dependent on hunting. Hunters competed against the swiftness of animals and sought technical advantages to complement their stealth. A major advantage came in the form of the laminated bow, which contained materials that could withstand enormous stresses, and store and transfer energy efficiently.

What's the secret of the composite bow? I have experienced the weapon's power on the shooting range, but I don't fully understand it. Back in his workshop, Batmunkh talks me through the bow's production, from one year ago. All the raw materials are laid out before me. The curved ibex horn and birch frame are familiar, but two others are not. These are thin, whitish fibres about ten to twelve centimetres in length, and dark brown vitreous blocks.

Batmunkh holds the fibres and points to his lower calf. 'These sinews are made from tendons – usually from deer. I cover the back of the bow with them, building up a layer that's glued on with this animal resin.' He points to the dark, vitreous blocks.

Tendons link muscle to bone. They contain a collagen protein called elastogen, and have four times the tensile (stretching) strength of wood. Batmunkh lays the deer sinews along the outside length of the birch, giving immense tensile strength to the bow in the area of its greatest tension. This was exactly the point at which my own bows always broke.

While tension creates the force along the bow's back, its opposite – compression – is at its greatest on the bow's inside, its belly. Batmunkh hands me sawn strips of horn, straightened out

DESCRIPTION:	Remains of a Mongol warrior's composite bow
SIGNIFICANCE:	The most feared weapon in the Great Wall theatre of war for 2000 years
ORIGIN:	From the Genghis Khan Period, circa AD 1200
LOCATION:	Museum of the Great Hunnu Empire, Erdene, Ulaanbaatar; private collection of the late Mr Purevjav Erdenechuluun (access courtesy of Mrs Nemkhehbayer)

through boiling. This horn outperforms wood when compressed: it can yield four per cent, compared to wood's one per cent.

On a finished bow, since the back is covered in tree bark for protection against moisture, you can't see the sinewed back, nor the glued interface between the birch and the horn. But on the bow's belly you can see thick horizontal bindings of glue-coated sinew, running the full length of the bow. These provide added strength and stability. It looks like fibreglass and is incredibly hard.

Nomads discovered the existence and qualities – strength, elasticity and adhesiveness – of animals' anatomical components as they butchered and cooked them. Nevertheless, it remains a mystery when and how they harnessed these qualities to craft weapons that gave them such advantages, in both hunting and warfare.

In the Great Wall theatre of war, composite bows in the hands of Mongols, along with their brute strength and marksmanship, made the weapon decisively advantageous in long-distance combat manoeuvres on various battlegrounds, from overcoming their first resistance along what border walls existed at that time, built by the Jin and Western Xia dynasties, to besieging and winning walled towns and cities that lay ahead in their path. Bows were their old friends, stalwarts, whose fatal use put fear into their unfortunate foes, for no other archers could compete with the Mongolian's composite bow, nor his strength and skill in using it.

Part Two

FOUNDATIONS

Objects from the third century BC to AD 221

From around 300 BC, conflicts began to create a single China. The ruling regimes became fewer, and controlled larger territories and populations. By 221 BC, and for the first time, one man, Emperor Qin Shihuang, ruled a unified land. Scale featured in all his plans. City walls were firmly established urban structures, while long point-to-point defences were newcomers. Qin Shihuang's vision was to link and extend the 'long walls' he had inherited from the former warring states into a single 'Endless Wall'.

His longevity, however, proved short. The Han Dynasty rose in 206 BC and extended their rule westward, and the Wall with it.

The Qin–Han period saw the laying of state foundations, the beginning of 'Chinese-ness'. Characters, coinage and cart-axle lengths were standardised, and dissidents destroyed. Society and urban life matured, the economy grew and transcontinental trade emerged along the Silk Road. Taxes were levied, censuses conducted, laws established and official histories compiled. Statecraft emerged.

One Great Wall was built, and another upon it. They, too, were national foundation stones, strategic precedents, which would be built upon in perpetuity.

9.

THE IRON AGE FACTOR

Mould for casting iron chisels

I witnessed the process of iron smelting only a handful of times in my twenty-five years at the Great Wall. The first occasion was the most striking, though at the time I didn't realise its significance.

I was wandering through a small fortified town tucked inside the 'inner' Great Wall of the Ming, in northern Shanxi Province: within a wall beside the Wall. Guangwu seemed to me to be a true enclave of antiquity, and more vividly so when I stumbled across a very ancient trade being practised there. Although it was 1995, I could have easily been observing a scene from 195 BC. Ironware was being remade from scrap.

With some minor differences, the oil-drum furnace was a makeshift version of an ancient smelter, and to Chinese no doubt a reminder of the 'backyard' furnaces that were set up during the Great Leap Forward of the late 1950s, as China tried to increase its iron and steel production by melting scrap.

What I saw was a very elemental process. An old man was using fire, wood, coal, air and water to melt metal and reshape it into something useful. He pumped a continuous stream of air into the base of this mini furnace, keeping the fire glowing

orange. Inside the drum was a crucible containing the scrap metal to be melted. Finally, he poured the molten iron into rough
moulds, and made some finishing touches with his simple tools.

But since when have such tools been 'simple'? Not since
500 BC or so.

We think of pliers and hammers as everyday items. But watching this man at work made me realise that our ability to create
such things was truly momentous. We find a heavier than usual
rock – iron ore – and then heat it and melt it down, separating
pure metal from other mineral impurities. Then we pour it into a
container, casting it in the specific shape of a tool. Of course, the
period in which humans made this discovery is known universally
as the Iron Age.

Our present object – an iron mould for casting two chisels – is
one of the oldest featured in this series. It was excavated in 1953
at Gudonggou, not in Shanxi, where I intensely watched smelting
for the first time, but in the neighbouring province of Hebei. It is
displayed in the stunning permanent exhibition called 'Ancient
China' at Beijing's National Museum of China, although most
visitors walk right past it.

They are captivated instead by the older and more visually stunning 'bronzes' on display nearby. But those objects, although metal, are very different. They are gorgeous, and intricate. Being cast
in bronze – an alloy of copper and tin – they were made mainly
for ritual use, so were rarities even back then, in the Bronze Age.

What I am looking at from Gudonggou is vastly different. It's
unattractive. It's plain. It was a utility. And although iron is relatively plentiful, occurring as a high-grade ore, that made it extremely difficult to soften, let alone melt. This is what makes our
object even more special technologically. It's the earliest known
iron mould for casting basic tools.

This mould was found together with eighty-six other similarly

DESCRIPTION:	Iron mould for casting two chisels simultaneously; excavated in 1953 at Xinglong County, Hebei Province
SIGNIFICANCE:	Mass production of iron tools (harder and sharper), enabling large-scale construction projects
ORIGIN:	Made circa 280 BC at a foundry of the Yan State, about 100 kilometres north-east of today's Beijing
LOCATION:	National Museum of China, Beijing

utilitarian artefacts. Clearly, it was a cache of tools from a foundry, and it's been dated to approximately 280 BC. Archaeologists in China have found scores of sites yielding ironware dating from circa 300 BC or earlier. They are widely distributed, from Guangdong in the south to Inner Mongolia in the north. Finds are scattered throughout the territories of the seven most powerful states of the Warring States Period (476–221 BC).

The Iron Age was a worldwide revolution. It seems to have happened in numerous locations independently, sometimes sooner, sometimes later. But it was far from equal in quality. Today, there are approximately 3 million English-speaking people in North America, the United Kingdom and Australasia who have the family name Smith. As many Western names do, this one reveals the occupation of the first Smiths. The word *smite* of course means 'to hit with a firm blow', and that's the way 'smithies' shaped iron 'bloom' (softened yet impure iron). In China, however, due to more advanced levels of innovation, iron could be melted and cast in the same way as bronze, despite the fact that iron has a much higher melting point. Casting of iron was achieved by the Chinese an astonishing 1000 years ahead of the West.

How was it done? A constant blast of air was pumped into a furnace. Anyone who has kindled a campfire knows how gentle blowing nurtures the flames. Next, heat was sustained by advanced insulation, using heat-proof clays. Finally, the melting point of the iron ore was cleverly reduced by adding phosphoric-rich chernozem soil, or 'black earth', common in Manchuria, to the iron ore and charcoal mixture. These methods permitted early Chinese metallurgists to raise the temperatures of their 'blast furnaces' to around 1000 degrees Celsius and produce molten iron.

In Europe, the spongey 'bloom' was the best that could be produced in a furnace; it then had to be hammered into shape by smithing. The product was rough. But in China, casting in moulds permitted the mass production of precisely shaped tools and other wares. Products were refined until they were perfect for the job, and this enabled large-scale building works to take place.

But how might the iron mould itself react to contact with molten iron? Would it not crack, even melt, with the thermal shock? Professor Christopher Cullen, emeritus director of the (Joseph) Needham Research Institute at Cambridge University, a specialist in the history of science in China, explains: 'A large piece of solid metal, which conducts heat relatively well, does not reach melting point just because some liquid metal above melting point is brought into contact with it. The mass of the mould is in general larger than the mass of the object cast in it.'

This object's function – the reproductive capability it permitted – is a milestone in technological innovation and had a marked impact on Great Wall building. Imagine how many chisels were cast using this mould, day after day, week after week, year after year. Operating at such scale, this tooling revolution opened a new frontier in construction.

Previously, most Walls had been made by ramming earth to compactness. In some areas, surface stones were used as building materials. But the construction technique remained limited, due to a lack of tools with sufficient sharpness and tensile strength. Workers were unable to efficiently quarry small, manageable pieces of rock from large, immovable outcrops or rock faces. You couldn't use a bronze tool to work a much harder stone surface. That changed during the middle years of the Warring States Period.

As neighbouring states contested for wider power, battles were commonplace. Technology provided a greater array of weapons, some made from the new material of iron. Our iron mould can thus be seen as a technological response to a need for better defences. From the late fourth century BC to the early third century BC, many coexisting states built long walls; most were for 'civil' defence. While much of the lengths of these structures were made of earth and field stones, at least some appear to have been made in a new way, using quarried rock. The iron chisels produced at the Xinglong foundry may have been used to quarry rock in an area that corresponds to the Yan State, which was centred on today's Beijing region.

However, there was still one major problem to overcome before the true potential of iron tools could be unleashed, as Professor Cullen points out: 'Simple "cold-casting" of iron produces a very hard but brittle high-carbon product that you would not want to hit hard with a hammer, or against anything hard, lest it should shatter. So if you want to cast an iron tool that will be useful, you need to heat-treat it carefully, which changes its microstructure so you get "malleable" iron.' The Chinese did this from the fourth century BC.

The Yan State is thought to have built defences that measured approximately 800 kilometres in total length. It's an important structure because it was one of the three pre-existing long walls that, under Emperor Qin Shihuang's orders, were joined together around 215 BC to form a structure that was described as a *Wanli Changcheng*, or Great Wall (see Object 11). The other two long walls were the Emperor's own Qin State Wall and the Zhao State Wall, built by King Wuling (see Object 7).

Remnants of the Zhao Wall can be found in the dry hills of the Wulaite Qianqi, north of Baotou in today's Inner Mongolia Autonomous Region. Some sections are composed of angular blocks that appear to have been forcefully freed from rock faces using efficient tools, such as hammers and chisels. As I run my hands along that Wall's sharp edges, I can feel the proximity of history, created by quarrymen using hard, strong and sharp iron tools produced twenty-three centuries ago.

10.

SURE FOOTING

A bronze stirrup

Cars and good roads are a relatively recent feature of life in China. Until the post-millennium car boom, most Chinese transported themselves on rickety bicycles via potholed roads. It's something that most of us have experienced.

Do you recall pedalling along and spotting a hole in the road ahead that was unavoidable? You probably 'rode' the bump by standing on the pedals and lifting yourself out of the saddle, thus avoiding the impact to your backside and spine. What you did was instinctively use your natural suspension. You let your leg muscles absorb the shock.

Before the bike, humankind's mass transportation method was the horse. (I've already explored one aspect of man's relationship with this incredibly useful animal – see Object 7.) But today, few people have ridden horses for long, and even fewer at speed. So you may have to imagine the following. A horse's locomotion is similar to a human's, only it's faster and takes bigger jumps as it runs. So how do riders absorb the constant shocks that are transmitted, let alone the major jolts when horses negotiate very uneven ground? Just like cyclists, they lift themselves out of the saddle. They use their coordination and instinct – horsemanship – to protect themselves from the immense shocks.

However, for most of man's horse-riding history, whether hunting, travelling or fighting, he never had the benefit of stirrups. Battles fought by the armies of the ancient world – the Babylonians, Egyptians, Assyrians, Greeks, Persians, Macedonians and Romans – all featured armies riding horses without stirrups. The bloody conflicts of the entire Warring States Period, the Qin and Han dynasties too, were all fought 'pre-stirrup'.

How? Some riders probably needed 'leg-ups' to mount, and all rode with their legs simply dangling down while gripping with their knees to remain saddled. Amazingly, the stirrup appears to have been invented only in the early fourth century. Our object is one of the earliest known examples. It's a fine specimen in cast bronze, and is believed to have been made during the stirrup's opening century, circa AD 350.

A few days after examining this 1660-year-old object in a museum in Ulaanbaatar, I observed the contemporary use of stirrups. On Mongolia's Eastern Steppe, the largest pristine temperate grassland in the world, I needed water, so I called by one of the few *gers*, or tented farmsteads, one might see in a whole day to ask permission to use the local well. I chanced upon a warm-hearted family with three children, and was invited inside to drink milk tea.

Before long, the family's two daughters proudly mounted their horses and gave us a riding display. Their little brother was determined not to be left out. His sister had no choice but give him a turn. She helped him climb onto the saddle by interlocking the fingers of both her hands to make a 'hand stirrup'. Then he took the reins and rode beside her, with his tiny feet way above the stirrups.

For the next year or so he'd be getting more practice in the saddle, coordinating his movement to the horse's natural motion – in

DESCRIPTION:	A bronze stirrup
SIGNIFICANCE:	Invention providing greater stability for mounted archers and comfort for riders
ORIGIN:	Made circa 350 AD, Northern Xianbei Period
LOCATION:	Museum of the Great Hunnu Empire, at the Genghis Khan Statue, Ulaanbaatar

other words, developing his riding skills. By the time he was seven or eight his legs would be long enough to reach the stirrups. He'd be able to mount alone and ride for longer periods. If he hunts any of the swift animals that roam the steppe, the stability that stirrups provide will give him a better chance of bringing home some meat. From lad to youth, he'll be moving from no stirrups to stirrups, from no suspension to shock-absorption – the same journey his ancestors made about 1660 years ago.

The stirrup proper is credited by some as a Chinese invention, based on the earliest evidence dating from the Western Jin (AD 265–316). A tomb discovered in 1958 at Jinpanling, near Changsha, Hunan Province, and dating from AD 302, contained seven figurines of horsemen forming a guard of honour, some of whom have stirrups. I examined them at the National Museum of China, where they are displayed within the 'Ancient China' collection, and a few things were immediately apparent. First, the cast stirrups are 'single' – that is, they are only fixed on one side of the saddles. Second, not all seven horsemen have them. Third, those who do have them don't have their feet in them!

It appears likely that single stirrups were simply an aid to mounting. This idea is confirmed by the fact that the Jinpanling horsemen are not using their stirrups once seated. And they are probably not present across the whole group because stirrups were difficult objects to produce; they were confined to the higher-ranking members of the guard. In other words, although we see cast stirrups dating from AD 302, their full potential had not been realised. The tomb figurines' stirrups can therefore be regarded as an intermediate stage in their development.

Researchers credit the origins of the stirrup to steppe nomads, who may have been the first to use a simple leather loop, or perhaps a bone 'pedal', to assist them as they mounted up. This design was probably improved upon – in cast metal – by the Jin horsemen, and soon after was greatly improved by their larger-scale production and their double use, which helped balance riders and permitted a much smoother journey, and more accurate discharge of missiles.

Advantaged by developing the invention, the Chinese may have enjoyed parity with, or even short-lived superiority against their nomadic adversaries, who possessed innately superior riding skills. Before long, however, the Chinese faced nomadic cavalrymen who had also begun using stirrups, as our object from the north evidences. Use of stirrups thus spread to all in the Great Wall theatre of conflict, and eventually across Asia to Europe, but not swiftly: their production depended on metallurgical casting expertise.

Stirrups greatly accelerated the pace and ferocity of cavalry warfare. Marksmanship improved, which in turn triggered the need for more, and heavier, armour (see Object 19). Meanwhile, the use of infantry forces waned, while clumsy chariots were banished to the annals of history.

'Prior to the stirrup, nomads could cross the steppe and desert by horse, but only with great difficulty because they had to hold on with their legs, and then they had to dismount for effective combat,' says Professor Jack Weatherford, author of *Genghis Khan and the Making of the Modern World*. 'The stirrup made long treks on horseback much easier because the rider could eat and even sleep for extended periods without fear of falling. The greatest change, however, meant that for the first time the nomads could fight from horseback as the stirrup freed up their arms and hands. It steadied the rider enough that he could fire while attacking at speed. Stirrups changed herders into warriors.'

11.

AN EYEWITNESS REPORT

Sima Qian's Records of the Grand Historian

What criteria do we use to gauge the success of a book? That depends on who we are. Publishers measure copies sold, frequency of reprints, translations and international editions. Agents look for sustainability: what's the likelihood of a sequel, or two, or more? Critics emphasise the importance of good reviews and literary awards. Authors want all of the above. Readers buy – but that's only the beginning.

I've asked a random collection of readers how they judge a book, and most give a similar answer. They ultimately rate a book's worth on whether they find what they are looking for – inspiration, information or whatever – within its pages.

Me too. Approaching ancient China's twenty-four 'official' histories (*Ershisi Shi*), which sit at the heart of the culture's vast corpus of historical writing, I'm hoping to find what I'm looking for: insights into the Great Wall's story which I can't find in the field. Later in this series we'll meet a completely fictitious work about the Wall's builders and a century-old account of its first exploration, and few other textual sources too. But I'm only including one ancient 'history book': *Records of the Grand Historian*.

It's regarded as the first of ancient China's twenty-four *Zhengshi*,

DESCRIPTION:	*Shiji (Records of the Grand Historian)*, authored from the late second century BC to the early first century BC, by Sima Qian (Qing Dynasty edition, printed 1875)
SIGNIFICANCE:	First eyewitness account of the Great Wall; first accurate 'military intelligence' on the state's main enemy, the Xiongnu
ORIGIN:	Originally written on bamboo slips, studied over the centuries in more than sixty editions; the oldest extant edition dates from the sixth century
LOCATION:	Rare Books Collection, Peking University Library

or official dynastic histories. Judging its achievements against the benchmarks of success mentioned above, it scores highly on all fronts. It's been reprinted an estimated sixty times since it was written, with a brush, on bamboo slips back in the second century BC (before the widespread use of paper). It first went international circa AD 600, with a Japanese edition, and set the standard for the future compilation which every legitimate ruling dynasty aimed to produce about its predecessor.

This work about China's opening historical chapter has its own history, which puts it among the world's earliest works, alongside Homer's *Iliad* (eighth century BC), Herodotus' *Histories* (fifth century BC) and Thucydides' *History of the Peloponnesian War* (fifth century BC). *Shiji* was written by Sima Qian, who lived between around 145 BC and 86 BC.

In it I find what I'm looking for as a reader and researcher: a first-person account relating to the Great Wall. Just a few relevant paragraphs lie buried, here and there, within its half a million characters, spread across 130 chapters. Given the scale of Sima Qian's task (inherited in 110 BC from his father, Sima Tan) – to complete a chronicle of China history from its beginnings to the present day – we cannot expect to find too much space devoted to border walls. But what little we get is worth its weight in gold: a few hundred characters on the Wall at the time, as well as a few thousand characters describing the reason for the Wall's construction: the enemy.

Opening an 1875 edition of 'Records of the Grand Historian' in Peking University Library's collection of rare books, my wife and researcher Wu Qi finds Chapter 88, and writes a translation for me in her notebook:

> I've been to the northern border and returned via the
> Direct Road. On the way I saw the ramparts of the
> Great Wall which Meng Tian built for Qin. He

hollowed out the mountains and filled in the valleys
and built a road there . . .

For me, this is the crown jewel, for it begins with 'I'. Sima Qian's
words are much more than an account of who built what, when
and for what purpose: we're following in the footsteps of the first
person to see the structure and record that experience. We're lis-
tening to the first eyewitness in the Wall's history. As Grand Scribe
(*Taishi Ling*), Sima Qian accompanied Emperor Han Wudi on his
inspection tours of the north and west in around 110 BC, and it's
possible that this was when he observed the Wall.

Elsewhere in his 'Records', Sima Qian provides the first and
most detailed ethnography of the Western Han's great nomadic
adversary, the Xiongnu people (see Object 3). To do this, he conducted interviews and built relationships with key people, including prominent military officials. With information gleaned from
army commanders Li Guang, Su Qian and Wei Qing – all of
whom led long campaigns against the northern nomads – he presented a comprehensive picture of the Xiongnu's lifestyle, military
methods, social hierarchy, rituals and beliefs.

> As children, they can ride goats, and can shoot birds
> and mice with their bows and arrows. When a lit-
> tle older they can shoot foxes and hares for food. As
> adults, they bend the bow well and all can serve as
> cavalry. They herd domestic animals and hunt in times
> of peace but, when needed, everyone sets off on inva-
> sions and practises military skills . . .
>
> They herd domestic animals such as horses, cows
> and sheep, and some rarer ones such as camels and
> other equines. Their movements are made in search
> of pastures and water, and they have no fixed places

of abode nor walled towns, and do not engage in the cultivation of crops.

Previous writing on the northern barbarians had demonised them – in *Shanhai Jing* ('Classic of the Mountains and Seas'), written the fourth century BC, for example, the foreigners were presented as distorted and grotesque beings. Sima Qian brought them from the realm of imagination and mystery, presenting them as realistic enemies on the edge of the Empire. In this respect, his descriptions represent the first recorded military intelligence on the Han state's main enemy, the Xiongnu.

Perhaps most significantly for scholars of the Great Wall, Sima Qian names the structure. He uses four characters – *wan li* and *chang cheng* – in close proximity in a sentence in Chapter 28, thus bringing together the terms that would later make up the structure's famous name:

> When Qin had unified All Under Heaven, Meng Tian took 300 000 to go north and drive out the Rong and Di barbarians and take control of the territory to the south of the Yellow River. He built a Long Wall [*changcheng*], taking advantage of the lie of the land and making use of the passes. It began at Lintao and went as far as Liaodong, extending for 10 000 li [*wanli*]. Crossing the Yellow River, it followed the Yang Mountains and twisted northwards. His army was exposed to hardships in the field for ten years when they were stationed in Shang Province, and during this time Meng Tian filled the Xiongnu with terror.

These two excerpts, although brief, not only provide evidence but are loaded with detail and insight. From them we learn that 'the

Wall' was masterminded by Qin, managed by General Meng Tian and built by a workforce numbering 300000, who also forged an approach road, the *Zhidao*, or 'Direct Road', leading to the frontier region where the Wall was to be built. We even get a rough geography: from Lintao (Gansu) to Liaodong, via the Lang Shan. Sima Qian mentions an obviously rounded figure of 10000 *li* (one *li* equals about 550 metres). This traditional and literal use of *wan* should be interpreted as being 'endless', making a more erudite translation of *Wanli Changcheng* 'the Endless Wall'.

With passing time, this turned out to be both an increasingly inappropriate and appropriate term. Synonymous with a place of no return, it elicits the heartbreaking legend of Lady Meng, warning of death and sorrow for its future builders and their loved ones (see Object 2). Yet, as dynasties rose and fell, and some of them built Great Walls for themselves – adeptly renamed *biancheng*, or border walls – and collectively the structures increased in length, becoming seemingly more endless. By pre-modern times, with all the Walls abandoned, the original four-character term gradually re-established itself as their evocative brand name, making it more famous.

Today, precious few of the tens of millions of the Wall's annual visitors, from near and far – most of whom are preoccupied with sharing their own first impressions of the Wall by WeChat, WhatsApp, Instagram or some other social media platform – are aware that the very first message was sent some 2125 years earlier, and written down on wooden strips by a man named Sima Qian.

12.

WRITERS AND FIGHTERS

Polyhedral wooden record

How are you reading this? On paper, or a screen of some kind? And when was the last time you wrote a letter, report or an essay on paper? If you answered 'A screen' and 'I can't even remember' to these questions, then you – like most people, I suspect – have entered a new era, and paper is almost a thing of the past.

With this *mugu*, or 'wooden document', we're backtracking to a time when refined paper was an item of the future; wood was the main surface for writing on. This object is an oddity both in its shape and in its rather puzzling content, but it's classified as belonging to a category of wooden strips called *mujian* that vividly preserve details of the Western Han's Great Wall operation – an episode elucidated by a group of more conventional two-faced *mujian* (see Object 15). As one might expect from an oddity, this one conceals a different story.

From the Shang to the Northern and Southern Dynasties period – approximately 1900 years – long strips of thin wood were the most commonly used writing surfaces, whether for scrawling brief notes or transcribing great works of history. Sima Qian's *Shiji* (Object 11), for example, would have been a truly voluminous and heavy read, as expressed by the idiom *xue fu wu che*, literally meaning 'possessing five cartloads of knowledge', or more eloquently 'erudite and scholarly'. Sima Qian gave a measure of Emperor Qin Shihuang's thirst for knowledge by remarking that he worked his way through one *dan* (approximately twenty-seven kilograms) of various wooden documents per day.

'The *mugu* was discovered in 1977 during excavation of ruins of a *fengsui*, or watchtower, on the Han Wall at Yumenhuahai, about 100 kilometres west of Jiayuguan in Gansu Province. Most people encountering it in the museum have little idea what it is, let alone appreciate its significance; it is listed as a State Level First Class Antiquity,' says Yu Chunrong, curator at the Jiayuguan Great Wall Museum.

The *mugu* is hexagonal in cross-section and possesses six surfaces for writing, compared to just a single side of a conventional wooden strip. Thicker at its top end, thinning towards the other, it's about thirty-seven centimetres in length. Overall, it looks rather like a chunky, cumbersome, oversized chopstick. Its surfaces are covered with a total of 212 characters in the *lishu* (chancery or clerk's) script, written in black ink. This peculiar, enigmatic object takes us back to the Western Han, circa 90 BC, to a watchtower on the dynasty's frontier Wall, and into the mind of one man; we'll call him 'the writer'. He's an officer, probably of *suizhang* rank, and in charge of a small squad of men deployed at the tower.

The first puzzle about the *mugu* is its strange mixture of content: it features two unconnected and contrasting texts in adjacency. One part has 133 characters, comprising an incomplete letter – partly a testament, partly a valedictory – issued by the third-longest reigning emperor in imperial history, Han Wudi (who reigned between 140 and 87 BC). The original document was addressed to his youngest son and chosen heir, Crown Prince Fuling, born in 94 BC, who would become the Zhaodi Emperor, reigning until 74 BC. It reads:

DESCRIPTION:	A polyhedral *mujian*, or wooden border document; its six faces are inscribed with a total of 212 Chinese characters
SIGNIFICANCE:	A marker of literacy, newly required of Han army officers engaged in frontier defence work
ORIGIN:	Made in Yumenhuahai, today's Gansu Province, towards the end of Emperor Han Wudi's reign, circa 90 BC, and excavated at a watchtower on the Han Wall
LOCATION:	Jiayuguan Great Wall Museum

This announcement is for the Crown Prince. My
health is ailing and soon I must depart this world
for the earth, never to return . . . Crown Prince, you
should be a benevolent ruler, paying attention to the
needs of ordinary people, reducing their burden of taxation, protecting talented people, staying close to the
great thinkers, being a model for all to follow, respect-
ing your ancestors . . . striving to uphold the mandate
of heaven you will inherit, then the Huns will not dare
to challenge you . . . I do wish to say more before it is
too late . . .

Running on from this is a second, unconnected part of the text,
totalling seventy-nine characters. Its content offers little of value,
although it is mildly entertaining. It's likely to have been a communication sent from our man, the writer, surnamed Shi, to a
superior at a nearby watchtower. It reads:

Highly respected brother, I should kneel before you
to express my respect, at your feet where I belong as
an insignificant, I'm awed at your example of guarding
the border in the inclement weather on frugal rations,
and though your heart is bitter you remain unceasingly
observant in your frontier defence duties. Should you
or your men pass our watchtower, we will generously
accord you our great hospitality.

Veritable juxtaposition. Clearly, neither text is in situ. Part one
is likely to have been issued as an internal military circular – or,
more aptly, a 'linear', as it would have been relayed along the
Wall. This testament cum valedictory is unique, preserved in no
other form, on no other surface. The note which follows is mere

grovelling praise from a lower to a higher rank. Read separately, the messages make some sense. Together, they seem like non-sense.

I think we should be less preoccupied with the content of the *mugu* and more concerned with the reasons for its creation. To this end, the key questions we must answer, if we are to under-stand the object's purpose and its place in our Great Wall story, are: what was the writer doing, and why? To me, literacy seems to be a good motive: his position, which saw him in charge of a watchtower and a number of men, demanded it. He needed to read incoming messages and send them out, and to have a skill that the men he commanded didn't.

From the abundance of *mujian* found at the Han Wall in Gansu and Inner Mongolia, we have much reason to believe that in the mid-Han Wudi period (circa 120 BC), literacy grew to be regarded as an essential military qualification in officers, alongside the more traditional martial attributes of valour, strength, discipline, a sense of duty, theoretical knowledge and practical experience in the art of war, as well as archery and martial arts skills. The Han Wall became more than just a barricaded frontier: it was also a busy signalling line and communications route. Those in positions of authority – the *suizhang* at each watchtower, at least – needed to be able to read and write.

But literacy requires practice. Our writer, making his own at-tempts to improve, used his knife to whittle down a tree branch and create a large surface area for writing exercises. Just as pri-mary school children often do today in China, he sought some handwriting of quality to copy, first picking up a clutch of adjoined *mujian*. These happened to have important content, which had been circulated throughout the army: news that the Crown Prince had been chosen. The original document would certainly have extended to more than several *mujian*. Our writer copied what text he had, but still had space left. So he picked up another document, which just happened to be unimportant. That didn't matter; it still allowed him to practise his writing.

As it happens, the most sweeping reform of the Chinese writing system occurred during the Han Dynasty, just at the time our officer was engaged in his *lishu*-character handwriting practice. These are geometrically constructed characters and are written according to certain rules, known as a stroke order. The writer built up his characters stroke by stroke, with each stroke having a name, number by number. Previously, character scripts were rounded, and based on expression of meaning by showing a picture. Known as *guwen*, or 'ancient script', these came in a series of different fonts, as we'd call them nowadays, but they were curved and difficult to copy and remember. *Lishu* characters simplified writing, allowing it to become a more common skill.

The frontier built and operated by Han Wudi required manning not only by men trained to fight, but also by soldiers with important new skills: the ability to write, send, receive, read, understand and interpret military orders and intelligence. This oddly shaped chunk of wood found in the sand, tantamount to a sheet of scrap paper screwed up and tossed to the ground, tells us that one man spent an hour or so of his spare time, in the shadow of a tall watchtower on the Han Wall, preparing himself to be a better soldier – not by sparring, swordplay or target practice, but with brush and wood in hand, writing.

13.

PAST GLORIES

'Map of China and the Barbarian Lands' stele rubbing

There's no more effective reminder of the staying power of the Great Wall than to see it routed across a contemporary map. My latest map of modern China shows both the country's high-speed railway lines, all built over the last five years, and the remains of the Ming Great Wall, built five centuries ago. This juxtaposition of megastructures is not an anachronism. The Wall isn't marked as an imaginary line, nor is it decorative. Long and continuous sections of the Ming structure still stand, and I can use my map to find them.

Once there, no matter where I am, where I climb to, how good my eyesight is or how crystal-clear the visibility might be, I can see maybe thirty kilometres of the whole structure at best. Wherever I stand, I'm aware that there is so much more beyond, behind and before me. My map can give me what first-hand experience cannot: a subcontinental view. The power of *scale* makes maps unique tools when we wish to understand the Wall's totality.

The object I'm searching for is the cartographic 'before', and it's to be found on older maps that preserve the Wall's historical geography. But how far back into history must I travel to see the earliest surviving map that shows a Great Wall?

There appears to be nothing earlier than the *Huayi Tu*, or 'Map of China and the Barbarian Lands', a large map carved into a stone slab. Dating from the 1130s, it measures 114 square centimetres. I'm looking at a vermillion rubbing of the map held by the National Library of China. It's an impressive and mysterious depiction. For one thing, it's titled *Huayi Tu*, which translates directly as 'China–Barbarian Map', which I regard as a synonym for the Great Wall 'conflict'. It follows, too, that this is a dedicated 'Great Wall' map per se. For Cao Song (828–903), a Tang poet, it represented a national zenith. In his poem 'Perusing the *Huayi Tu*', he wrote:

> In brush strokes the Earth is shrunk
> Unfurling the map I feel peace
> The Chinese occupy the place of prominence
> Under which distant stars lie the border areas?

The Wall is drawn boldly, the dominant symbol on the map. It's represented by a battlement-like symbol that was adopted and varied by successive cartographers to depict the Great Walls of various dynasties over the centuries. Two continuous sections are marked. The Wall enters at the map's north-eastern edge. It proceeds westward and then curves down, towards the south-west, within the great bend of the Yellow River, terminating near Mintao. Further to the north-west, on the far side of the Yellow River, a second but shorter segment of the Wall is depicted, stretching from Juyan to Yumenguan.

The cartographer's focus, then, is the *Hua–Yi* (or 'China–Barbarian') conflict, and this fact is reinforced by the position and contents of box-like chunks of text that surround the map proper, describing the appearances and characteristics of the peoples on the peripheries. Spatially, they are 'outside', whether they be beyond the Wall to the north, across the sea to the east, or over the mountains and deserts to the far west. One block of text to the immediate right of the

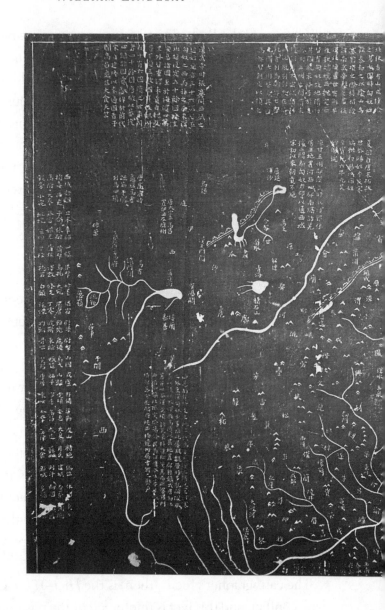

DESCRIPTION: The *Huayi Tu*, or 'Map of China and the Barbarian Lands'

SIGNIFICANCE: The earliest extant image of any Great Wall

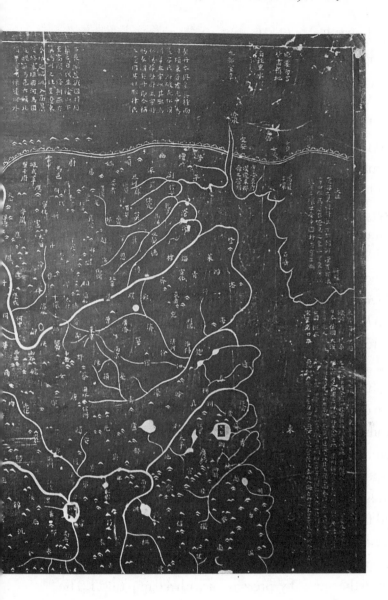

ORIGIN:	Based on a map drawn AD 801, copied onto a stone in AD 1136
LOCATION:	National Library of China, Beijing; the original stela is thought to be in the collection of the Forest of Steles Museum, Xi'an, Shaanxi Province

title describes the Wall as *Gu Changcheng*, or the 'ancient Great Wall', confirming that the Wall was already obsolete at the time of the map's original production, during the Tang Dynasty.

But was the Wall marked as an imaginary relic or a physically visible one? And which dynastic Wall does it show? To learn the answers, we need to appreciate a little more about this map's genesis.

Text on the map tells us the stone was engraved later Shuo Qixue in 1136, and that he based his work on a previous work, by Jia Dan (730–805), a scholar-official and cartographer who was commissioned to draw a map by the Dezong Emperor (who reigned between 780 and 805). The very large map that Jia Dan constructed was said to have measured 9 metres by 10 metres; it was apparently covered with a grid of squares measuring one *cun*; each *cun* equated to 100 *li*, which made it a 1:1500000 scale map.

It's rational to assume that one reason the original Tang map was downsized and copied onto stone during the Song was to preserve what might eventually have been lost – as, indeed, the paper copy was. However, that was not the primary motive. Engraved slabs were produced specifically to function as templates for reproduction later named Shuo Qixue copied Jia Dan's map onto a stone in response to political changes that created social and market demands: a need for multiple paper copies.

The size and illustrative style of the stone suggest explicitly that it was not intended for display, but as a surface for reproduction. Such a copying process involves at least five stages. The first step is to fix the paper to the stone, by 'pressing' it with a damp towel. The second is to force the paper into the carvings by means of *da zi*, a hitting action using a stiff brush. Third is drying. Next comes the first application of ink by 'thumping'; this stage is repeated two or three more times to attain an even application. Finally, the paper is carefully peeled off the stone. The whole job takes about an hour.

The rubbing I inspected was produced in the first half of the twentieth century. Despite repeated efforts, I have never been allowed to see the actual stele. 'Nobody, not even Chinese, let alone foreigners, is allowed to see the stone, and it's forbidden to discuss it because it presents political problems,' said the curator's office in the mid-1990s. The probable reason is that the map doesn't show Taiwan as an island. In fact, it doesn't show Taiwan at all.

Jia Dan made his large map in 801. Its size indicated it as having been designed for imperial use – just imagine what a rigmarole it must have been to unfurl and hang up such a large map. Shuo Qixue engraved his downsized *Huayi Tu* in stone in order to enable the creation of copies of more manageable size, for use by a wider audience. The cartographic business was lucrative. Interestingly, just as we use both sides of a sheet of paper to save trees and cash, Shuo Qixue used both sides of this stone: the opposite surface has another map carved upon it. The dual use hints at commerce. But who, then, were the map's customers, and what had changed to produce the demand?

Wu Shu, a Song Dynasty official in the Bureau of Military Affairs, which was responsible for the maintenance of the state's annually updated maps, stated:

> All maps are for the sole use of His Majesty and the
> military. Others found using them privately, or in
> secret, and foreigners found with them should be
> punished. All maps are to be stamped, inventoried and
> stored securely. Authorised persons desiring to consult
> maps need to obtain his Imperial Majesty's permission.

During early-twelfth century Song China, however, there appears to have been a liberalisation of attitudes concerning one genre of cartography – historical maps – for the sake of furthering patriotic education. Jia Dan's Tang map was 'declassified' and could now be reproduced as an educational tool. The Southern Song government wanted to remind their people that although land south of the Great Wall was overrun with Mongols, it remained Chinese.

Beginning in the mid-tenth century, Qidan ethnics and then Tanguts supplanted Han rule in the empire's north. By 1127 advances by Jurchens had toppled the Qidan–Liao empire, forcing the Song to pull back south of the Huai River. Han people evacuated southwards en masse, escaping the advancing tide of 'barbarian' rule. Never before had so many Hans been compressed into such a small territory.

They made the best of it. Necessity spurred scientific, agricultural, commercial and cultural benefits. Trades flourished and a market economy emerged.

The Southern Song government aimed to strengthen its control of the denser population and increase resistance against northern invaders by greatly enlarging its civil service. Determined to build on the firmest of foundations, it instigated a vigorous imperial examination system that contained a broad range of subjects; its goal was the recruitment of quality scholars. A scramble to enter the bureaucracy and climb the ladder ensued.

As the demand for knowledge increased, the craft of stele rubbing enabled the reproduction of copies that could be used as study materials. History was a prized field of knowledge, a means for the student to learn from past events. *Huayi Tu*, being a summary of Han conflicts with the northern nomads, was poignantly relevant as the Jin continued its attacks on the Southern Song. Rubbings of this map provided a poster-style lesson, summarising and disseminating basic knowledge on Han–barbarian relations.

While that was its use back then, what does it show us now, 900 years later?

From a geographical standpoint, the map's rendering of China's land is immature. Any Chinese primary school pupil today could draw a better map. They have the shape of a rooster in mind when sketching their mainland, and are sternly reminded not to forget their countless number of islands, especially Taiwan. Jia Dan's China does feature the Yellow, Yangzi and Huai rivers, as well as the Taihu, Boyang, Dongting and Qinghai lakes, but his drawing of the country's overall outline, and especially it's coastline, is amorphous. It lacks even minimal protrusions to show Shandong and Liaodong, while the shape of Korea's peninsula remained unknown.

Although the Great Wall's route does appear to be a sweeping approximation, we can still work out its dynastic origins. Immediately before the Tang there was the Sui Great Wall, and before that several 'lesser' Great Walls built by Northern Dynasties, all of which were much further south than this one, and much shorter. This is a true '10000 *li* Great Wall' of subcontinental scale, stretching from the Gobi to Korea. Only one dynastic structure matches up with such an identity, and that's the Western Han Dynasty Great Wall. Until it was explored by Aurel Stein in the early 1900s (see Object 14), it was thought to have its western terminus at Yumenguan, as marked on the *Huayi Tu*.

Rubbings of the *Huayi Tu* collected in the National Library of China and Washington D.C.'s Library of Congress (thought to have been made circa 1933), among other institutions, preserve a full-length image of the Western Han Wall. At the time of the map's reproduction, during the Southern Song, it served as a graphic reminder of the halcyon days of centuries past, when the Wall was the border and the barbarians were kept outside it.

For the poet Lu You (1125–1210), the *Huayi Tu* was a map of times past, not present – part nostalgia, part lament, showing a glorious then and a grim now. Seeing it caused him much anguish:

Living for seventy years my heart has stayed
as it always was at the beginning,
By mistake I see the map, and my eyes fill with tears.

14.

CHARTING ARCHAEOLOGY

Stein's sketch map of the Han Wall

As I read Aurel Stein's handwritten diary, and refer to his popular published account, *Ruins of Desert Cathay*, and his detailed field report in *Serindia*, I draw on my own considerable experience of the desert region in question and reconstruct the scene. It is April 1907.

Stein wasn't at all perturbed about riding back to camp in the dusk. After two rides along this stretch of fragmented fortifications, a much improved map was shaping up in his mind, one that he would soon transfer to paper. Besides, he could rely on his loyal dog, Dash, to sniff out the route they had taken on the outward ride, nine hours earlier.

Stein was riding Badakhshi, a young stallion named after its motherland, an Afghan province on the far-flung western edge of the Qing Empire. He was accompanied by Tila Bai, the local Uyghur who was in charge of all the horses and camels. The caravan had carried Stein's expedition all the way from Kashgar, along the southern rims of the Taklamakan Desert and the Lop Nur salt lake.

Their camp was near, but not within 'the Fort', a structure much larger than the umpteen *paotai*, or watchtowers, that Stein was investigating along this ancient frontier. It was square, with high, thick walls and a large central enclosure, but was swarming with mosquitos and *tao-zi*, or midges, so they shunned it, preferring an outside spot for their several nights' stay. This fixed camp functioned as their central base, from which to ride out, explore and excavate; it saved them precious time, relieving them of the need to make and break camp, and transport all their paraphernalia.

Time was pressing. The summer heat would soon make desert travel impossible, and there was a mountain of archaeological and survey work still to be done. Stein's reconnaissance rides aimed to reveal in advance 'the task awaiting at each ruin', and to enable selection of the 'most suitable camping places', close to springs.

It had been a worthwhile day. Stein had ridden as far east as watchtower T. XVII, observing and taking compass bearings. But the onset of evening brought him no rest. On the homeward plod he further pondered the relationship between the remains of the fortifications and its host landscape.

As the sky reddened in the west, they reached T. XV, from where Stein could clearly see the next watchtower in the string; he estimated it to be three miles (five kilometres) distant by line of sight. While the availability of water was a logistical consideration that influenced the placement of watchtowers, it was becoming clear to Stein that the towers were located on higher ground so they could be linked visually, a system he later described as 'optical telegraphy'.

It had been some weeks since Stein's caravan had reached and resupplied at the Dunhuang oasis, where the name of the Han Dynasty garrison town had been discussed. It translated as 'Blazing Beacons' – a reference to the beacon signals that were relayed along the fortifications to warn of enemy action. Archaeological evidence was backing up that interpretation: Stein had found some 'queer little mounds' beside T. XIII – five large bales of reeds, which he'd worked out were faggots to be ignited as signalling beacons. At a number of towers he'd found *mujian*, with two flat faces; in time, they would reveal details of ancient signalling 'codes' (see Object 15).

Somewhat more puzzling was the discontinuity of the 'agger', as Stein first called the Wall. Having followed it for several weeks, he was beginning to wonder whether its apparently fragmented layout could be explained solely by disintegration over the centuries. He was becoming convinced that the structure's route, and its long gaps, had a relationship to the terrain. He'd been marking these on his map: 'Sai' (bare, stony plateaus or sandy patches), 'Togruk jungle' (Euphrates poplar forest), the scrub of 'Tamarisk cones', tussocks of 'Kumush' (tall savannah grasses) and troublesome marshy 'Nullahs'.

Badakhshi was invaluable in sensing the dangers of the marshes. He'd stop, back off or veer away as soon as his hooves sensed moist, sagging ground. Tila Bai's gestures implied that no horse would ever traverse a 'Nullah', for fear of sinking. It had surely always been the case: not even the Huns, twenty-one centuries earlier, could get through these marshes on horseback, and without equine transport they were impotent.

Stein speculated that 'Chinese engineers', as he called the Wall builders, had saved on labour and materials by incorporating these marshes into their defence plan. Meanwhile, he noted that the building of the Wall 'had been carried out unfailingly over every bit of firm ground capable of offering a passage for the enemy's inroads and right down to the edge of marshy inlets'.

Men and beasts alike were relieved to return to the high ground of a rocky 'Sai', from where the position of Fort Camp reappeared. It was dramatically marked by its campfire's leaping orange flames. In the final furlong they trotted across firm ground; a plume of steam was a welcome sight. Stein rocked his horse to a canter before reining him to a halt, sprang out the stirrups and strode directly over to the fire. He was eager to check that the fire was burning on dung and tamarisk, and not on 'rubbish', as the labourers had at first called the various wooden objects from the past that Stein had found lying in quantity around all the towers.

The day's finds were laid out on a table: another clutch of painted wooden slips unearthed by Chiang Ssu-Yeh, Stein's field secretary and principal interpreter, who had been working with the Indian surveyor Naik Ram Singh at T. XIIa in the west. However exciting these were – some showed Aramaic script – Stein put his own cartographic duties first. He retreated to the privacy of his closed tent – his 'purdah', as it was jokingly referred to – and got to work.

He opened his pocket notebook, dipped his fountain pen in the ink and began to write:

> April 18, 37 F, light haze, E breeze. Sent Naik & Sieh back to finish T. XIIa. Set out with Tila for T. XIV. To NE across great depression two Pao T'ais visible, prob. XV and XVI. A little to S. of them but further off binocular shows some large ruin (?). No sign of buildings to N or NW. To S240W across two marshy Nullahs, a small tower, approx. in line with T. XIII, latter clearly visible; perhaps also T. XII. The two Nullahs seem to contain a good deal of Toghruk jungle. Fort with camp E165S about 2 ½ m. off in straight line.

Next he focused on his map, much of which had already been sketched out in pencil. Based on the day's observations, he used his dividers and protractor to amend the positions of T. XVI and T. XVII – which he described as a 'palace-like ruin' – half a mile (0.8 kilometre) south, and a little further apart.

Stein inked over his pencil marks, using some of the cartographic symbols he had learned during a compulsory but useful year's

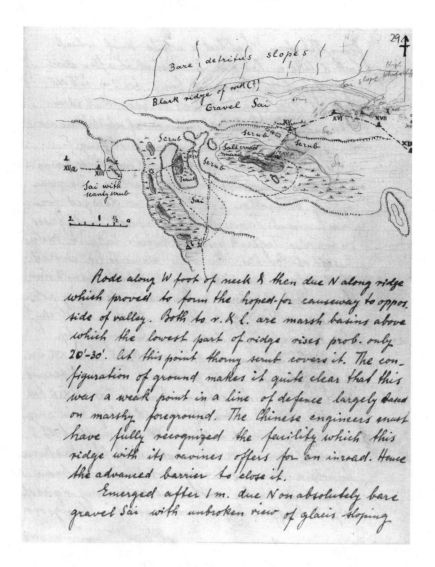

Rode along W foot of neck & then due N along ridge which proved to form the hoped-for causeway to oppos. side of valley. Both to r. & l. are marsh basins above which the lowest part of ridge rises prob. only 20'-30'. At this point thorny scrub covers it. The configuration of ground makes it quite clear that this was a weak point in a line of defence largely based on marshy foreground. The Chinese engineers must have fully recognized the facility which this ridge with its ravines offers for an inroad. Hence the advanced barrier to close it.

Emerged after 1 m. due N on absolutely bare gravel Sai with unbroken view of glacis sloping

DESCRIPTION:	Sketch map in ink of the Western Han Great Wall
SIGNIFICANCE:	The basis for the publication of the first detailed 'large-scale' map of Han Wall, showing the positions of remnant Wall, watchtowers and surrounding terrain
ORIGIN:	Drawn in the field in April 1907 by Aurel Stein (1v862–1943), British explorer and archaeologist
LOCATION:	The Bodleian Library, University of Oxford (MS Stein 199 fol. 29)

stint in the Hungarian military in 1885–86, spent in the forested hills surrounding his native Budapest. As a young man of twenty-three, he had already studied the ancient Persian and Sanskrit languages, and gained valuable curatorial experience in three of Great Britain's finest institutions: Oxford's Ashmolean Museum and Bodleian Library, and the British Museum. He revelled in his posting at the army's Ludovika Academy's school of cartography, where he mastered the science of field surveying and the art of drawing maps. He used his accurate watch to roughly measure the longitude and a quadrant to measure the latitude – using the North Star by night or the solar zenith by day – and an altimeter for elevation and plane-table for distances. He appreciated the fundamental importance of fieldwork to the making of maps, especially in places for which no others existed.

Soon into his fieldwork on the 'Chinese Limes', as he later preferred to call the Han Wall, Stein had decided that 'a large-scale map was needed to show properly and accurately express this intricate figuration of the ground'. He used red ink to denote sections of the Wall, the locations of the various watchtowers and the routes he had taken. Finally, he added a red triangle to mark the position of Fort Camp. The finished work was combined with eleven other small maps to produce the large-scale map. In time, this became a half-metre-long fold-out in volume three of the detailed report of his Second Chinese Expedition, *Serindia*, published in 1921, some fourteen years after he had completed his sketch map that night at Fort Camp.

Stein's masterpiece – titled *Detailed Map of Ancient Chinese Limes West of Tun' Huang*, surveyed by Sir Aurel Stein and R. S. Ram Singh – plots the locations of thirty-eight towers spanning what was, in 1907, a completely uninhabited void. Covering 6240 square kilometres, it was the most detailed map of any Great Wall, and would only be equalled in its accuracy by the work of Chinese surveyors in the 1980s.

Assessing Stein's fieldwork and archaeological follow-up on the Han Wall in her 1995 biography *Aurel Stein: Pioneer of the Silk Road*, Annabel Walker wrote:

> In contrast to the callous calculation of his approach at the Dunhuang caves [from where he obtained large quantities of manuscripts through purchase and pressure], his method here [on the Wall] was a model of integrity. There was no treasure likely to emerge from the haunts of poor soldiers . . . the wealth of the wall lay in its abundant antiquarian evidence: details of the soldiers' lives, of the way the wall had operated and of the topographical considerations that influenced its construction. A site could hardly have been devised to attract Stein more, with his interest in both historical and geographical factors and his ability to synthesize the two. He was absorbed by a desire to understand as much as possible about the place.

Stein's legacy lay waiting to be appreciated by those few explorers and Wall scholars who would follow him across this same desert. A century on, in 2006, I was one of them: his 'large-scale' map was my guide as I made my way to the fortifications he had photographed and numbered. My mission was 'rephotography' (see Object 50) – a desire to document any changes with my camera.

As I did, I used my GPS to record the precise locations of Stein's sites. This revealed the extraordinary accuracy of his 1907 mapmaking. I found that his Fort Camp, which he later evidenced as being the Jade Gate mentioned in Han documents, lay within a radius of just one kilometre of its true position, as pinpointed by today's satellite technology.

15.

ALARMS FROM THE NORTH

Wooden records bearing signalling instructions

If you wanted to communicate with your descendants, 2000 or so years in the future, how might you do it? By leaving them a message of some sort. The type of message you leave, what you write with and on, and the place you leave it and the future human activity in the vicinity will be major factors that determine whether or not your message gets through.

This fascinating object presents specific advice on maximising your chances of success; it speaks from experience. If you write with ink on wood, it suggests, and bury your message in a desert like the Gobi, it will have a very good chance of being received and understood some 2000 years on.

Our object is composed of seventeen interlinked wooden strips, *mujian*, bearing 600 characters. It unfurls as a large booklet and reads as a regional signalling code. Daytime alarm signals were made by hoisting *peng* (lantern-shaped bales of straw), by igniting bales of *yan* (vegetation to make smoke) or by *biao* (the raising of one or more flags). Night-time signals were made by *ju* (flaming torches), while *jixin* (igniting faggots) could be used at any time.

The booklet is exactly the same size of my Macbook Air when opened fully flat, measuring thirty centimetres in width and forty centimetres in length. It has a remarkable resemblance to the character *ce* – 冊 – a pictograph dating back to the earliest Chinese writing, dating from the Shang, found on oracle bones, which suggests that around 3500 years ago the Chinese were already using long, thin strips of wood, often bamboo, as a medium on which to write. However, rather than showing only two adjoined strips, as the character does, this booklet has seventeen. And instead of being 'bound' with one string, it has three.

Dubbed *Saishang Fenghuo Pingyue*, or 'Regulations on Frontier Beacon Signalling', by the team of archaeologists who unearthed it in 1974, this object belongs to a distinct category of *mujian*, historical texts called *hanjiandu*, or 'Han Dynasty border documents'. Following their initial discovery and investigation by Sir Aurel Stein in 1907 (see also Object 14), these wooden records were unearthed in their tens of thousands at various archaeological digs throughout the twentieth century, primarily in the vicinities of the watchtowers strung out along on the Western Han Wall.

The population of Han China was enormous – around 60 million – while that of the nomadic peoples to the north was around 1 million. The latter chose where to strike, and possessed superior cavalry and archers. For the Chinese, having enough soldiers in the right place at the right time to fend off an attack was difficult, so they created a system that allowed them to deploy reinforcements in response to special signals. The plan relied on literacy skills, wood availability and messengers.

Archaeologist Wei Jian of Renmin University, in Beijing, directed an excavation between 1999 and 2002 along the line of frontier watchtowers of the Juyan region, north of the Hexi Corridor, which discovered more than 500 such wooden documents. 'After Sima Qian's *Records of the Grand Historian* and *The Official History of the Western Han*, the large quantity of Han wooden slips found in Gansu and Inner Mongolia provide vivid insight into

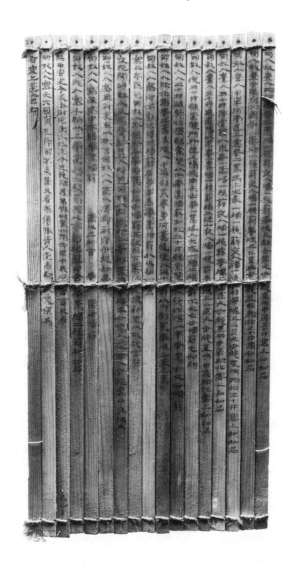

DESCRIPTION:	Seventeen interlinked *mujian*, or wooden border documents, bearing 600 characters
SIGNIFICANCE:	A record of the regulations for frontier signalling
ORIGIN:	A Western Han Dynasty frontier watchtower, Juyan region, circa 110 BC; excavated in 1974 from 'T44 F16' at Pochengzi, in today's Inner Mongolia Autonomous Region
LOCATION:	Gansu Provincial Museum, Lanzhou

frontier fortifications and their operation; using excavated *mujian* to reconstruct episodes of Han border life is a possibility,' he said.

To make sense of this booklet, we first need to know the local geography of Juyan. This Xiongnu word refers to a 250 kilometre by sixty kilometre area of fortifications with a north-east to south-west orientation in today's Ejina Banner of Inner Mongolia, which adjoined those in the Hexi Corridor. The watchtowers were built approximately 1.3 kilometres apart. The 'outside' is to the left, or north-west, but there is no actual wall as such between the towers. Rather, the multiple channels of the Ejina River were borrowed as natural defences. For administrative purposes, the region was subdivided into three stretches from north to south: Tianbei, Jiaqu and Sanshijing. The personnel manning the towers here were on the very front line, and were required to report any Xiongnu activity immediately to the regional military headquarters in the hinterland, Juyan Dusiwei. We can be certain that this booklet was created there – from a template.

A high-ranking officer would have written out a master copy. Next came the copying out, a job for several of the lower-ranking but literate officers (see Object 12). The text states that all the regulations were to be memorised by all personnel. To comply, every tower was issued with one 'textbook', meaning a total of several score were required. A large quantity of wooden strips had to be cut and trimmed, using locally available woods – some *hongliu*, or tamarisk, some *huyang*, or Euphrates poplar, and some *suosuo* or saksaul.

Using thin brushes (also found by the archaeologists), the production group began their task. Our officer writes: '*Xiongnuren baitian ru . . .*' ('When the Xiongnu approach during the daytime . . .') in a vertical manner – a directional practice dictated by the slip's elongate shape. This mode of writing – from top to bottom, from right to left – was used for Chinese until recent decades.

Strip after strip they wrote – it took seventeen to contain the entire code. The men began to know it themselves – almost. When the writing was finished, they had to bind the strips together in sequence with a twisted hemp string, set by set, ensuring that the order was correct. There was likely a cursory inspection, but no real proofreading. The completed booklets were delivered by messengers. Each roll's strip bore the marks of a 'top-priority' document: a black dot at the top.

At a tower on the Jiaqu section, the men gathered around their *suizhang*, or tower commander, to hear him read the code aloud. 'Juyan Dusiwei orders requires all of us here at Pochengzi to learn by heart the signals we need to make!' he said. The men recited the words after him: '*Xiongnuren zhouru* . . . When the Xiongnu approach by day, hoist two *peng* lanterns and ignite one *jixin* bale. *Xiongnuren yeru* . . . When the Xiongnu approach at night, ignite one *jixin* bale and sustain the signal until daybreak.'

Other towers in the Juyan region had slightly different signals, which were specified in their own copies of the signalling code. The design of local signatures ensured that headquarters could receive a signal and know which section was under threat, and organise an appropriate response.

Poets of later dynasties lamented that 'beacon fires on the Han Wall burned incessantly' (see Object 22), yet despite the border unrest this signified, it was actually rebellion from within that toppled the Han, early in the third century. Juyan, a hostile field on the Gobi's edge, saw its fortifications abandoned, left for the desert to claim. Sand blew, swamping the Han's past there, covering the towers' history for nearly two millennia, until the arrival of twentieth-century archaeologists with their trowels and brushes.

Their excavations of these *mujian* allow us to glean vivid details about Han frontier operations. We have no such detailed insight on the Ming Wall (which is fifteen centuries younger) because paper had replaced the use of wooden strips, and paper struggles to survive the centuries unless carefully stored.

For us, though, these border documents relay another relevant signal. Although the communications devices we use today are remarkably quick – to write, to send and to receive messages – it's difficult to see how they can possibly survive the tests of time and reach our descendants 2000 years from now.

16.

A HAN-HUN WEDDING

Lady Wang Travels Beyond the Wall *marriage print*

The Economist magazine ranked Melbourne as 'the world's most liveable city' in 2014. Two thousand years ago, the choice might well have been Chang'an, for to live in the Middle Kingdom at that time, was, in name and practice, to live at one of the world's great epicentres. During the late first century BC, the population of the Han capital at the eastern end of the Silk Road was nearing half a million. It was one the world's largest metropolises, and thus a magnet for those who wanted to be the best.

Men and women migrated to Chang'an. But the empire that this sophisticated city claimed to control was not as safe as it seemed. As they had done since the time of their own establishment, in the very late third century BC, the federated Xiongnu people threatened the frontier. Only Han Wudi, who reigned from 141 to 86 BC, had stood up to them offensively, pushing them well back, constructing defences and keeping the border secure, if at immense financial cost. All other Han emperors had submitted to the Xiongnu's demands for goods. They were forced to buy peace to keep the Xiongnu 'outside', north of the Han's lengthy fortifications.

This is where Wang Zhaojun enters the Wall story. She would

DESCRIPTION:	*Wang Zhaojun Chusai*, or *Lady Wang Travels Beyond the Wall*, a print of approximately sixty centimetres by thirty-five centimetres
SIGNIFICANCE:	Centrepiece of the *Heqin*, or 'harmonious marriage alliance' policies between the Han and the Huns
ORIGIN:	Printed in the Republic of China, circa 1920
LOCATION:	Wang Zhaojun Tomb and Museum, near Hohhot, Inner Mongolia Autonomous Region

become the most prominent imperial feminine 'seal' of a three-point appeasement policy known as *Heqin*, or 'harmonious marriage alliances', which the Han used repeatedly in order to avoid costly war and almost certain military defeat.

Our image of Lady Wang could have been chosen from thousands. It's a print, barely a century old. It shows a rather odd party of elegant young ladies, accompanied by some rough-looking old men, making their way through dark hills. It looks like a kidnapping. Lady Wang is in red, while the Xiongnu chieftain Huhanye (their 'Shanyu', literally 'Son of the Endless Skies', who reigned from 58 to 31 BC) is the warrior-ruler wrapped in a snow leopard's pelt. It's one example from a plethora of works – by poets, playwrights, painters and filmmakers – generated by an extraordinary industry that has been running for 2000 years, producing a distinctive genre of its own, dubbed *Zhaojun chusai*, or 'Zhaojun Travels Beyond the Wall' works. The image shows a single frame of an actual historical event of 33 BC, which has been the focus of a never-ending post-mortem conducted by historiographers, essayists, artists and political spin doctors.

Lady Wang's wasn't the first marriage of convenience of its kind, nor would it be the last. But it was different, and the most famous. For one thing, it was two marriages: in accordance with the Xiongnu's custom of inheritance, she fulfilled hymeneal roles to successive shanyus. She also produced children, achieved a tentative peace for Han China and stirred intense national debate.

At its core, the rationale of *Heqin* was the belief (or hope) that a blood relationship between the two states would create peace. Liu Jing, principal adviser to the Gaodi Emperor who reigned between 206 and 195 BC (actually Liu Bang, who founded the Han), stated that the betrothal of a princess to Modun Shanyu should be seen as a long-term investment. It would, he argued, potentially generate a grandson for the Han emperor, a boy who would surely honour and obey his grandfather, show dual allegiance to his father's and his mother's states, eventually become ruler himself and unite the Xiongnu and their land with the Han and theirs. In reality, problems arose for several reasons: because a genuine princess was not offered, and because the Xiongnu had no regard for the Confucian virtues of filial piety. A major schism proved to be the Xiongnu's levirate custom, whereby a widow was obliged to marry her husband's brother – or, in Lady Wang's case, her husband's successor.

Wang Zhaojun's story was the fifteenth and final *Heqin* marriage of the Western Han, and was first recorded in the official history of that period, the *Hou Han Shu*. As a girl, Wang had been selected as a county belle to join the Yuandi Emperor's 'side court', or harem. Her beauty and musical skills may have got her into the Weiyang Palace, but getting into bed with the Emperor was another matter. He had so many concubines (estimated to be around 3000) that he couldn't remember them by name or even face. To assist his nightly selection, a court artist prepared what was tantamount to a concubine catalogue.

Artist Mao Yanshou found a way to make some extra money from the women he painted. Knowing that they all wanted an early night, he knew they'd be willing to pay for it by having their beauty enhanced in the catalogue. Wang Zhaojun, however, had nothing to offer, so she was portrayed with a blemished face.

The Shanyu and his entourage arrived in Chang'an with a list of their demands. In return for various goods – food, wine and textiles – as well as due regard for themselves as an equal state, they would observe the Wall as the border. This deal was sealed with a royal woman. She was of great importance, and not only for the Shanyu's pleasure and pride. His ownership of a royal Han woman was a gift that no others around him could obtain, a possession that reinforced his position as ruler.

The Yuandi Emperor relied wholly on his catalogue to select

one of his less attractive women. Only when Wang Zhaojun was presented to the Shanyu did he discover her true beauty and his big mistake, but by then it was too late for him to correct it. Off she went on her journey of no return, north of the Wall, to a felt-walled *ger* on the windswept steppe. By Chinese standards, it was an unliveable place.

Having been neglected by the Emperor and victimised by court corruption, Lady Wang was betrothed to a barbarian on the edge of the known world. Yet she was credited as selflessly executing her role as '*Hu*-pacifying Chief Consort', keeping the Shanyu content and conforming with the custom of marrying the next Shanyu when her husband died.

Wang Zhaojun died, but she wasn't allowed to rest in peace. Her *Heqin* marriage began to preoccupy Chinese historiographers, essayists and thinkers. A policy that had seen the Son of Heaven rely on a concubine for imperial security brought national humiliation, while Wang herself – long-suffering in her loyalty to her husbands and in her duty to China – was seen as exemplary, ironic, tragic, patriotic and, ultimately, legendary. She became a symbol of the *Heqin* policy.

Her lot struck a poignant chord with poets, such as Bai Juyi (AD 772–846):

> Full in her face, barbarian sands, wind full in her hair;
> gone from her eyebrows are the last traces of kohl,
> gone is the rouge from her cheeks,
> hardship and grieving have wasted them away,
> indeed now she has the face of the painting!
> As the Han envoy departs, she gives him these words:
> 'When will they send some yellow gold as ransom?
> Should His Majesty ask how I look,
> don't say I'm any different from those palace days!

Twelve centuries later, twentieth-century politics put a new spin on Wang Zhaojun's achievements. She was praised as a civiliser, the one who cemented Han–Xiongnu kinship, a champion of peace and harmony among the minorities in a multi-ethnic People's Republic. In 1960, Premier Zhou Enlai suggested that her story be used by writers to encourage more Han women to marry men from ethnic minorities (see Object 47).

Despite this propagandistic adoption of Wang Zhaojun's story, we might ask: what did *Heqin* achieve, and for whom? What did it mean for the Wall?

Each side, of course, had different aims. The aim of the Han was to maintain power and avoid their land being occupied, and their people enslaved, by barbarians. To keep the Shanyu at bay, they offered three commodities annually: grain, wine and textiles. They viewed the tribute as bait, a means of corrupting the Xiongnu.

Food, even in its largest recorded annual quantity, amounted to a trifle that could not be distributed far. It was enough for the Shanyu, his family and guard. Wine went further: tribal chieftains, on whose support the Shanyu relied, had a great love of alcohol. The Shanyu used the 10000 *shih*, or 20000 litres, as currency to keep them happy. Textiles, too, were highly valued. Conclusion: the Shanyu, his family and top brass had a good deal, while the ordinary nomads received nothing.

Sounds a familiar story, doesn't it? Yet rather than vent their discontentment on the Shanyu, the empty-handed continued to raid the border area, stealing their own share of Chinese products. These actions benefited the Shanyu, which is why he turned a blind eye to them, defaulting on his side of the *Heqin* treaty: to observe the Wall as a border that was not to be violated. Raids were a useful, menacing reminder of Xiongnu violence against the Han, and topped up the Shanyu's bargaining power when the time came for deals to be renegotiated. Raids threatened to become more frequent and larger if the quantities of tribute were not increased.

From this perspective, we can see that the Xiongnu, as a state, was not predatory as such – that is, it was not aiming to wipe out its productive Han neighbours. It aimed merely to live off them and ensure a sustainable relationship. It was very much in the Shanyu's personal interest that Han China remained functional, maintaining its ability to provide the good life to his few, who nominally controlled the rest. A parasite needs a good host.

And as for the Wall? Emperor Han Wudi's great military offensives and his investments in lengthy defensive additions worked well but almost bankrupted the state. His reign was virtually free from Xiongnu border aggression, but the afterglow was short-lived. His successors tilted towards *Heqin* in order to save money: Walls and wars were too costly.

17.

MECHANICAL ADVANTAGE

Trigger mechanism of a crossbow

Every morning, the National Museum of China in Beijing plays classroom to hundreds of school students, who rush through 5000 years of their culture's art history, capturing their favourite antiquuities with a click of a smartphone as they go.

One day, acting the foreigner with no knowledge of Chinese history, I pointed to an unimpressive-looking relic in the 'Ancient China' exhibition and turned to a group of students. 'Do you know what that is?' I asked.

'I'm not too sure,' murmured one.

'It's some kind of on/off switch,' added another.

'We should read the explanation,' said another. 'It's a crossbow!'

'A crossbow? I can't see a crossbow . . .' A debate ensued.

The cryptic object they were struggling to place in context was the bronze trigger mechanism of a crossbow. Although highly complex to produce, crossbows were in fact manufactured, being made in mass quantities by the use of machinery, beginning several centuries BC.

Based on finds of bolts and triggers, the crossbow probably debuted on the Chinese battleground of the Chu Kingdom, in around the seventh century BC, and soon became the most favoured weapon at the Wall, above sword, spear and bow. It was prized for firing from elevated positions, through openings in battlements, for its sheer power (range) and for its general 'user-friendliness'. It was already a prominent weapon by the Qin Dynasty, and formed the bulk of the Han's firepower against the Xiongnu. Thereafter, in diverse sizes and elaborated forms, it consolidated itself as the stalwart, and was used against the Mongols. By the time of the Manchu conquest, in the mid-seventeenth century, it had accrued a long service record approaching 2500 years.

The crossbow was the world's first mechanical weapon, and it gave the Chinese a huge military advantage. Moreover, it was so difficult to manufacture that even when China's nomadic enemies captured it, they could not replicate it. The design was protected by its complexity.

State foundries produced trigger mechanisms by the hundreds of thousand during the reign of Han Wendi (180–157 BC), when the weapon's crucial mechanical heart was a banned export. Nonetheless, examples were smuggled to Korea and Sogdiana (in Central Asia), where they were copied. By the twelfth century, the use of crossbows in southern Europe produced such carnage that the Catholic Church's Lateran Council, which convened in Rome in 1139, banned the killing machine on humanitarian grounds. It was deemed so lethal that it should not be used by Christian against Christian.

Steppe nomads were makers and masters of the composite bow (see Object 8), and few Han Chinese archers could match their enemies' skills. Technology came to their rescue with a simple device that was strong enough to hold an adapted bow.

The trigger is a multi-part assembly that easily fits into the palm of one's hand, and its advantages were demonstrated to me in the village of Yaoyuancun, one hour's drive east of Beijing. There, I entered a workshop and was transported back in time, to an earlier

DESCRIPTION:	Bronze trigger mechanism
SIGNIFICANCE:	The mechanics at the heart of the crossbow, the first killing machine
ORIGIN:	Three Kingdoms Period, circa AD 280
LOCATION:	National Museum of China, Beijing

era of weapons history. Sitting amidst piles of tools and the raw materials for making bows and crossbows was Yang Fuxi.

'The Han crossbow evolved by mounting an extremely heavy draw-weight composite bow onto a stock,' he says, 'but the special component is here, the trigger. It is this invention that made the crossbow easy to use, even for someone with inferior strength and skill.'

The trigger I'd seen in the museum was replicated by Yang Fuxi and neatly embedded into the stock of a crossbow. Beneath the stock, under the mechanism, was the so-called hanging knife, or trigger. The advantage of the trigger lies in its ability to store power, and release it on demand.

In ancient times, the manufacture of two moving pieces on two shafts demanded quality casting and precise machining. The meticulous production process was carried out in some quantity, at least low-volume industrial scale. Armies of several thousand crossbowmen, half of them firing while the others reloaded, could unleash heavy outbursts of bolts.

Several variants to the basic crossbow design evolved, including a large-scale version for launching several large bolts, and a 'machine-gun' crossbow, which could fire ten bolts within fifteen seconds. The advantage of these weapons is like that of hot weapons against cold, tanks against cavalry, or nuclear weapons against conventional bombs.

I compared the bow and the crossbow. Drawing a bow, even to half of its 27-kilogram weight, put my arms, shoulders, chest and abdomen under great muscular strain, with the brunt of the stress borne by the three fingers I used to pull back the bowstring. Trembling from the strain, I could hold the full draw position only momentarily. To use this weapon effectively, it was clear I needed brute strength, much practice and plenty of accumulated skill.

Loading the crossbow was so much easier. I used my feet to hold its 'wings' against the ground, and pulled the bowstring back with two hands, securing it behind the trigger's notch. It took strength, but it was a strength I had – in my arms, legs and lower back. With the crossbow loaded, I lifted it, placed its end against my shoulder, took aim and waited for the right moment to fire. I was relaxed. It was as easy as one, two, three. Use of the crossbow demanded technique, not strength. Its manufacture relies on technique, tradition and time.

In 1720 the Yang family migrated from Manchuria to Beijing on imperial orders to establish an archery workshop within the precincts of the Imperial City. By 1823, however, the bow's use was on the wane, as guns increased in prominence and popularity. The Yangs moved to Dongsi, joining other bowyers at *Gongjian Dayuan*, or 'the Archery Workyard', where they made weapons for public sale.

Nine generations later, into the 1950s, Yang Wentong was still making weapons in the time-honoured way – on one occasion he presented a prized specimen to Chairman Mao himself. For Yang, however, political regression, not technological advancement, would put an end to his craft: imperial connections became taboo under the political extremism of Maoist China of the late 1950s. Family history was no longer a source of pride but something to be hidden. During the Cultural Revolution's movement to smash the 'Four Olds' – the traditional customs, culture, habits and ideas of China – Yang Wentong hid his last remaining bow in a pile of firewood. His son, Yang Fuxi, became a factory worker, then a driver.

More than thirty years later, in 1993, Yang Wentong started to rejuvenate his family's craft by teaching Yang Fuxi the complex, time-consuming techniques. With local government support, growing interest among weapons enthusiasts and collectors (who pay up to US$8000 for his masterpieces) and recognition of his skill as an intangible national heritage, Yang Fuxi, with his son Yang Yi, have continued to revive this aspect of ancient China's military history, rescuing it from extinction.

On a bare winter field, I draw my bow, savouring the twang and swish as my arrow flies into the distant haze, straight and true. I raise my crossbow and squeeze its trigger, savouring its sweet mechanical click. These sounds have been much more than a year in the making. They are echoes of history, embodied in an art that has taken the Yang family 300 years to perfect, and preserve.

Part Three

INTRUSIONS

Objects from AD 221 to 1368

Cyclical conflicts destroyed, recreated and destroyed the geopolitical entity of China, ruled by one. The land was divided among a few and then among many, until the late fourth century, when a nomadic group exploited the division and came south to rule a large portion. Reunification was achieved between the late sixth and tenth centuries by the Sui, the glorious Tang and then, the hapless Song. From the millennium onwards the country faced the Liao, then the Jin, which forced a retreat south, and then the Mongols, who, in conquering the Southern Song, ruled all of China.

These eleven centuries feature three phases of border history. In the period of division, before AD 589, several 'Lesser Great Walls', considerably shorter than their predecessors, were built by some minor dynasties. During reunification – actually an interbellum from the late sixth to tenth centuries – only one of the three dynasties, the Sui, constructed a Great Wall.

Surprisingly, the Liao, the Western Xia and the Jin each constructed 'Conquest Dynasty Great Walls' as they edged south, keeping watch behind them. But neither these nor an empire full of fortified towns and cities were enough to stop the Mongols.

18.

BECOMING CHINESE

Figurine of an armoured horse and rider

I recently saw one of the largest ancient helmets I've ever seen. It was extremely long, more than half a metre, and comparatively narrow, with two large round holes for vision pierced in its heavily rusted iron segments, topped by a high, crest-like brim. This macabre hulk, known as a chanfron, was not made to protect a man's head but the head of a horse.

It had been a long search for this crowning piece of barder, or horse armour, which I came across at the National Museum of Korea, in Seoul. I'd been on the lookout for a glimpse of the real thing ever since I first saw a striking depiction of iron-clad cavalry in a most unexpected place. It featured as a Northern Wei ceiling mural of Cave No. 285 at Mogao, near Dunhuang, in north-west China's Gansu Province, one of the largest 'monastery style' caverns at the 'Caves of Ten Thousand Buddhas'.

The cavalry in the mural were Tuoba Xianbei horsemen. They interested me because they wrote the opening chapter of what transpired to be a remarkable and recurring episode of the Great Wall's story: that for approximately 800 years out of 2200 years of Chinese dynastic history, Hans were ruled by non-Hans who originated from the north, outside the Wall, founding 'conquest' dynasties within it. Their success stories constantly reminded Han regimes of the need for an astute border defence policy.

Having seen the chanfron, the awful head of the beast as it was, I yearned to gain a fuller picture of the monstrous horseman's appearance. I found spectacular and complete sets of barder across Europe – for example, at the Royal Palace Armoury in Madrid – but they were in steel, were made for ceremonial occasions, and dated from the late Renaissance, circa sixteenth century. Component parts in iron, dating from its initial appearance 1000 years earlier, in the middle of the first millennium AD, and used by the likes of the Tuoba Xianbei horsemen, were much rarer. I found no trace of it in any of the great museums along, or on either side of, the Great Wall.

Few segments of iron barder have survived because it was utility military equipment: if it didn't rust, it would be reused and eventually consigned to the scrapheap. My rusty find in Seoul, at some 1500 years old, is therefore quite remarkable.

The trail warmed up as I found a related object, and a potentially more enriching one for our Great Wall studies: a pottery figurine of a warrior saddled upon his armoured horse. It stood closely in place and time to other leads in my story: the object was displayed at the Shanhaiguan Great Wall Museum, not too far across the Yellow Sea from Seoul, and like the Mogao mural, it dated from the early sixth century of the Northern Wei.

After the fall of the Han Dynasty in AD 221, China divided into the Three Kingdoms, experienced a brief unification under the Jin Dynasty, then fragmented into the Sixteen Kingdoms, many of which were takeovers by various nomadic groups. In the late fourth century, the Tuoba Xianbei, as herders, impoverished by deprivation of opportunities to raid a well-organised and productive Han China, exploited the chaos and rode south-west to conquer and unify many of the minnow kingdoms. They established the Northern Wei Dynasty.

Our mounted warrior gives a face to the Touba Xianbei people, the first nomads to establish a Han-style ruling dynasty. Along with the help of other foreign faces, which we will meet in our next two objects, these three will usher us one by one into the period of chaotic division, through the stability of the reunification, and up to the millennium and a second major conquest dynasty, which marked the start of the most sustained era of nomadic rule in China's history.

The warrior was one of scores of similar figurines found in the tomb of Princess Ruru, who died aged thirteen back in AD 510 in Ci County, near Handan, about 400 kilometres south-west of Beijing. What looks solid and chunky is in fact hollow, light and fragile, a typical burial article. In colour, the figurine's mottled surface looks like a cloudy grey and white sky, with traces of sunset pink, showing that it was originally once painted. It's about the size of an old-fashioned doll, and perhaps because we know that it accompanied a young teenage princess in the afterlife, it exudes a somewhat romantic feeling of perhaps having also functioned as one of her toys in life. Over its 1500-year history it did suffer a broken hind leg, which thankfully the restoration department has repaired. I always feel dreadfully nostalgic at the sight of broken toys, for they remind us how all children move on, leaving behind what they once cherished. The Touba Xianbei moved on, not only south, but also to a major change in lifestyle.

Two things strike me as I examine the figurine up close. It's clear that by cladding your fast and nimble bare-fleshed steed in iron armour, you are going to handicap him considerably. This sacrifice of the horse's natural qualities is clearly conveyed by the horse figurine's wide stance. Its fore and hind legs are splayed

DESCRIPTION:	Pottery figurine of a Xianbei nomadic warrior on an armoured horse
SIGNIFICANCE:	Portrait of the first nomadic conquerors of Han Chinese territory
ORIGIN:	Tomb of Princess Ruru, Ci County, near Handan, Hebei Province, circa AD 510
LOCATION:	Shanhaiguan Great Wall Museum

for stability, which indicates the considerable weight of the full barder, estimated at more than 100 kilograms.

What necessitated such a burden? In the same way the machine gun took the skill out of the rifle, so the crossbow's mechanics helped level the balance of firepower on the battlefield for the less skilful. Crossbows from the Han Dynasty onward gave warriors greater range, if not accuracy. Meanwhile, in the Three Kingdoms Period of the late third century, the renowned strategist Zhuge Liang invented an automatically reloading crossbow that was particularly favoured in relatively close combat, as it could spray fifteen bolts in quick succession at the enemy. The increased likelihood of horses being hit made barder mandatory.

My second observation is that while the figurine's artistic styling is Buddhist, the subject is military. This creates the rather odd contrast of a serene, compassionate-looking rider mounted upon a heavily armoured horse. To me, this arrangement shows the very different two-stage journey of the people who made it, and whom it depicts.

Another 'first' achievement of the Tuoba Xianbei was their adoption of Han ways. Their seizure of territory in the late fourth century forced many Hans to flee, fearing being ruled by 'barbarians'. It was a victory tainted by a loss of the Han's productive force. After initially developing a hybrid Tuoba–Han regime, the Xiaowen Emperor (who reigned between 471 and 499) accelerated his dynasty's Sinicisation by personal example. He abandoned his own family clan name, Tuoba, and replaced it with a Han name – and he required all others to do the same. Chinese language and dress were adopted, intermarriage with Hans was encouraged, and shamanism renounced.

As our warrior's serene expression indicates, the Northern Wei embraced Chinese Buddhism; the belief's distinctive architectures, sculptures and fine arts transformed the territory. Tall pagodas were constructed to mark temples, and giant statues cut into cliff faces. Underground, too, from the single tomb of a princess in the east to the Cave of Ten Thousand Buddhas in the west, colourful, lifelike art and sacred texts shed light on an aspect of the human experience that previously had been a mysterious step into darkness. Through its tenet of rebirth, Buddhism provided an explanation for death, a concern neglected by the indigenous Han philosophies of Confucianism and Daoism.

For us, however, the most significant and surprising landmark left by the Tuoba Xianbeis on their journey to becoming Chinese was their use – largely through recycling – of an extant Great Wall defence in the north. This had been built centuries earlier, during the Han Dynasty, but part of it was now revamped to fend off assaults from the new occupants of the steppe region, the Rouran and the Tujue.

In its smile, stance and style, this figurine shows us how the Tuoba Xianbei became the Northern Wei. His story tells us that while wars were won with valour, weapons and barder, the Tuoba Xianbei made peace and prosperity by adopting Chinese ways. In doing so, they not only changed their own identity but also gave new meaning to 'Chinese-ness'. Originally, it was defined as a Han story, but now it was redefined as diverse.

To me, the serene smile of the warrior on the iron-clad horse says: 'First we beat them, and then we joined them.'

19.

THE GAP YEARS

Tri-coloured glaze figurine of a camel

What's the longest gap in the Great Wall? This question might see you reaching for a map of China, locating the Wall and proceeding along its battlement symbol to find and then estimate the length of its gaps. You might ponder: 'Was the Wall there originally? And if it was, what happened to it?'

My question is deliberately ambiguous: it doesn't refer to spatial gaps in any of the walls' geography, but temporal gaps in its trans-dynastic construction. The Great Wall has been under construction in for most of its existence, with only a few relatively short breaks – after the Western Han during the Three Kingdoms Period, for example, and now.

As the seventh century dawns, we are poised on the edge of the longest chronological gap in Great Wall construction. The Tang (AD 618–907) was China's longest-lasting dynasty (291 years), outliving other lengthy rules such as the Western Han (190 years) and the Ming (276 years). But unlike these blood-brother ethnic Han dynasties, whose rule pervaded 'all China', the Tang never built a Great Wall of its own.

(I should note that the Tang did build a long wall of sorts, but it was a rather feeble effort, compared to its much lengthier

DESCRIPTION:	Tri-Coloured glazed pottery figurine of a group of musicians on a camel.
SIGNIFICANCE:	Insight on Tang China's control of the lucrative 'Silk Road' trade route.
ORIGIN:	Xi'an, Shaanxi Province
LOCATION:	Ancient China Exhibition, National Museum of China, Beijing.

relatives. As it was less than 100 kilometres in length, I include it in the 'disputed' group of structures that do not possess the basic requirement of a Great Wall: extraordinary length.)

Why include in this book an object from a dynasty that built no part of the Great Wall? I believe that the reason for this long pause in Wall-building is integral to the overall Wall story. In order to understand 'the Wall', you need to understand something much broader: the relationship between the Chinese and their northern nomadic neighbours. Just as questions arise over the reasons for spatial gaps in today's Wall, very intriguing questions arise when we try to understand why there was no Tang Dynasty Great Wall worth mentioning. What alternative strategies or policies did the Tang use to defend their frontiers?

I began my quest in literature. Li Bai (AD 701–762) refers to the 'Great Wall' in his epic poem 'Fighting South of the Rampart':

> Last year we were fighting at the source of the Sangkan;
> This year we are fighting on the Onion road.
> We have washed our swords in the surf of Parthian Seas;
> We have pastured our horses among the snows of the Tian Mountains.
> The King's armies have grown grey and old
> Fighting ten thousand leagues away from home.
> The Huns have no trade by battle and carnage;
> They have no fields or ploughlands,
> But only wastes where white bones lie among yellow sands.
> Where the House of Qin built the Great Wall that was to keep away the Tartars,
> There, in its turn, the House of Han lit beacons of war.
> The beacons are always alight, fighting and marching never stop.
> Men die in the field, slashing sword to sword;
> The horses of the conquered neigh piteously to Heaven.

Crows and hawks peck for human guts,
Carry them in their beaks and hang them on the branches of
withered trees.
Captains and soldiers are smeared on the bushes and grass;
The general schemed in vain.
Know therefore that the sword is a cursed thing
Which the wise man brandishes only if he must.

Poetry is a language of its own, but to me this poem speaks of geography, mentioning a handful of places, some of which I know, some I don't. It refers to great distances stretching to a new frontier, where the old business of battle is fought, now as it was before. It speaks of territorial expansion, and questions the purpose of it.

The poem prompted me to reach for an historical atlas of China and Central Asia, so I could see the extent of the Tang Empire. In outline it looked like a large bone, with bulbous knuckles in the north-west and south-east, linked by a thinner segment of land. The eastern mass was the heartland of China, centred on the Yellow River, while the other mass was referred to as the 'Western Regions'. Between the two ran the Hexi Corridor.

The map summarised, and simplified, a very complex historical period, and poignantly emphasised a trade link of paramount economic importance. Unprecedented prosperity was enjoyed in the heartland of Tang China, so glittering that it was dubbed the 'Golden Age'. A plethora of visual arts from the period evidence the good life of the Tangs. The object I have chosen does exactly that.

This large, bright, joyful figurine shows us a band of foreign musicians – we might even assume them to be expats from the Western Regions who are working abroad, part of a permanent foreign community of around 5000 residing in the imperial capital of Chang'an, populated by 1 million inhabitants. Created in stunning tricoloured glazed pottery, the piece depicts the symbiotic relationship that existed between powerful and populous Tang China, home to four of the world's five largest cities, and its Silk Road neighbours. It was a mutually beneficial relationship, oiled by lucrative exchanges of goods. This kept the merchant class happy, while taxation poured into government coffers, funding huge military offensives and shrewd political frontier campaigns.

The fruits of this 'soft power' from the Silk Road helped foot the bill of the hard power drives in other directions. Specifically, we are talking about the land north of China's heartland: the steppe. Well off the main transcontinental trade route, successive groups of northern nomads were ostracised, their access to the Silk Road trade route blocked by the Chinese masters of its eastern end. Between the sixth and eighth centuries, the Tujue Empire stretched across this vast region, which was targeted and subjugated by a very well financed Tang military. The Silk Road economic boom paid for these wars of aggression, and others.

In comparing the new Tang approach to the more conventional one of a Wall built and operated by the preceding Sui Dynasty, Emperor Tang Taizong (AD 626–649) congratulated one of his generals who had won victories against the Turks by saying, 'You are a better Great Wall than the ramparts built by Sui Yangdi.' The Emperor went on to rule for two decades which became known as 'the Zhenguan Era of good government', laying the foundations for the Tang's Golden Era, the prelude to three long centuries of solidarity, unitary rule, prosperity and expansion.

20.

MILLENNIUM MAN

Silver funerary mask of a Qidan nobleman

Six billion people recently experienced the pivotal point in time-keeping which we dubbed 'the millennium', while 'only' an estimated 265 million experienced the one before, in AD 1000 – still a huge number of people. Of them, few can show us their true faces. This funerary mask personifies one of them, a man of very great distinction. It's the visage of a Qidan tribesman, a nobleman, who witnessed the millennium before last. For me, seeking out the transformative episodes of the Great Wall's tortuous story, he was in the right place at just the right time.

The Qidans built one of the most mysterious of all the Great Walls. The Liao Wall, which remains as a parallel trench-mound structure, streaks across hundreds of kilometres of Mongolia's Eastern Steppe. Along its course, I found nothing that might reveal the personality of these people, apart from a few pottery sherds. Then I met this Qidan nobleman of the millennium in one of Ulaanbaatar's most remarkable museums. His funerary mask illuminates the changing world of the Liao, nomadic tribesmen turned empire builders.

First, a post-mortem. This Qidan lived between around AD 980 and 1030, and was buried on Mongolia's Eastern Steppe. As far

DESCRIPTION:	Beaten and chased silver funerary mask of a Qidan nobleman
SIGNIFICANCE:	Portrait of a Qidan, the founders of the Liao Dynasty (AD 906–1125), first builders of 'alien regime' Great Wall
ORIGIN:	Eastern Mongolia, circa early eleventh century
LOCATION:	Museum of the Great Hunnu Empire, Erdene, east of Ulaanbaatar

as a funeral went, you got what your family could afford. His were nobles, so they commissioned a silver mask.

A mould was made of the man's face; it was then inverted and covered by a large, thin metal sheet, perhaps heated to render it malleable. A metalsmith used a hammer to shape it. Like a crude three-dimensional rubbing, the sheet assumed the size, shape and features of the deceased man's face.

One thousand years later we can recognise this Qidan's long, thin visage, his hollow cheeks, his small puckered mouth, which is rimmed by a sparse moustache and a scraggly beard, his large, high nose, and his small, squinting eyes, which are set deep in their sockets.

Undoubtedly the most famous funerary mask of antiquity is that of Egypt's King Tutankhamun (1341–1321 BC), discovered in 1922 by archaeologist Howard Carter. It is unique. This Qidan funerary mask is one of a genre, and they have been found in gold, silver and bronze inside tombs scattered across a swathe of today's north and north-east China and Eastern Mongolia – the former empire of the Liao. Many have been smuggled worldwide, where even silver masks are expected to fetch more than US$100000 at auction. This one was saved from such a fate by the Mongolian antiquary Purevjav Eredenechuluun, who in 2011, just a few months before he passed away, told me of his patriotic quest: to save Mongolia's cultural heritage from disappearing overseas. He had been working to acquire antiquities to put them on display for the Mongolian people.

Our millennium man lived during the Liao Dynasty, a critical point in our Great Wall journey – its midpoint, in fact. His people, the Qidans, nomads turned pastoralists, 'reintroduced' Wall-building proper after the 300-year lapse during the Tang. Their establishment of the Liao heralded the start of a series of unprecedented events in the Great Wall theatre of war, for China and the region's geopolitics as a whole. Over 470 years, the whole region progressively fell to the sustained advances of northerners. One after another they came: first the Qidans, then the Jurchens, and after them the Mongols.

This funerary mask gives a face to those who set in motion what we could call the era of northern rule. From the fourth century, the Qidans had been rooted to the grasslands, but they took advantage of the permeable border policies favoured during the Tang, and when it collapsed they made their move from steppe to plain. They steadily increased their domain, eventually reaching the edge of the North China Plain, where they chose to build one of their capitals, which they named Yanjing. Geographically, that lies under today's modern Beijing; thus, the Qidans became the first 'Beijingers'. Their empire stretched from the Siberian and Manchurian forests in the north and east, through the steppe and Gobi Desert at the centre, to the North China Plain in the south; over such territory, a major challenge for the Qidans was to rule a multi-ethnic population. They set up two systems of government: the northern division contained mainly Qidan nomadic and pastoral herders living in *gers*, while the southern division comprised crop cultivators, mainly ethnic Han, living in sedentary abodes.

Back to the mask. We cannot look into this Qidan's eyes, but we can try to look through them. What did this middle-ranking Qidan nobleman see on the social and political frontiers of his world? He witnessed a change in his people's way of life, from *ger* tents to fixed abodes, as well as the waning in importance of age-old tribal and family ties, which were supplanted by the array of relationships one develops in a town or city.

He saw the Qidans change from being looters and raiders to being builders, traders and diplomats. Perhaps diplomacy was the Qidans' greatest achievement. As the Qidan Liao coexisted with the Song, they enforced a change in attitudes. During the early years of the reign of Song Zhenzong (AD 998–1022) the Qidans were dubbed 'cowards of the north', 'hideous barbarians' and 'wolves'. (The legendary border region alarm signal termed *lang yan*, or 'wolf smoke', may derive from this era; see Object 28.)

Later in Zhenzong's reign, under military and diplomatic pressure, the Qidans' customary sourness and derision was dropped in exchange for polite accommodation, kinship and respect. Our man of the millennium witnessed the Qidans becoming a 'brotherly kingdom', a 'northern state' and eventually 'the Great Liao'. He experienced the era of national 'signage' being edited in their favour, respectfully, with an imperial decree abolishing place names with derisory meanings, such as those which included *lu*, meaning 'coward', and *hu*, 'barbarian'. He participated in the ascent of his people, going south, seizing land and enforcing an elevation of their position in the eyes and minds of the Han.

21.

THE 75, 15, 10 FORMULA

A pottery hand grenade

While walking in the lee of a fine section of rammed-earth Wall in Ningxia, I found many glazed potsherds (see Object 6). When I walked outside the Wall, and a little further away, I found an odd-looking fragment that was different. It too was glazed and curved, thick-walled, but it had several broken spiky nodules. I estimated that, when whole, it would have been about the size of a large apple. I was holding a fragment of a hand grenade.

I guessed it had been thrown long ago from the top of the battlements – maybe as a test throw, or perhaps to halt some charging nomadic cavalrymen. But all I'd found was a fragment of its shell, the container. I found a perfect example in Shanhaiguan's Great Wall Museum, but even that specimen was missing the most interesting component – the propellant, the gunpowder – and this is the Song story we'll now explore.

The invention of gunpowder was one of mankind's greatest accidents: alchemists who were trying to concoct imperial elixirs accidentally discovered its astounding properties. What they formulated by mixing potassium nitrate (KNO_3, commonly called saltpetre), sulphur and carbon did not prolong life; it did the exact opposite, shortening it with abrupt efficiency. *Huo yao*, or fire medicine, if mixed in proportions of seventy-five per cent saltpetre, fifteen per cent sulphur and ten per cent carbon, not only burned exceedingly well, it exploded with a flash and thunderous noise. The formula is mentioned in *Wujing Zongyao*, or 'A Collection of the Most Important Military Techniques', written around 1044, having been commissioned by the Song Renzong Emperor during his campaigns to resist Tangut and Qidan threats. Better weapons were sought that would put the Song ahead in the arms race.

From the outset, the nomads had held the technical advantage with their excellent composite bows and horse/archer combination. The Chinese copied them, and then came up with the mechanically ingenious crossbow mechanism (see Object 17) and the stirrup. Now, it seems, in the Song, they are poised again to call the shots by pioneering a new era of arms: 'hot' weapons that relied on gunpowder.

This all sounds neat and logical – until we consider what actually happened during the Song. The dynasty presided over the largest loss of territorial sovereignty in Chinese history: first from the Northern Song to the Southern Song, and then from the Southern Song to the Mongol-founded Yuan Dynasty. This suggests that the advantage of gunpowder existed only in theory, and not in practice.

Glazed grenades like the one I found provide some clues. If delivered on target, they could be lethal, but otherwise they were just bangs and flashes. What matters most in any weapons advantage is the accuracy of delivery. While close combat depended on strength, skill and bravery, longer-distance weapons that projected missiles – whether cold or hot – relied on a wider combination of qualities, including strength, skill, speed, adeptness, instinct and coordination.

Archers and crossbowmen were thoroughly trained, and then

they honed their skills until they were instinctive. Crack archers could quickly and precisely adjust the range and trajectory of their arrows and bolts to hit moving targets. Their weapons became extensions of their own arms. Weapons that projected burning or exploding missiles were more complex and more hazardous. They were slower and more dangerous to load, and thus were less suited to moving targets.

The Song arsenal generated a bizarre array of new weapons for firing and tossing missiles of all shapes and sizes, but generally they were better suited to use in urban environments, particularly counter-siege situations. Such conflicts featured large deployments of besieging troops, and cavalry en masse that presented itself as a large single target, whether static or charging.

Frontier warfare was different. Grenades were not suited to elaborate mechanical launching. For one thing, trebuchet-type weapons were too bulky, too complex and too expensive to be deployed at regular intervals along the frontier's defences. Moreover, they were only suited to striking large and static or slow-moving targets, while in the Great Wall theatre of war most incidents were characterised by sudden attacks and retreats. Mechanical launchers could not be finely tuned, and lacked that irreplaceable human skill of nimbleness, adjustment and instinct.

No, it must be that grenades were thrown from the Great Walls in the time-honoured way, demanding strong and nimble arms, especially when the target wasn't static. A throw's weight and trajectory depended on the circumstances: how fast the target was moving, how long the fuse had been burning for, and even what the prevailing weather conditions were. Most vital of all was the thrower's sense of anticipation. Showers of grenades, all aimed at a single target area, would surely have been an especially deadly tactic.

To enhance the thrower's grip, the grenade had nodules on its

DESCRIPTION:	A glazed pottery hand grenade
SIGNIFICANCE:	Perfection of gunpowder formula during the Northern Song, circa 1044
ORIGIN:	Ming Dynasty, circa fourteenth century; found in the early 1990s during reconstruction work of the Juyongguan Great Wall, Changping District
LOCATION:	Shanhaiguan Great Wall Museum

surface – the disastrous potential consequences of a mis-throw are obvious. The nodules would have also enhanced the shrapnel effect when the porcelain case fragmented. And why were the grenades glazed? To ensure that, once prepared and stored for use, the arms were not affected by damp, rain or snow. And perhaps also to make them look even more impressive.

It may seem strange that even during the Ming, some four centuries after the Song gunpowder revolution, the delivery of a grenade still relied on a nimble and powerful arm. Another four centuries on, during World War I, grenades were still thrown by hand, illustrating the very long time it took for a mechanical technology to be developed that would offer a superior launch method.

Song weaponry was more suited to defence than attack. The advantage of gunpowder was theoretical rather than practical, and in 1127 the Song and its tens of millions of Han Chinese retreated south, where – paradoxically – they created a dynasty of unprecedented innovation, population growth, increased productivity and bustling commercial life. Yet it was short-lived, and destined to fail: there was nowhere further south to which it could retreat. As Winston Churchill said of Dunkirk in 1940, hoping to temper Britain's euphoria at rescuing half a million Allied troops from Normandy's beaches, 'Wars are not won by evacuations.'

22.

MAPPING HISTORY

'Handy Maps of the Past Dynasties,
Chronologically Organised'

If you're setting up home anytime soon, you might be well advised to save a few cubic metres of living space, and a tree for the planet, and forget about buying what has long been considered essential within the home of any educated family: a bookcase. You'd be better off buying a tablet or an ebook reader.

In August 2012 the UK arm of the world's largest bookseller announced that sales of its ebooks had overtaken sales of its printed books for the first time. Like it or not, wherever you're reading this, and in whatever language, you're witnessing the biggest change in publishing since it took off in Song Dynasty China some 900 years ago.

The printing revolution is interesting enough, and relevant to our story. Over the centuries, the reprinting and copying of maps has left us with numerous editions of *Lidai Dili Zhizhang Tu*, or 'Handy Maps of the Past Dynasties, Chronologically Organised'. The oldest, an original Song edition, is housed at Toyo Bunko, the Oriental Library in Tokyo. This historical atlas is essential reading at this stage of our off-Wall journey, because it depicts a Great Wall symbol on each of its forty-four maps. I consult one closer to my home, a Qing copy kept in Peking University Library's Rare Books Collection.

Although it's a printed edition, the first stage of its production was the copying out, by hand, of every line and character, as book printing required the carving of wooden printing blocks – in reverse – for every page. This was a laborious, costly task, and only worthwhile if subscriptions were sold in advance, to cover the cost of months of labour by scholars and artisans – literate men with wood, chisels and especially dexterous hands. True craftsmen.

The original book therefore gives us an insight into printing, one of China's 'four great inventions' (the others were the compass, paper and gunpowder). This technology became the foundation of the publishing industry, which catered to the emergent educated class's demand for knowledge, the best means by which to get up the social ladder and become wealthier in an increasingly competitive world. The Chinese preoccupation with examinations, still prevalent today, began back then, in the mid-1100s.

In turning the pages of this 'Handy Atlas', therefore, we are not only surveying the historical geography of China from the Song back into a semi-mythical time, we're also witnessing the birth of popular education. Woodblock printing would put more knowledge into the minds of more people than ever before, just as digital technology today has opened up a new era of information dissemination, allowing any author to reach potentially billions of people.

The atlas is one of nine cartographic objects that I've chosen for the Great Wall 50. Visually, it is the dullest: it's monochrome and unimpressively small, just twenty-three by thirty centimetres, dwarfed by the likes of the original *Huayi Tu* (see Object 13), imperially commissioned during the Tang and said to have measured seven by three metres. Yet these differences demonstrate this atlas's very different social purpose, and call to mind its target audience.

The atlas was designed and produced to appeal to a particular

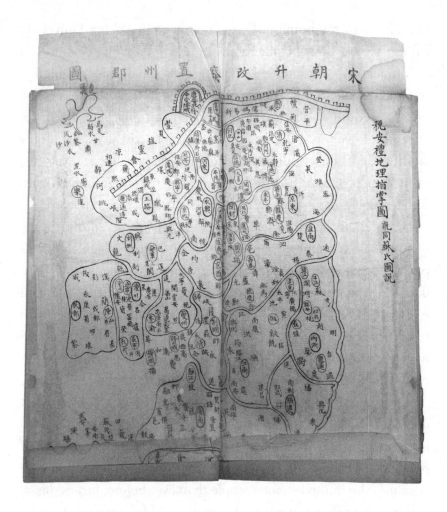

DESCRIPTION:	*Lidai Dili Zhizhang Tu*, or 'Handy Maps of the Past Dynasties, Chronologically Organised'; a hand-copied edition from the Qing Dynasty
SIGNIFICANCE:	An historical atlas showing the presence of Great Walls before the twelfth century
ORIGIN:	Compiled by Shui Anli during the Southern Song Dynasty, circa 1140
LOCATION:	Rare Books Collection, Peking University Library

market. It was printed cheaply, without frills, because it was meant to function as essential study material. Its first buyers were probably the parents of aspiring young men about to sit civil service entrance exams in the early 1140s – their first step towards becoming government officials. The editor of this atlas was not trying to impress an emperor, or court officials, or the military's top brass. He was doing quite the opposite – summarising and simplifying history for students.

The editor's challenge was to present history in a simple and clear form that examinees could easily remember. The product had to condense a wealth of historical information into as few pages as possible. It had to fit on a modest table, not a minister's desk; when opened, it's exactly the same size as a *National Geographic* magazine. The author, said to be Shui Anli, prioritised visuals rather than characters. This would be a new way of looking at history, simplifying and clarifying it by means of maps – one for each era. The *Lidai Dili Zhizhang Tu* is the world's oldest known historical atlas. Europeans didn't think of presenting history on maps in a single book until the sixteenth century.

So, let's consider the historical information the atlas contains. We see a battlement symbol representing a Great Wall on each and every page. What these depictions represent, or misrepresent, requires some careful thought.

As we turn the atlas's forty-four pages, a pattern emerges: things become repetitive. The shape of China remains more or less the same, as does the route of the Great Walls. It seems the author is ignorant of the fact that the size and shape of China's sovereign territory changed from era to era – and, post-Qin, from dynasty to dynasty. Similarly, the presence of a Great Wall is generalised. Rather disappointingly, these maps shed no light on the various routes of the different dynastic Great Walls, or of the pre-dynastic long walls which preceded them. Superficially at least, the atlas is monotonous and, for the Wall scholar, inaccurate.

To make the most of this atlas, we need to focus on what we do have. One thing to note is the mandatory inclusion of a Great Wall, not always as an active defence but as a geographical marker. For example, it's anachronistic, if not an historical blunder, that one of the atlas's spreads shows 'A Map of the Nine Regions of the Shang Dynasty' which depicts a Great Wall: there were none at that time, circa the late second millennium BC. The cartographer aimed to orient maps users by including a Great Wall symbol as a boundary of China. On later maps in the atlas – for example, that of the Song – the Great Wall's presence indicated its existence as ruins. It therefore functioned as an historical marker, just as contemporary maps of the People's Republic show the line of the Ming Great Wall's ruins.

But generalisations have pitfalls. Including a Great Wall as a standard geographical feature led users to think that China had always had a Great Wall – that it was something built and repaired, passed on, inherited and maintained. In fact, only sixteen out of sixty-six legitimate dynasties ever built or rebuilt previously existing Walls. Constructing functional Great Walls was a recurring strategy, but certainly not permanent or chronologically continuous. Nor were the Walls geographically static, as the atlas suggests.

Yet the greatest irony of the atlas is the map showing contemporary Song China. As elsewhere in the atlas, the Great Wall is indicated by a stylistic rampart, etched with turrets, which stand like disciplined sentries along a battlement stretching between the Gobi Desert and the ocean, giving the reader the impression of total defence across the empire's northern periphery. Barbarians are mentioned 'outside' the Wall, but their actual territorial gains inside the Wall are ignored, undrawn, unacknowledged.

By the time of the atlas's printing, the Western Xia, Liao and Jin had successively taken vast areas of the Song's north, forcing the border south. This map is evidence of how maps can be manipulated by political orders for self-protection. Wouldn't it have been folly for an emperor to authorise the production of maps that showed his government's incompetent loss of territory? That would be tantamount to revoking his own mandate from heaven.

Professor Jerry Brotton, of Queen Mary University, London, and author of the bestseller *A History of the World in Twelve Maps*, summarises the pros and cons of our Song atlas: 'The overwhelming majority of maps put the culture that produced them at their centre. [Their] perspective literally centres individuals, it elevates them like gods, inviting them to take flight and look down upon the earth from a divine viewpoint . . . gazing at what can only be imagined by earthbound mortals . . . the map's dissimulating brilliance is to make the viewer believe, just for a moment, that such a perspective is real.'

The 'Handy Atlas' is thought to have been printed in the tens of thousands during the Southern Song; if that's correct, it would have permitted an unprecedented number of people to 'take flight' and see the history of China from the air. But its phoney geography concealed the true, grim state of Song China's contemporary defences: the barbarians were in fact well south of the Great Wall border. The future was set to become grimmer in the face of the most unified nomadic threat ever to materialise in the north.

23.

HARNESSING SUN AND WIND

Gold-tipped trident of a spirit banner

While most Chinese people typically associate the likes of Meng Jiangnü, Qin Shihuang and Qi Jiguang (see Objects 2, 11 and 36, respectively) with the Great Wall, I frequently hear a different name when I ask people of other nationalities whom they associate with the structure. The most common response is Genghis Khan.

Even when I don't ask the question, his name often appears anyway. I've frequently been up on the 'tourist' Wall at Badaling or Mutianyu and have heard first-time visitors, overwhelmed by the scene, musing: 'It's incredible, but it didn't stop Genghis Khan . . .'

Of course it didn't – the Ming Wall (1368–1644) was built after the time of Genghis Khan (1162–1227). Rather, it aimed to prevent history from repeating: to stop the Mongols, once they had been ousted from China, from invading again. And even if some of the tourists are speaking more knowledgably, referring to 'it' as the earlier Great Walls that were operating at the time of Genghis Khan – built by the Western Xia and the Jin – those border defences didn't stop him either.

The Mongols, as nomads, built little of permanence, yet the world's largest construction – the Ming Great Wall – was in some sense built for them, if posthumously. Like it or not,

Genghis Khan's name is irrevocably linked to the Ming Wall.

On the Mongols' continent-wide conquest of Asia, they became seasoned victors in surprise attacks, open battles and in siege warfare. According to some researchers, they conquered so many fortified cities that they made defensive walls obsolete. I disagree. The legacy of the Mongols' brutal success forewarned the Ming restorers of Han rule that the longevity of their dynasty depended on their success in keeping the Mongols out. They prompted the Ming to 'reinvent' the border defence system – and thus to build the greatest of China's many Great Walls. In 2005 the president of Mongolia, Nambaryn Enkhbayer, during a state visit, said: 'Yes, it is a "great" Wall, but I must add that it takes a great people to have a Wall like this built for them.'

Our next four objects tell us how 'the Mongols' transformed themselves from a family clan to that 'great people', a nation. Formidable firepower, armour and transportation all played vital roles, yet they were resources that could only be effectively pointed at larger enemies if combined sizably in scale and organised reliably and adeptly, an extraordinary process of unification. Without this, arrows, armour and horses might only be used in the usual way, by tribe fighting against tribe.

The leader of our group of four objects is a fork-like metal object called a *sulde*, or 'spirit banner'. Its symbolism shows us how nature and spirituality inspired a sense of destiny in the mind of a warrior, empowering him to rule his own, to become stronger by conquering others, and to unify them into his larger own.

When a steppe warrior died, the Mongols did not build any visible structure as a memorial, not even for their Great Khan. Graves were never marked: they were of no real importance, for they contained only a body. The soul of the person was believed to live on, forever entwined spiritually in the horsehair of the spirit banner.

We don't know which warrior, clan or tribe owned this spirit

DESCRIPTION:	A gold-tipped trident, the upper part of a Mongol *sulde*, or spirit banner
SIGNIFICANCE:	A symbol of unity on which Mongol military success depended
ORIGIN:	Mongolia, circa late twelfth century
LOCATION:	Museum of the Great Hunnu Empire, Erdene, east of Ulaanbaatar

banner but there's no better object with which to study the spirituality of the Mongols and the journey they took under Genghis Khan's leadership to conquer the Western Xia, the Jin and the Southern Song.

Like many historical artefacts, it is incomplete. What remains looks like a large trident. The frame, made of iron, is now severely rusted. In glorious contrast, the three untarnished golden tips flare up symmetrically. Each one has been worked into the shape of a flame. The central tip achieves almost perfect symmetry, while its surface and edges bear many more small curled flame designs. The two flanking spear tips, near mirror images of one another, flare outwards, balancing the trident.

Following the rusty stem downward, we see that it becomes hollow: the pole to which it was once attached is now missing. Also absent is a large round disc that served as a frame to which strands of long horsehair were attached. All artists' impressions of Mongols at war show a large spirit banner like this one, its thick horsehair swirling in the wind as it is held high during a charge, inspiring the nomadic warriors to victory.

Professor Jack Weatherford explains the mysterious significance of the spirit banner in his book *Genghis Khan and the Making of the Modern World*:

> Through the centuries on the rolling, grassy steppes of inner Asia, a warrior-herder carried a Spirit Banner, called a 'sulde', made by tying strands of hair from his best horses to the shaft of a spear, just below its blade. Whenever he set up camp, the warrior planted the Spirit Banner outside the entrance to his 'ger' to proclaim his identity and to stand as his perpetual guardian. The Spirit Banner always remained in the open air beneath the Eternal Blue Sky that the

Mongols worshiped. As the strands of hair blew and
tossed in the nearly constant breeze of the steppe,
they absorbed the power of the wind, the sky, and
the sun, and transferred them to the warrior. The
wind in the horsehair inspired the warrior's dreams
and encouraged him to pursue his own destiny. The
streaming and twisting of the horsehair in the wind
beckoned the owner ever onward, luring him away
from this spot to seek another . . . to create his own
fate in his life in this world.

The nomads' greatest weakness was disunity. They lived in small,
clustered encampments of cramped *gers*, and fierce family argu-
ments easily erupted, often becoming hostile. Everything was in
short supply, including people, and especially women. Inheritance customs saw widows become wives to their husband's oldest
surviving brother: the practice meant a clan did not have to offer
gifts to outside clans in order to win a wife. Female fertility was
a resource not to be wasted. More children increased a family's
chances of survival in this harsh environment, but the levirate
custom led to mistrust and killings as siblings and half-brothers
contested for dominance.

Mongoliin Nuuts Tovchoo, or 'The Secret History of the Mongols', written circa 1230, narrates the life and times of the boy
Temüjin who became Genghis Khan. It contains 'The Parable
of the Five Arrows', in which Alanqu'o, a mother of five sons,
heard the oldest two wondering who fathered their three younger
brothers:

One spring day, after boiling mutton, Alanqu'o sat
down her five sons in a row. She gave each of them an
arrow, asking each to break it. They broke them easily,

and threw them aside. Next, she took five arrow shafts and bound them together. She gave the bundle to the first son, saying, 'Break them!' All tried in turn, but none of them succeeded. 'All of you were born of this same belly, alone you can be broken by anyone; together, and of one mind, like bound arrow shafts, nobody can vanquish you.'

Temüjin would have known this parable, and thus been acutely aware of the danger of internecine warring. His own life was full of conflict and retaliation with surrounding clans. He was born of an abducted Merkid woman. His father was poisoned by Tartars. He killed his half-brother. He was captured by Taiitchi'uts. He escaped. His wife Borte was kidnapped by Merkids. He rescued her; she was already pregnant. In 1189 he became Temujin Khan, chieftain of his own tiny Mongol tribe. Over the next twenty-five years, he slowly subjugated other steppe tribes one by one, making his Mongols the largest, and finally the only one: a powerful nation.

Temüjin Khan's strategy for winning the allegiance of hostile tribes that he defeated was unprecedented. He abandoned nepotism, instead rewarding outsiders with rank and rewards if they pledged loyalty to him. According to Professor Ugunge Onon, translator of 'The Secret History', he entrenched this practice by promoting three types of prestigious inter-tribal relationship: marriage, sworn brotherhood and deep friendship. Eventually, his core command group consisted of men from nine tribes, among them Shamans, Buddhists, Muslim and Nestorians.

'After Genghis Khan had unified the people of the felt-walled tents,' 'The Secret History' says, 'they assembled at the Onon River in the Year of the Tiger [1206]. After hoisting a white banner with nine pennants, the title of Great Khan was bestowed upon him . . .'

At this *khuriltai*, or 'council', Genghis Khan announced the names of ninety-five men, each of whom was placed in command of 1000 households (*tumens*), a reward for their loyalty in establishing the Mongol nation. The spoils of war would provide the material reward for their continued loyalty.

Even before Genghis Khan set out on his campaign of expansion, the creation of the Mongol state in 1206 put all neighbouring lands and their peoples in peril. States to its south could no longer bank on safety brought about by enemies fighting each other. A new spirit banner was made, from the hair of black stallions, especially for war. It would be carried by Genghis Khan's army in their battles against the Jin, won in 1220, and during the twenty-year campaign against the Western Xia, during which he died near Liupanshan, in today's Ningxia.

According to Jack Weatherford:

> The union between the man and his Spirit Banner grew so intertwined that when he died, the warrior's spirit was said to reside forever in those tufts of horsehair. While the warrior lived, the horsehair banner carried his destiny; in death, it became his soul. The physical body was quickly abandoned to nature, but the soul lived on forever in those tufts of horsehair to inspire future generations.

In this way, the spirit banner came to represent the past and present of its holder, and the future of its inheritors.

A solemn procession, led by the spirit banner, guided Genghis Khan's body back on a forty-day journey across the Gobi Desert and steppe to the place of his birth, in view of the sacred Mount Burkhan Khaldan, in today's Henti Aimag, between the Onon and Kherlen rivers. There he was buried secretly.

Genghis Khan's spirit banners became revered icons. Like other national treasures – such as the seals of the Khans, and 'The Secret History' – they remained in Mongolia for safekeeping. The white banner went missing early, but the black one was kept by the Lama Zanabazar, who built a monastery for its veneration, near Genghis Khan's birthplace at the sacred mountain.

Centuries later, during the 1930s, the monks of the monastery were murdered by Stalin's troops; it was a fate that befell some 30 000 Mongolian monks. The black spirit banner disappeared. The Soviets became so paranoid at preventing a nationalist revival that they cordoned off much of Henti, designating it a 'highly restricted area'.

In 1990, with the impending collapse of the Soviet Union and its satellite states, including Mongolia, a democratic revolution erupted which saw the return of Mongolia proper. New spirit banners were made. Embodying the soul of the Mongol nation founded by Genghis Khan, and Mongolia's past, present and future, they are now displayed as solemn symbols of state inside the Presidential Palace in Ulaanbaatar.

24.

SHARPSHOOTERS

Mongol arrowheads

Most national armed forces have an elite regiment, a crack division. The French have the Foreign Legion, the British the SAS, the Americans the Navy Seals. The ancient Mongol army was different. They had no ordinary, standard forces. They only had one regiment, and it was a crack regiment: their cavalry. It was one of history's smallest armies, but it was entirely elite, with every warrior physically equipped and mentally prepared only for victory. The army had just 95 000 men, each of whom carried around sixty arrows. If fully deployed in battle, this Mongolian cavalry force was capable of unleashing some 5.7 million arrows at the enemy.

Our next object – a collection of arrowheads from the National Museum of Mongolia, in Ulaanbaatar – focuses our attention on the Mongols' awesome firepower. The collection contains specialised arrowheads for various purposes, and analysing them illustrates how the Mongols became such feared killers with their composite bows (see Object 8).

The largest arrowheads, each about the size of one's palm, with a flat, diamond-shaped surface, were designed for hunting game. They weigh between 200 and 300 grams apiece. Fixed to a shaft the length of a tall adult's arm – from fingertips to armpit – they were shot from heavy draw-weight bows by very strong archers.

Practising archery by aiming at stationary targets makes one good at hitting a stationary target. But in battle, targets move, so the Mongols considered hunting experience the optimum preparation. Children began on foot, playing with the bow and arrow by waiting silently and motionless near rabbit and marmot burrows. Youths graduated to riding horseback, stalking and chasing fast-running game, including the fleet-footed gazelle, which made the transition from the hunt to the battlefield a natural one. Their practice ground, the steppe, was hostile and vast, a test of endurance; China's plains, although alien, were comparatively easier.

The Mongols observed how predators in the natural world hunted their prey, particularly how wolves hunted gazelle (see Object 28). They copied these survival-of-the-fittest skills: they pursued slowly, with stealth and patience; they utilised the terrain to their advantage, causing panic; and they timed their attacks for when the enemy was least ready. By adulthood, Mongolian archers, having spent years in the saddle hunting and herding, were truly an elite force.

The armies of native Han Chinese dynasties, because of their sedentary way of life, did not experience such paramilitary hunting apprenticeships. Most had only a modicum of combat experience. Conquest dynasties established by the Qidans, Jurchens, Mongols and Manchus, however, once they became more sedentary, paid strict attention to maintaining their soldiers' hunting skills, in order to retain their martial supremacy. The emperors of the Qing were great advocates of the hunt. 'If the officers and soldiers of provincial garrisons are not made to go out and hunt every year to practise their martial skills, they will eventually become lazy,' professed Emperor Kangxi, while Emperor Qianlong stressed the need to cultivate what he termed *wei jiaoyang manzhou zhidao*, or 'the Manchu Way', by maintaining the tradition of the hunt, a retreat into the wild.

The other arrowheads in our collection were used in combat. During Genghis Khan's campaigns in North China, he offered his enemies a choice: surrender and be spared, or resist and be annihilated. In this we see the mind war which the Mongols waged. They touted their confidence in victory, taunting their enemies, setting free those who had seen their brutality so they might convince the next targets to surrender. Fear was a vital weapon in their arsenal.

Within the zone of an engagement, 'whistling arrows' were unleashed primarily for signalling, but they also induced fear in those under attack, draining their nervous energy. Via a small hole in the arrowhead, a high-pitched fizzing sound was emitted when the arrow was unleashed, warning of the onslaught to come, and giving the enemy a final chance to surrender.

Finally, in our collection are arrowheads designed to kill. These are distinguished by their smaller, thinner, more pointed forms, although there were several kinds. The larger types were for use from a distance; with their slightly heavier weight and their slower velocity, they were designed to penetrate armour. At closer quarters the Mongols used smaller, lighter arrowheads that were specifically designed for deep piercing.

The type of arrowhead a soldier used depended not only on the distance of the engagement, but also on a number of other variables, including the battlefield's features, the cohesiveness of the enemy and their fortifications. The Mongol army was divided into ninety-five units of 1000 soldiers each. As *The Secret History* records, these were not individuals but household units of men, women and children. While men formed the frontline cavalry force, women brought up the flank and were responsible for resupplying the cavalry with fresh horses and arrows.

For many years I was confounded by my inability to find arrowheads during my Wall and Wall-side explorations. Their absence seemed conspicuous. Why were there none to be found? The an-

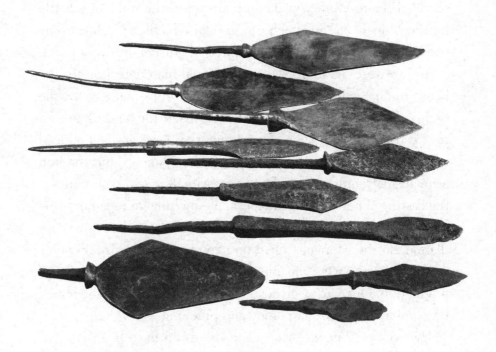

DESCRIPTION:	Arrowheads from the Mongol period
SIGNIFICANCE:	Firepower of Mongol military success
ORIGIN:	Mongolia, twelfth century
LOCATION:	National Museum of Mongolian History, Ulaanbaatar

swer is simple. Arrowheads took much time to produce, and demanded expensive resources in great quantities. If it was at all possible – that is, when victory was won – the Mongols collected and recycled them. Women picked up arrows in the wake of a battle for the Mongol cavalry. Each warrior carried a file for refurbishing used arrows, and then they were stored in quivers, ready for reuse.

Arrows were made from three principal materials: iron for the head, birch for the shaft, and eagle or vulture feathers for the flights. Deer sinew and fish glue were used for binding the arrowhead to the shaft. The natural materials were easily produced and readied for arrow manufacture by the Mongols, but the iron arrowheads required manufacturing. Metallurgical techniques – the casting of new arrows, and perhaps smelting for repair of badly damaged ones – were virtually non-existent within the native population, so the Mongols relied on captured artisans from enemy populations who were capable of metalworking to set up their own production. Once an arrowhead had been cast, it had to be honed for combat by filing, sharpening and pinching.

The Mongols' need for arrowheads would have been particularly acute immediately after Genghis Khan's unification of the steppe tribes in 1206, as they readied themselves to attack the Jin and the Western Xia. Once the Mongol war machine gained momentum, capturing people and resources as it went, the pressure of arrowhead production would have eased considerably.

It's estimated that each Mongol warrior, during the long campaigns across Asia in the first half of the thirteenth century, killed between 100 and 400 people. This unprecedentedly efficient and brutal killing machine, many generations in the making, rode tens of thousands of kilometres, fought hundreds of battles and unleashed untold millions of arrows against their enemies.

25.

CAVALRY WEAR

Mongol armour

Go into any supermarket in Ulaanbaatar – in fact, any general supplies store, anywhere in Mongolia – and you'll find much shelf space, sometimes entire aisles, occupied by vodka. Dozens of brands are offered, and virtually each one associates itself in name or image with Genghis Khan. The impressive frosted bottle that caught my attention was Chinnghis Silver, Pride of Mongolia. Its embossed metal label depicts a silhouetted Genghis Khan, heavily clad in plate armour, mounted on a spirited horse, with bows and quivers full of arrows behind him.

I was intrigued because something about the Great Khan's portrayal matched what I'd just seen. I had spent an afternoon in the National Museum of Mongolian History examining a *hatangu degel*, literally 'a robe as strong as iron', or a coat of plates, and armoured boots. These components of an all-covering suit of armour were vividly represented on the bottle's label.

To my mind, this was stereotypical armour. It was metal, worn to stop missiles. Uncomfortable, yes, but you'd be protected, not punctured. And it was heavy – about twenty-five kilograms in total, by my guess. Armour like this was originally the preserve of the Khan and his generals, and only later became readily available to the cavalrymen who campaigned west into Central Asia, and south into China's heartland. Seeing it inspired me to look back at the Mongols' armour, or the lack of it, for the various types speak to the style of combat that prevailed at the time.

According to *Mongoliin Nuuts Tovchoo*, or 'The Secret History of the Mongols', in 1201, when Temüjin Khan, who had sustained a neck wound from an arrow during battle with the Tayichiud, regained consciousness in his *ger* in the night, he was craving *airak*, or fermented mare's milk, but there was none in the camp. His deputy commander, Jelme, set off to steal some from the enemy's camp, across the valley. Rather than donning his armour and setting off with a group of armed men, he did the opposite: he stripped off, went alone and carried nothing – and he returned before dawn with a bucket of curds.

Roaming through the *ger* encampment in the dead of night, Jelme was exploiting a taboo: his nakedness. Rather like a shield, he knew, his nakedness would act as his defence, literally deflecting looks away from him. If anyone did see him, they'd assume he was one of their own, out from his bed to relieve himself. This bizarre incident teaches us a subtle lesson about the use – or not – of armour; different types had advantages or drawbacks in various situations.

During combat, the steppe tribes at this time were limited to armour made mainly from natural materials, if they had any at all. The minimalist style featured jackets made up of around 150 pieces of leather, each about half the size of a credit card, stitched together. Once made, each leather piece was coated with hot fish glue, the superglue of its day, whose properties had been long known to nomads. It set rock-hard when it cooled. Such armour was extremely lightweight, and, being lamellar, it allowed an archer on horseback flexibility of movement. Furthermore, its use did not greatly burden the horse: such a waistcoat in Ulaanbaatar's national museum weighs only six kilograms.

At this early stage, some armour may have featured what initially appears to be a luxury lining: silk. Over the centuries, Han Chinese had from time to time engaged in strictly regulated trading with their nomadic adversaries as a pacification policy, or sometimes as a means of buying peace. Only harmless commodities for civilian use were permitted; anything that could be used militarily – for example, anything metal, which might be reworked into spearheads, arrowheads, swords or armour – was banned. Wine, medicines, tea and textiles formed the bulk of legally traded goods and gifts. Almost certainly by accident, the Mongols discovered a military use for the most unlikely of garments: silk underwear. They learned that an arrowhead, even at great velocity, did not puncture finely woven silk. Rather, it would push the fabric ahead of itself, into the flesh, encasing it in a condom-like protection. This prevented any poison on the arrow's tip from entering the bloodstream, and allowed a relatively swift and clean withdrawal.

The armoured waistcoat and boots exhibited in Ulaanbaatar's National Museum are classified as state treasures, and they represent the zenith of the Mongols' personal defence apparel. Although they come from different regions, the two pieces date from the 'mid-Mongol' period, around the early fourteenth century, during the Yuan Dynasty, and form two components of a complete protective suit that would also have included a helmet, shoulder guards, vanbraces (protection for the forearms) and a tasset (protection for the thighs). This full coverage reflects a change in warfare style adopted from necessity, as the Mongols' campaigns took them further south. Combat now had a slower pace. It often involved protracted sieges of walled towns; when clashes occurred, they were direct engagements which demanded complete protection. A full set of armour – from helmet to boots – might have weighed forty kilograms. Gradually, as the Mongols gained access to the resources of conquered lands and

DESCRIPTION:	Armoured waistcoat and boots
SIGNIFICANCE:	Defensive apparel of Mongol cavalry
ORIGIN:	China/Mongolia, Yuan Dynasty, early fourteenth century
LOCATION:	National Museum of Mongolian History, Ulaanbaatar

the skills of their artisans, this kind of armour became available to all their soldiers.

The 'coat of plates' is a metal lamellar design of thin iron plates attached to a woollen felt-wadded garment, with dual functions. First, it protected the warrior's most vulnerable area, his torso, which, being large and containing vital organs, was the most likely to be struck and sustain serious injury. And second, its backing provided some warmth. Although campaign winters were much warmer than those on the steppe, *Jiangnan*, or South China conditions, were notoriously damp and chilly for several months each year.

The boots are also a combination of utility and protection. Stout boots were a must for riders who spent long hours in the saddle, and who had to mount and dismount quickly while engaging in close combat. These unique objects are also among the first known safety boots. Small metal plates (from China) are sandwiched between locally made pressed wool felt on the inside, for warmth and comfort, and hide from Central Asia on the outside, for robustness and to block the wind.

Collected in 1953 by Dashragha, an old herder woman in Arkhangia Aimag, a province of north-central Mongolia, these size forty-two boots are ruptured. Dashragha did it herself, so she could give plates from the boots to local men going off to serve in the army – a way to empower the new soldiers with the courage of the boots' previous owners. These dead man's boots allow us to follow in the footsteps – or, rather, to stand in the stirrups – of the Mongols, who from firm footings like this conquered China on horseback.

26.

HORSEPOWER

The Mongolian horse

At every museum I visited during my off-Wall journey in search of objects that would bring the Great Wall's story to life, I had a specific target in mind. But I also took the opportunity to ask curators for their own suggestions, hoping to meet 'fascinating strangers' I knew nothing about. At Ulaanbaatar's National Museum of Mongolian History, I asked Professor Saruulbuyan for his thoughts.

On a previous visit, museum staff had brought out the suction pads, lifted away the glass of exhibition cases, and allowed me face-to-face meetings with antiquities. I sensed the weight and felt the sharpness of arrowheads by touch. I experienced the peace of mind – and strength – of warriors who encased their bodies from head to foot in heavy armour.

'It seems you've omitted one object, the most important one – the Mongolian horse,' stated Saruulbuyan. 'Mongols could have fought bare-chested, bare-handed, but they couldn't have walked barefoot. Without the horse they couldn't have traversed such great distances over hostile terrain.'

Yet the horse is an anomaly among antiquities: it's a live animal. I might have sidestepped that problem by choosing an antiquity that depicts a horse – there were many such totems in the museum – but surely, in shying away from the living subject itself, I'd be ignoring the best source of evidence. Since I was interested in the horse as a means of transportation and movement, and the most direct evidence for that was the horse itself, then I simply had to include it. It's a living continuity.

The global stable contains several hundred breeds of horse, and the Mongolian is one of the least impressive in terms of height: it's just fourteen hands, about one metre and forty-five centimetres fully grown. But it's robust, stocky and incredibly strong, and possesses tremendous endurance. Cantering at twenty kilometres per hour, a distance of 160 kilometres per day was well within its capability. And each warrior had as many as three fresh horses corralled at the rear, part of a huge reserve herd which, used in rotation, could ensure that the advancing force kept up a high speed.

Mongolian horses provided more than just transport, of course. In a survival situation – when crossing the tract of desert separating today's Mongolia from China, for instance – a warrior could drink the blood from a nipped vein in his horse's neck for a protein-rich drink. Elsewhere, the animal could be butchered, boiled and eaten.

The horse had always been revered as a means of nomadic transport, but Genghis Khan and his heirs used it for the ultimate conquest. Horses carried Mongols to battle in distant lands, and the victors benefited greatly from the looting that followed. Horsepower literally took the Mongols from poverty to wealth. However, although they were aware that they could obtain much from the Chinese whom they defeated, they knew they needed their own Mongolian horses – and this was the reason they took so many with them. Horses demanded maintenance, and the primary requirement for that was good pasturage. The further south they travelled, the more difficult that became, to the great detriment of the horses' health.

As its name suggests, the Mongolian Horse is native to Mongolia's heartland – its steppeland and mountains – which are cool, high-altitude places, carpeted with lush, sap-rich grasses. But to the south of today's Inner Mongolia, the terrain, altitude, climate and vegetation were different. Beyond lay the North China Plain, the first of many landscapes unknown to the Mongols, and to its south was the Han territory of the Southern Song, with its genuinely alien terrains and unfamiliar climates.

China's ancient Wall builders had traditionally incorporated natural features such as narrow mountain ridges, cliffs, gorges and marshland into their border defences, a strategy understood and described by writers from Sima Qian to Aurel Stein, and now termed *jie shan*, or 'borrowing the mountain'. Aware that the North China Plain presented a 'straw mat' to invading cavalry, the earliest Northern Song strategies against the Qidans and Jurchens had included use of revamped (probably) Northern Qi Walls, 'military management of rivers' – which involved the damming of channels to deepen upstream depths, and the sabotaging of bridges to deny the enemy's use of them – the deployment of portable 'deer antler' obstacles (like a *cheval de frise*), horse traps using caltrops, and the planting of saplings to cultivate thick, impenetrable palisades.

In 1134 the Song were finally forced to retreat much further south, foregoing the Yellow River, which froze annually and had failed to stop the Jurchens from taking the Northern Song capital of Kaifeng. Instead, the Southern Song exploited a chain of three geographical features as their border. In the west, the Sichuan Basin was, in the words of the Tang poet Li Bai (AD 701–762), 'harder to reach by road than heaven'. Meanwhile, the wide, ice-free Han Shui tributary of the Changjiang (Yangzi River) defended the central region. In the east, and flowing to the coast, was the Huai River, with similar qualities.

DESCRIPTION:	*Equus ferus caballus*, the Mongolian horse
SIGNIFICANCE:	Enabled the Mongol conquest of China
ORIGIN:	Indigenous to Mongolia
LOCATION:	Throughout Mongolia

One century later, as the Mongols had taken the Jin from behind, they approached the south proper, the last stronghold of the Southern Song. The farther south they travelled, the further out of their depth the Mongols' horses were: they became lacklustre, lethargic and diseased. Genghis Khan's campaigns against the adjacent Western Xia and the Jin in the north had allowed him to pull his armies back onto the Inner Mongolian Steppe to let his horses recuperate, but the campaign launched against the Southern Song by his son Ögedei Khan (who reigned from 1229 to 1241) meant that 'commuter' warfare like this was no longer an option; the distance was simply too great. The Mongol war machine was forced to slow down. Horses were deprived of their staple of quality grass, and the men were deprived of meat and dairy foods. They considered grain and vegetables to be for animals. War became slower and seasonal.

The Changjiang was up to 800 metres wide in its lower reaches, the largest water barrier the Mongols had ever seen. They had to use captives to build pontoon bridges. Further south they met an almost impenetrable maze of tortuous waterways, interspersed with swampy ground. Their horses had thrived beside cold, fast-flowing rivers back in Mongolia, but in the subtropical climate of South China they succumbed to hoof-rot, as the men did to trench foot and malaria, as well as a host of other diseases to which they had no resistance. Möngke Khan, leader between 1251 and 1259, died of cholera.

The Mongols faced even greater difficulties during the second half of their China campaign. Their bows, too, disliked the humid and wet south. Laminated in the aridity of Mongolia, they 'exploded' – an archer's term describing when the laminated faces sheer away – when subjected to long-term 90 per cent humidity.

The Mongol–Song War that began in 1235 finally concluded in 1279. These forty-four long years were ominous for the Song (the number 'forty-four' sounds like 'death-death' in today's Mandarin), and opened a new era in nomadic history, for the Mongol conquest was a first: no other nomads had ever managed to take all Han territory under their rule. The Southern Song had given the Mongols their most protracted and toughest war. Of their 100 million population, 11.5 million died in the war, making it one of the bloodiest conflicts in history, even by twentieth-century standards.

Kublai Khan, who reigned from 1260 to 1294, was told by a Chinese advisor: 'While you can conquer a nation on horseback, you cannot rule it from horseback.' The Mongolian horse, one of the shortest in the world, had proven itself to be a colossus, having taken the Mongols to their limits: geographically, to the far southern end of China, spatially, from emptiness to urbanisation, and politically, from ruling fewer than 1 million to conquest of a dynasty a hundred times larger.

The Mongols ruled China under their Yuan Dynasty until 1368, when they were ousted and pushed back to their distant, northern homeland by a Han restoration. Horses once again grazed contentedly on the lush steppe, ready to be saddled and ridden in future attacks. It remained to be seen whether the Mongols could unify to exploit their full strength, or whether the new masters of China, the Ming, could build a Wall great enough, or do something else, to stop their well-proven horsepower.

Cancan. Quianpa. Chaulion. Tabu. Comu. Chemquim.

Hontu. Pungon. Xiparlo. Cochem.
Puchi. Tribon. Penbi. Xentaho. Holem.
Hoen. Patum. Culij. Colem.
Triuan. Quentim. Oma. Ceaui.
Loheu. Qu heto. Hocheu. Tanfo. Yom.
Indu. Muixhim.
Xicim.

Chana- queu. Taiton fu.
Tuchy. Aichij.
Ymulij.
Faliquem.
Fulij.
Cohenhu.

Huchio. Tlach io. C.Sanci.
Quialij.
Pulij.
Quigancu.

KIAM XII.
Tiancheu.
Limu.
Quiquij.

C.Sucho. Cuenfu.
Hoyam.

Tianchewo. Honbor. C.Quincho.
Cuchencau. C.Paquin.
QVINCII.
C.Mamohu.

Mulon.

C.Paut im.
C.Tonheo.
Suidio.

Quionquim.
Jhafom.

C.Cic bio.
C.I.

Murus Quadringentarum leucarum, contra Tartarorum, inter montium crepidines, ab hac parte eruptiones, a rege Chine extructus.

The Great Wall as featured on the China map in Ortelius' world atlas, Object 1

Rubbing from a bronze mirror
showing cavalry, Object 7

Silver funerary mask of a Qidan
nobleman, Object 20

Batmunkh, a traditional Mongolian bowmaker, draws a bow of his own making, Object 8

Young Mongolian riders learn to balance themselves on horseback with the aid of stirrups, Object 10

萬女箟孟

喜長看見孟姜
花園露体撈扇

第三回

閘門

捉拿萬喜漂
削去造長城賞
銀一千两

韓幹呈馬圖

Detail of a trident tip from a
spirit banner, Object 23

Close up of a *mujian* or wooden border document bearing signalling instructions, Object 15

Silk painting of the Ming Dynasty
Imperial City, Object 27

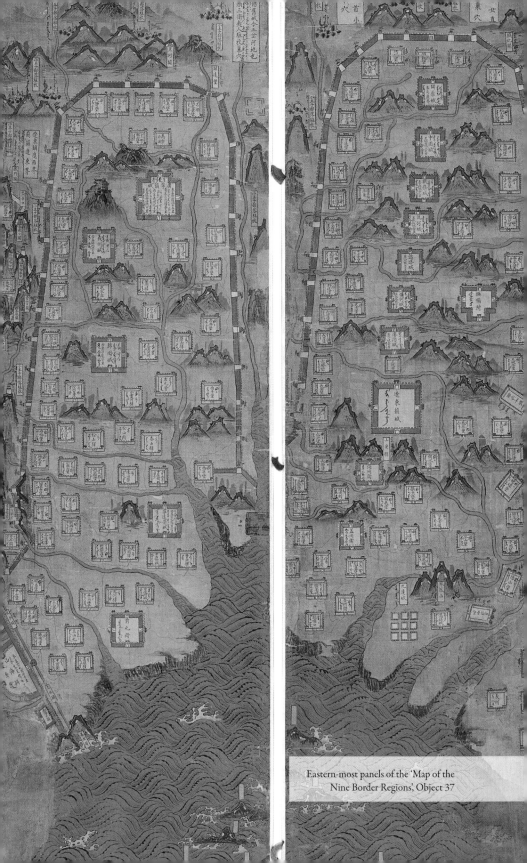

Yang Fuxi demonstrates use of a cross-bow in his workshop, Object 17

Making an ink rubbing of a stone-in-scribed construction record, Object 35

Close up of a tri-coloured glaze
figurine of a camel, Object 19

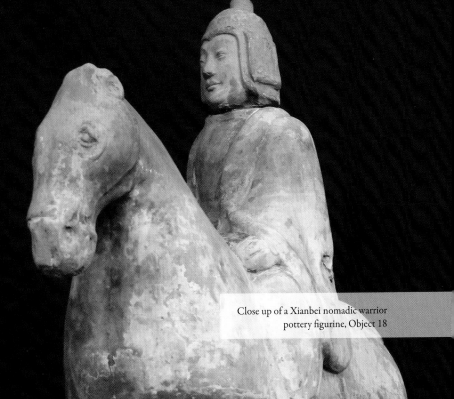

Close up of a Xianbei nomadic warrior
pottery figurine, Object 18

Rock bombs found by the author near his
farmhouse close to the Great Wall, Object 33

William, Wu Qi and Wang Xuenong
discussing Great Wall objects in his study

Part Four

CORE

Objects from 1368 to 1644

As the Mongols were ousted by the nascent Ming, Hongwu, the dynasty's founder, sent his princes to defend the frontier. The most capable became Yongle, the 'Emperor on Horseback', and chose the site of the former Mongol capital for building Beijing, the 'North Capital'. But how would this city on the frontier be made safe?

Yongle led expeditions deep out on the steppe, but he died alongside most of his army on the disastrous fifth adventure. His legacy was a vulnerable capital. The mountains to Beijing's north became lynchpin sections of the world's largest building site, which extended along the whole frontier, from desert to sea. Beijing's population grew to three-quarters of a million, making it the world's largest city.

In 1448 the Zhentong Emperor led a frivolous sortie just outside the Wall, and was captured and held to ransom. In 1550 Mongols attacked the Wall, defenders abandoned it and looters got through. In 1644 the Wall witnessed a decisive battle – not fought on the outside but the inside, and not between Ming and Mongol but between a rebel army and Manchus. Imperial cowardice, court corruption and military treason caused the Ming's demise. What was an almost perfect Great Wall looked on as a mere bystander.

27.

FRONTIER PALACE

Silk painting of the Imperial City

Who in their right mind would build a magnificent new capital within the Great Wall theatre of war? Successful invaders from the north had done so, repeatedly. But defenders, native Han dynasties? Never.

Property values, as real-estate agents profess, are not just about buildings; location matters. A mediocre building in a good spot may fetch more than a luxurious building in a bad one. So, why abandon your secure capital, Nanjing, and go to the trouble of building one of the most beautiful capitals in history in a very unsafe place? The only possible reason is that you expect something big is about to change – or perhaps you are going to make that change happen yourself.

Following victory in the four-year civil war against his nephew, the new Ming emperor, Yongle, who would rule from 1402 to 1424, abandoned Nanjing, the capital established by his father, the Hongwu Emperor, whose thirty-year reign had ended in 1398. Yongle broke with the time-honoured tradition of siting capital cities in good locations. For 1600 years Han imperial seats had sat safely in the heart of their territory: this land was a buffer against invaders, as it might take weeks to traverse it on horseback.

For example, Xi'an – which literally means 'Western Safe' – clearly pronounced the advantage of its location. For 1200 years the vicinity had been chosen by all the major Han dynasties – Zhou, Qin, Han and Tang – as their seat of rule. By contrast, the site chosen by Yongle, on the northern edge of the dusty North China Plain, and not even beside a major river, had only previously appealed to nomadic invaders coming from the north. Cities of various names – Yanjing, Zhongdu and Dadu – had been built there on the same spot, one after another, and all because their builders all had northern roots.

Our object is a magnificent scroll painting on silk showing Ming Beijing's Imperial Palace, nowadays known as the Forbidden City, Yongle's jewel in the crown of his 'north capital' at the edge of the Han Chinese world. Superficially, it appears to have no direct connection to the Ming Great Wall. But if our field of view expands, and if we fast-forward just one century, to 1513, we'd see the Great Wall looming at the top of the painting. And if this were an interactive work, we might see plumes of 'wolf smoke' – the alarm signal sent from the frontier's watchtowers, notifying of an enemy approach (see Object 28) – rising on the northern horizon and being relayed across the plain to the city.

The connection, therefore, is the city's very proximity. The Imperial Palace is ridiculously close to the border region. And by moving it there, from the centre to the edge, Yongle inadvertently influenced the building of the Wall to the immediate north of the capital for the rest of his dynasty, some 220 years. We can learn how and why by exploring the painting – by walking through it, from bottom to top, in the company of those in the know.

Running along the base of the painting are red gates and grey ramparts of the *Huangcheng*, or Imperial City Wall. Passing between guardian lions and carved marble pillars (*huabiao*), we enter the palace precincts, to be welcomed by Kuai Xiang, whose

DESCRIPTION:	Large painting of Beijing's Imperial City. Circa 1.7 metres in length; silk
SIGNIFICANCE:	Earliest illustration of Ming Capital on the edge of the Great Wall theatre of war
ORIGIN:	Beijing, late Ming Yongle Period (1403-1424)
LOCATION:	National Museum of China, Beijing. *Ancient China* permanent exhibition

placement hints of his importance: he was the palace's chief architect. He tells us about its superb materials, sourced empire-wide, and its craftsmen. There's no doubting its beauty, grandeur and quality. But, as any discerning investor might, we also want to know about the location. The architect sends us up to the next stage of our visit.

As we cross a bridge spanning the Golden Stream, the palace's large ceremonial halls, built along its central axis, loom ahead. Engulfing us now is a mist of richness: we are surrounded by golden roofs. Here, the palace's principal geomancer explains how the orientation of the architecture is balanced and harmonious from a *fengshui* perspective. Still we wish to know exactly how safe from attack the palace really is. We're sent along to the Board of War.

The Minister of War suggests that if we want to understand the palace's location in relation to its surroundings, we should ascend Jingshan, the artificial hill created by the excavation of the perimeter moat. There, we gain a bird's eye view. Naturally, we are seduced by the view south across the magnificent palace cityscape, a sea of golden-tiled roofs, but the minister points out the dangers as we look north.

On the horizon just fifty kilometres away, we see mountains which separate China proper from nomadic homelands. He concedes they form a natural barrier, but cautions that they contain passageways made by rivers, valley passes that, if exploited, give access to invaders coming from the north. Quite frankly, he says, it's too early to tell how successful Beijing will be; the safety of Yongle's capital rests on speculation. Just as Genghis Khan wrote a new chapter in the history of the nomads by coming to rule China, Yongle cherished an equal but opposite plan, and was eventually lured into attempting to make it a reality: he led northern expeditions onto the steppe which aimed to eradicate the perennial threats of the nomads, and thus do away with the need of a

Great Wall. If the *Mabei huangdi,* or 'Emperor on Horseback', could achieve this military goal, his city's status, safety and future as capital would be assured. But if he failed, the city's vulnerable location would be threatened, which might force a retreat to Nanjing.

Yongle was guided by his experiences and instinct, and ignored history. As a boy, he'd come north because his father had introduced the frontier defence policy known as *fan wang,* or 'guarding the border with the blood of princes'. The Prince of Yan was given one of nine border fiefdoms, around today's Beijing, to administer. He loved *Beifang,* the North, and excelled in the martial life of riding, hunting and combat, which later proved vital in his defeat of his nephew.

Once he became Emperor, Yongle naturally tilted towards the north, where his military allegiances were rooted. The Mongols, lacking the charismatic leadership of Genghis Khan, had become fragmented, and two groups remained troublesome to the Han: the Oirats and Tatars. Now Yongle prepared to confront them on their homeland of the steppe.

'The immense desert is my sword, the celestial mountains my dagger, using them I sweep away the filth, forever I pacify the Gobi,' wrote Yongle in the wake of an initial victory.

Fourteen years into the campaign, on his fifth Northern Expedition, Yongle's effort capitulated in an immense military fiasco. The Emperor on Horseback lost an estimated 200 000 men, even more draught animals and his own life, as he tried to maintain supply lines that stretched as far north as the Great Eastern Steppe and as far east as today's Manzhouli. Yongle had been defeated by distance and terrain. The lesson was clear: attempts to defeat the nomads were futile; they could only be contained.

Through his ambitious offensives, Yongle inadvertently laid the foundations for an unprecedentedly elaborate and extensive

Great Wall, which would, for the next two and half centuries, protect his vulnerably located Beijing. The concluding lines of a poem written by a general surnamed Xu in the 1620s, and inscribed on a stone tablet unearthed in 2001 at Beijing's Nine Windows Tower, summarise the Wall's eventual success: 'Now our mighty empire is safely nestled behind the all-powerful Coiling Dragon, there's no need for us to retreat south for protection.'

28.

INTO THIN AIR

The wolf smoke alarm signal

Were dead Wall builders buried in its core? Does the whiteness of the Wall's mortar derive from ground-up human bones? Can it be seen from the Moon? Were smoke signals warning of the enemy's approach really made by burning wolf dung?

Among the Great Wall's catalogue of legends, that of *lang yan*, or 'wolf smoke', is unique and intriguing: it exists to this day, being firmly embedded in the Chinese language as a phrase to warn of danger. In *Xiandai Hanyu Cidian*, or 'A Modern Chinese Dictionary', this ancient term is denoted as having entered the language in poetry as long ago as the Tang Dynasty, around the ninth century.

Twelve centuries on, explanations of the legendary signal still smoulder in villages beside the Wall. Farmers explain that when the so-called barbarians were sighted by soldiers stationed in the watchtowers, they emitted 'wolf smoke' as an alarm signal. It was black and thick, they relate, and it rose as a straight plume, high into the sky. As we know, there's no smoke without fire: surely the signal has some connection to the wolf? Was wolf smoke really made by putting dried wolf dung on signalling fires? Or is just a metaphor for the barbarians, who were likened in character to preying wolves?

While filming a documentary scene some years ago, I stood atop a watchtower to demonstrate that one of the main functions of a *fenghuo lou* – literally, 'a making-fire building' – was signalling. In the rubble of the tower's *pufang*, or sentry post, I ignited a small bale of straw. It burned rapidly, sending wisps of grey-white smoke into the milky sky. To turn up the contrast, I dropped a small black lump into the flames, telling viewers that to make the smoke visible, dried wolf dung was used. As the smoke blackened, however, I made a confession: 'I didn't have time to search for wolf dung, so I've cheated by using a smoke bomb, just like the ones used in war movie re-enactments . . .'

Joking aside, the question of dung immediately puts the 'wolf smoke' question to a stern practical test. The national survey of the Ming Great Wall, organised by China's State Administration for Cultural Heritage between 2007 and 2009, found that the Beijing Municipality had 388 kilometres of Wall, along which once stood some 1510 towers. If we estimate that each tower had a basket of wolf dung ready for use at each sentry post, and that each bucket of dried dung weighed two kilograms, then approximately 3000 kilograms of dung – three tonnes – would have been needed to supply the capital region's watchtowers alone. If we extrapolate for the whole of the Ming Wall, we are talking about a very large amount of dung – and therefore a very large amount of time required for its collection.

The Mongolian wolf is gregarious, living in a rigidly territorial pack that can number between ten and several tens of animals. Studies show that a pack's territory varies greatly, depending on the availability of prey, ranging from a few tens to a few thousand square kilometres. While searches for wolf dung may have been difficult and time-consuming when the Ming Wall was operational, the challenge five centuries on is very different. Wolves exist where there is prey, and prey such as gazelle exist where there

DESCRIPTION:	*Lang yan*, or 'wolf smoke'
SIGNIFICANCE:	A frontier alarm system that signalled an enemy attack
ORIGIN:	Watchtowers along Great Wall, including Ming defences
LOCATION:	Momentary existence, now dissipated

is steppeland. Vast areas of North China's steppeland has been destroyed by over-grazing, by the increase and spread of human populations (which have risen almost fourteen-fold from approximately 100 million in 1600 to 1.4 billion in 2014), and by a slew of environmentally destructive modern practices.

The wolf is also overburdened with negative connotations in Chinese folklore and psyche, even more so than in many other parts of the world. In English, for example, 'to keep the wolf from the door' means to ward off starvation or poverty. In China the same phrase would mean to prevent the wolves of the north – the barbarians – from attacking. The wolf became hated, and it is now regionally extinct, or on the brink of extinction, across large areas of North China, including much of the Inner Mongolia Autonomous Region, which shadows the ancient Great Wall theatre of war. It is not surprising, then, despite increased study of the Great Wall, that no Wall scholars or university researchers have probed the 'wolf smoke' question experimentally. Wolf dung is nigh on impossible to find.

Regardless of whether wolf smoke was generated using dung or not, it was a transitionary, fleeting object, and is now one of the Wall's idiosyncrasies. Might a local zoo be able to help by supplying wolf dung? No, because dung relates to what is eaten. As the writer Shi Tiesheng remarked, 'A wolf in a cage becomes a dog.'

In Mongolia, the wolf still sits at the top of the food chain, preying on a host of large mammals – from gazelle, ibex and marmots to sheep, goats, cattle and horses. During my own recent Mongolian expeditions in uninhabited desert and sparsely populated steppe, while I have seen 'fossilised' wolf tracks on saltpan flats beside a brackish lake, I found no coprolites.

According to Dr Kirk Olson, a biologist who has studied Mongolia's large mammals for ten years, although the wolf is revered in Mongolian history – it is said that Genghis Khan's ancestors were descended spiritually from the blue-grey wolf – in practice it is hunted and feared. 'Nobody is studying the Mongolian wolf, and sadly most of the images one now sees of it, show it fleeing or shot dead.'

A detailed and intimate portrait of the Mongolian wolf was presented to the world in a semi-biographical fictional work, *Wolf Totem*, written by Lü Jiamin. He lived and worked with herders in Inner Mongolia for twelve years, from the start of the Cultural Revolution until 1978. In his bestselling work (penned under the name Jiang Rong), contemporary China's most successful book in the West, the Han author sees parallels to the nomadic–China conflict in the contest between the wolf and its prey, between the pack and the herd, between the swift and the immobile, between the wild wolf and the domesticated dog. Unsurprisingly, as a Han aware of the idiom *'lang yan si qi'* – literally, 'wolf smoke all around', but meaning something like 'engulfed by the flames of war' – his curiosity leads him to burn the wolf dung he collects, as an experiment.

He wrote: 'The fire got larger as the wolf dung burned, smelling of urine and burned fur, but there was no black smoke, it was nothing special, it was just light-brown smoke like that from burning sheep droppings and wool; it was even lighter than burning twigs!' So the burning question was answered more than thirty years ago. 'Wolf smoke', it seems, was not made by burning wolf dung: rather, metaphorically, it warned of the approach of the wolves, attacking northern nomads.

For me, wolf smoke also conveys a new signal: the cry of the wolf, warning as much of modern catastrophe as it did in ancient times. Few have found wolf dung to burn because the wolves have almost gone, taking refuge in what few pockets of safety they can find. The wolf's prey has gone because its habitat has gone. And that happened because man arrived, to graze, then overgraze, to live and then overpopulate, to take water from the streams, then to suck it from the ground, to mine and move on to mine more, without any reclamation. Man has turned land that was once pristine grassland into a wasteland speckled with disparate tufts, pushing all that lived there towards extinction, and leaving us, the so-called highest mammal of them all, alone on a wasteland to contemplate our follies.

29.

A CALAMITOUS SORTIE

Iron gate lock

The objects I've chosen so far on our off-Wall journey are not just antiquities; most are also functionally quite remote from the average person's life today. This object, a lock, isn't. I've already used locks several times today – to secure my bike, my gym locker and of course my front door. This huge specimen, which is the largest lock I've ever seen, once secured the most important gate on the entire Ming Great Wall. It's no exaggeration to dub it the lock on Ming China's front door.

If we try to imagine the millions of stone blocks and bricks as the mass ranks of soldiers making up the Ming Wall, then this lock is unique, their supreme commander. It reflects pivotal decisions: for example, whether to remain locked and stand one's ground, or be opened and allow an army to go out, to proceed through the Wall. Examining this lock lets us ask the top brass a direct question: is it really possible to lock the enemy out?

To look for answers, I travel first to the China Great Wall Museum at Badaling, where the mighty lock is exhibited. I reach the mouth of the Juyong Pass at Nankou after fifty kilometres' driving. Still on sentry duty on the western and eastern shoulders of the pass entrance are beacon towers that once relayed

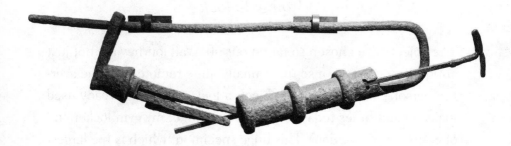

DESCRIPTION:	A large gate lock, cast in iron, 1.03 metres long, and weighing 16.7 kilograms
SIGNIFICANCE:	Thought to have been a main gate lock in the Juyong Pass at the Badaling Great Wall
ORIGIN:	Excavated in 1997 during road construction work on the Badaling Expressway
LOCATION:	The China Great Wall Museum at Badaling, Yanqing District, Beijing

signals between the Wall and the capital. As I proceed north up the nineteen-kilometre-long pass, the gradient steepens, the mountains gather in, the fortifications curl all around and remains of the Walls, in ruins or rebuilt, are traversed, one after another. Finally, at the top of the pass, on the crest of the ridge, just before the descent, comes the most important – and most famous – section of the Great Wall: Badaling. It is right here that the lock probably stood on duty, the supreme commander.

The gate itself is but a couple of arms' lengths in width. Despite its rebuilding, I can see what it would have been like originally. Holes in the masonry have been filled, but a large framework once supported swinging wooden doors here. At waist or chest height, holes in the tunnel wall would have once held a long bolt to ensure battering rams would not break the gates open. On those gates there were hooks on which the lock was attached. Everything indicates that this is a location of massive strategic importance – for both sides of the conflict.

So what precisely is this location, and what was at stake here? There is no better way to understand a *guankou*, or strategic pass, than by ascending the Wall at Badaling on a clear morning. Part view, part map, a 360-degree panorama illustrates the opportunities of the geography. For an invader, the pass is a key pathway between high mountains. At its southern end the North China Plain unfurls, a 'straw-mat' leading to Beijing. But if the defenders fortified this location well, and fought well, they had a clear opportunity to lock the enemy out and turn them back.

This is a place to ponder the history of the Great Wall, the history of China. Although I can see a lot, I know there's a lot more Wall to the west and east, and many other Walls before this Ming Wall. Why, then, many wonder, was there more or less the same old approach – Wall building in different shapes and forms – for so long? Did the Ming Emperors ever get fed up, disillusioned – cramped – by their stagnant approach towards the same old enemies?

The restoration of Han rule of North China in the early Ming saw the land return to its original owners for the first time in nearly 500 years. Ming rulers were rightly preoccupied with the northern frontier, and it's no wonder they made a border wall the corner-stone of their defence plans. As it evolved its success depended on a multitude of factors. Was it strictly a defence to stay behind, thus limiting expansion? Or could it be used more like a shield – as protection, but one from which defenders could emerge peri-odically to advance, to push the enemy further back?

Few lines, other than modern national borders, represent abso-lute divisions. During the early Ming, rulers tried to win control of the land beyond the Wall by establishing forward garrisons – or, in the case of the Yongle Emperor, by launching far-reaching north-ern offensives. Just twenty-five years after Yongle's failed fifth expedition of 1424, in September 1449, the gates in the Juyong Pass were unlocked to allow passage of a 500 000-strong Chinese army, en route to a direct engagement with the Oirat (Western) Mongols, who had reunited under Esen Khan, leader of 20 000 cavalrymen.

If we approach this event as a breaking news story, rather than one of history, we might hazard a guess on its outcome. Outnum-bered by twenty-five to one, what chance did the Mongols have? But in warfare not every significant factor is measurable. How do we measure the combat value of one man against another? Or the importance of leadership in battle?

If we add another historical fact – that the Ming force was led by none other than the Emperor himself – we might expect the odds to tilt even further towards a Ming victory. But the fact is that the Emperor was not in the mould of his great grandfather Yongle, the 'Emperor on Horseback', who had four decades' worth of battle experience. The Zhengtong Emperor (who ruled from 1435 to 1449) was aged twenty-two. He had been sheltered and misguided, he was martially incompetent and foolishly persuaded by his eunuch tutor, Wang Zhen, to saddle up himself and command an army of untrained peasants. What makes the story more astounding is that the final showdown in the conflict took place so close to the unlocked gate at Badaling, at Tumu Bao, just fifteen kilometres away from the Wall.

Not only was virtually every Ming soldier killed but the Zhengtong Emperor was captured, becoming the one and only Chinese ruler ever held for ransom by his enemies. His half-brother assumed rule, taking the reign name Jingtai, but refused to pay up. Zhengtong's ransom value depreciated to zero and he was eventually released. On his return to Beijing, he was kept in palace confinement, until 1457, when his half-brother fell ill. Zhengtong seized power and reigned for a second term, between 1457 and 1464, taking the title Tianshun.

The only Chinese emperor who reigned twice effectively ensured, much like Yongle had done, that his successors would be preoccupied by Wall construction. He showed that bold, brazen changes in strategy were ill-advised. When I saw the lock, I'd asked whether the enemy could in fact be locked out. In searching for the answer, I discovered that the defenders could not always be locked in.

30.

POINT AND SHOOT

A *blunderbuss*

Even leaving aside its great age – 635 years – it feels strange, even macabre, to have this blunderbuss lying across my lap as I write. Called a *shouchong*, it was one of the world's first metal guns made in quantity.

It's as long as my forearm, from fingertip to elbow joint. It's heavy enough to use as a light weight for strengthening the arms, and would also work very well as a cosh. It's cold bronze, a dark, muddy colour with green, coppery flecks, and has a rather unpleasant smell, like stagnant pond water. I can just about insert my thumb into the end of its long, straight barrel, which leads to a bulbous gunpowder chamber with a touch-hole for ignition. I know that the two are connected because when I blow down the barrel I can feel air coming out of the touch-hole.

Put simply, this was a device for containing and directing an explosion at a target. A violent but controlled chemical reaction occurred in its strong tube, and the brunt of its force – a vortex of shrapnel, heat, shockwave, noise, smoke and stink – thrust along the barrel and burst out through the muzzle at an enemy. It's terrifying to think that explosions from this weapon might have ended the lives of scores of people.

DESCRIPTION:	A *shouchong*, or blunderbuss, an early form of shotgun, 43.5 centimetres long, cast in bronze
SIGNIFICANCE:	Firearm whose use proliferated across northern China and throughout the Great Wall theatre of war during the fifteenth century
ORIGIN:	Cast in 1378 at Yizhou, Shandong Province
LOCATION:	Author's collection, Beijing

This little monster's name, blunderbuss – rather onomatopoeic to my ears for the damage that it threatens – is an alteration of the Dutch *donderbuss*, which means 'thunder pipe'. I'd owned it for years before I thought to scrutinise its dents, patina and scratches closely. The inspection revealed a faint 44-character inscription in three columns on the barrel, in what I'd describe as scratchy character script. Thirty-eight are legible under a magnifying glass, and I read:

> Long shotgun, number 748, weighing three *jin* and nine *liang* [1.95 kilograms], made in the eleventh year of the Hongwu Emperor [1378], under the supervision of Li Guo at the Yizhou Ordnance Factory.

So, sometime in 1378 this new weapon came out of a factory, and was taken to North China and the Great Wall theatre of war. A decade earlier, Han rule had been proclaimed by the founding of the Ming in Nanjing. Meanwhile, the Hongwu Emperor's generals were pacifying the north, pushing the remnant Mongol forces back and building defences where they were urgently needed, across strategic passes.

State ordnance factories initially monopolised the manufacture and sale of these high-tech weapons for both security and market reasons. Demand for more of the latest forced a reform from around 1376, when the government licensed military units to make their own. Early in the 1400s the Yongle Emperor established China's first specialised firearms and artillery division – the *Shenjiying*, or Divine Engine Corps – while a milestone treatise, the *Huolongjing* ('Fire Dragon Manual') was printed.

As the inscription on this blunderbuss shows, weapons were numbered. It's estimated that some 100000 such weapons – blunderbusses in various shapes and sizes – were cast during the

Zhengtong, Jingtai and Tianshun periods alone (1435–1464). The fifteenth century in China was one of firearms research, development and proliferation.

The long-running Great Wall conflict gave sustained impetus to Chinese weapons development; pressure is a great pusher of progress. Interestingly, sentry posts atop the first battle platforms on what little Wall there was in the early decades of the century were stacked with weapons virtually identical to those used on the Han Wall 1500 years earlier – swords, spears, bows and crossbows. But the last few decades of the fourteenth century was a time of rapid technological development, when cold weapons met hot.

Officers and visiting commanders had new inventions hanging from their belts: leather nooses for holding the *shouchong*, pouches for gunpowder, and wooden rods for ramming barrels. We're on the threshold of what was, quite literally, an explosion in weapons technology. 'Thermal weapons', such as boiling liquids, fire arrows and ignited animals, had been part of the Chinese arsenal for millennia; gunpowder weapons, such as grenades, mines, firearms and cannons, now redefined the meaning of 'hot weapons'. The former relied on stored energy; the new genre produced their own. These were the opening shots of a weapons revolution that continues today. Thirty generations on, today's descendants of Chinese blunderbusses are rifles which, in the hands of trained snipers, can put bullets through an enemy's head from two kilometres away.

So what was so revolutionary about the *shouchong*? What advantages – marginal or major – did it give its users in the fifteenth-century, especially those fighting in the Great Wall theatre of war? Might it have greatly boosted the morale and performance of soldiers fending off an attack from the Wall in a siege situation? Or, in a worst-case scenario, might it have been a decisive weapon for fighting on the Wall itself?

For one, it was a personal weapon, a firearm. Two, it ejected not only fire, shock, gas and chemicals, but a physical missile, a projectile, the precursor of the bullet. Three, because of very advanced and long-established casting techniques, its strong metal barrel permitted the use of large quantities of gunpowder, allowing the creation and control of a very powerful explosive force, which was channelled through barrel and muzzle and aimed at a target – it was the beginning of 'point and shoot'.

A forerunner of the *shouchong* had been the *huoqiang*, or firelance, made from bamboo tubes. These had limitations imposed by climate. In the south they worked a few times at most before they shattered, but in the north the aridity caused them to split. A fourth advantage, therefore, was that the blunderbuss was sustainable: it could be readied for use again and again. Finally, because it was new and mysterious, it held a definite element of terror for those facing it.

But how user-friendly was it, and how did it perform at the Wall, or forward of it, against fast-moving enemies on horseback? Loading the weapon was a particularly finicky process, firing it was potentially dangerous to the user.

The barrel was packed with a gunpowder projectile mixture. Flintlocks, matchlocks and triggers would not come until much later. Right now, the user of the *shouchong* had to spend considerable time loading the weapon. He'd carry set measures of gunpowder, or *ding liang*, in special pouches, specimens of which are found among the blunderbuss collection at the China Great Wall Museum at Badaling. Some pouches are roundish, leather-sewn containers, a little larger than a clenched fist. However, it was important not to overload the *shouchong* with too much gunpowder. Newton's Third Law of Motion – to every action there is an equal and opposite reaction – hints at the consequences.

So, after a soldier packed his *shouchong* with gunpowder, adding some solid matter to inflict extra damage, he would light a short, thin fuse. The explosive force, as well as propelling the matter out of the barrel, also produced an enormous recoil, threatening the firer himself with injury. If the *shouchong* was held in the hands at arm's length, recoil might thrust the entire weapon back at great speed into the user's ribs or abdomen. To control this, the *shouchong* was mounted on a wooden rod via its rear opening. This stand, the forerunner of the stock, transformed it into a much safer long-handled shotgun that could be pressed against the shoulder or, safer still, planted against the ground.

The blunderbuss's name in English is hardly a good advertisement for its accuracy, as it conveys a sense of clumsiness and blunder. Its target area – or 'point blank range', defined as the distance within which a trained shooter could be guaranteed to hit his mark with every shot – was only fifteen metres maximum. The user had one shot only. Then the blunderbuss needed reloading, a process that took one minute at least – if he had everything at the ready.

If my commanding officer had asked me whether I wanted a *shouchong* instead of a crossbow or bow, without second thought I'd have chosen one of the familiars, something that I trusted, that was straightforward and fast. The availability of personal firearms did not advantage the Chinese measurably in the Great Wall theatre. At most, it possessed limited terror and awe value.

The *shouchong* represents an important stage in firearms development, but it would be a long time before it could be adapted, harnessed and tamed for easy, quick and effective battle use. Even one and a half centuries after our Hongwu Period *shouchong* was cast, firearms on the Great Wall were still used only with considerable trepidation. Commander Qi Jiguang (1528–1588) (see Object 36) cautioned in his *Lianbing Shiji*, or 'Records of

Military Training', that while he had successfully employed fire-arms in the south, in the Great Wall theatre of war, where targets were mounted on horseback and fast moving, and where a northerly headwind prevailed, 'hot weapons' had suitability and reliability issues.

The Ming military benefited from the potential promised by the blunderbuss. It would be a few more centuries, and a fair bit more inventing, before political power grew from the barrel of a gun, to paraphrase Chairman Mao Zedong. In the early Ming, power still rested on the strength of bows and swords. It is the soldiers of today who are benefiting – and suffering – from the real progress.

31.

THE GIFT OF HORSES

'Presenting Horses' scroll painting on silk

In May 2012 an unprecedented event in China–Mongolia relations took place: the southerners sent their northern neighbours
a gift of horses. Coals to Newcastle, ice to the Eskimos, and now
horses to Mongolia? The irony is that for more than 2000 years,
horses had made a strictly one-way journey into China – as battle
horses in times of war, and as gifts in times of peace, or perhaps pa-
raded as tribute or herded in exchange for Chinese commodities.

We've already met the horse and archer in combination, as cavalry. We've seen how the stirrup made cavalry more effective. And
we've ridden the Mongolian horse to grasp its foundational importance as transportation, enabling the Mongols' Asia-wide conquests. Our final encounter with the horse is different again, and
somewhat baffling. Why were horses from 'beyond the Great Wall'
constantly sought by successive Chinese dynasties? The key word
here is *constantly*.

The question occurred to me when I was out of China, but
admiring Chinese art, at the Smithsonian's Freer Gallery in Washington D.C. As I faced a magnificent scroll more than four and a
half metres in length, titled 'Presenting Horses', I was struck by
the realisation that horses were an extremely repetitive subject.

An entire artistic genre of bronzes, pottery figurines and paintings has immortalised the horse as a prized possession in China for two millennia. The stampede that I see is led by the bronze 'Flying Horse of Gansu' – so swift of foot that it tramples a swallow – a stunning gilt specimen from Emperor Han Wudi's tomb, a cluster of Tang tricolour glazed steeds, and a rear guard of paintings from the brushes of Han Gan of the Tang, Zhao Mengfu of the Yuan, and the French Jesuit Jean-Denis Attiret during the Qing. Just as cars today are not simply four-wheeled transport, neither were horses merely four-footed conveyances. Their quality separated the elite from the common.

It was during the Golden Age of the Tang (from the seventh to the tenth centuries AD) that horses were at the acme of their artistic status, a position attained in part through the masterful brushstrokes of Han Gan (circa 715–781) and his maverick technique. Rejecting the tradition of studying the works of previous masters, he found inspiration by observing live models, and spent much of his time watching horses in the flesh, from stables to palace precincts. This scroll that I faced shows three horses groomed and blanketed with embroidered rugs, led by foreign emissaries, probably from Central Asia. The scene bears a certain resemblance to grooms parading their horses before a race.

While the inscription over the large red seal translates as 'Presenting Horses, Painting by Han Gan', the museum believes the work actually dates from the Ming, eight centuries later. Thus, the painting illustrates the consistently high status of the horse over many centuries – as a national treasure, a military resource and a revered artistic subject. It is also an endearing appreciation of Han Gan's approach to painting, which became a generic style to be copied (or faked) for appreciation or profit.

In most cases, however, horses lived for work, not artworks. They didn't migrate freely across border regions but had to be won through barter or battle. Histories and documents detail, for example, how much tea was exchanged for how many horses. The trading of these very different resources illustrates the fact that the nomads' horses were seen as superior: faster and stronger. They became a famous brand, and one of national importance. The adoption of cavalry warfare around 300 BC, under pressure from the Xiongnu, might be considered the start of China's never-ending demand for *qianli ma*, or 'thousand-mile horses': fine steeds with speed and stamina, which might allow the Chinese to compete with their enemies on equal terms.

Reports of so-called *tianma*, or celestial horses, in the fertile Ferghana Valley, today's Uzbekistan, were conveyed by imperial envoy Zhang Qian to Emperor Han Wudi in 138 BC. Subsequent imperial campaigns managed to secure only limited supplies of them, but enough to enable a full appreciation of their military value. General Ma Yuan of the Eastern Han, who lived from 14 BC to AD 49, professed: 'Horses are the foundation of military power, the great resources of the state, and without them the state will fall.'

One thousand years later, the quest remained unchanged. It was becoming clear that China's problem was not only the quality of the horses, but of the riders too. The Song Dynasty Grand Councillor Song Qi (998–1061), also a respected military adviser, noted:

> China has few horses, and its men are not accustomed
> to riding; this is our weakness . . . The court constantly
> tries, with our weakness, to oppose our enemies'
> strength, hence we lose every battle . . . Those who
> propose remedies for this situation merely wish to
> increase our armed forces in order to overwhelm the
> enemy. They do not realize that, without horses, we
> can never create an effective military force.

DESCRIPTION:	*Han Gan Chengma Tu* ('Presenting Horses, Painting by Han Gan'), scroll painting in ink, colours and gold on silk; thirty-five centimetres by 4.58 metres
SIGNIFICANCE:	An artwork from a vast genre, showing China's admiration of, and need for, war horses

ORIGIN:	Late Ming, purporting to be the work of renowned Tang artist Han Gan (circa AD 715–781)
LOCATION:	Freer Gallery of Asian Art, Smithsonian Institution, Washington D.C.

Ancient China faced four main problems in its efforts to provide its armies with enough horses. The fundamental challenge was procurement: horses were difficult to source, and even if some were obtained, they were seldom enough. Once procured, additional problems arose. Horses required care and maintenance, and any sizeable number created a distribution problem, particularly as large and suitable areas for grazing had to be found, and China was already intensively cultivated.

Horses were not indigenous to China's heartland. They prospered in the temperate and cold lands on its northern and western peripheries, directions in which China's influence diminished. Only at certain times did the political climate present windows of opportunity for China to get horses from these regions. For example, when peripheral societies acknowledged the superiority of China, they indicated their respect through the offering of tribute. If the society became a vassal state, it had to present tribute annually. And as any savvy gift-giver will tell you, it's best to give a foreign friend something they don't have in their own country. For nomads of the steppe, horses fulfilled this function perfectly. Received with thanks, horses were shared among the imperial family and favoured military families. Otherwise, it was only in rare times of peace that cross-border trading opportunities gave China access to larger numbers of horses.

But 'large numbers' on the steppe were not large numbers in ancient China, where everything, including a demand for commodities, was so much bigger. The horse deficit was a constant problem. As Song Qi observed, one strategy was 'to overwhelm the enemy'. While large nomadic armies were in the order of a few tens of thousands, contemporaneous Chinese armies were of several hundred thousand – at least ten, and sometimes twenty-five times larger.

The difficulty of supplying horses – and the ease with which they could be lost – became more acute when China went on the offensive, sending armies north of the Great Wall, to engage the enemy. Han Wudi's *Mobei* or 'North Desert Campaign' of 119 BC was victorious, but his army lost an estimated 80 per cent of the empire's entire horse population.

In the Ming, the Yongle Emperor was responsible for the successful production and drastic loss of horses. Nomads assessed wealth according to the number of steeds owned. Almost mimicking them, the Prince of Yan, the future Yongle Emperor, had written: 'In ancient times the official in charge of horses was known as the "Overseer of Horses". When asked about the wealth of a ruler, they answered by counting the horses. This shows that horses are the most important thing to a country.'

On taking power in 1402, the Yongle Emperor put his words into action. He'd seized an empire possessing only 40 000 horses, but through diverse means – large-scale tribute from vassals, capture, exchange and breeding programs – he increased it to an impressive 1.5 million. But he lost a large number of them on his final, disastrous fifth Northern Expedition, in 1424. A quarter century later, in 1449, during the offensive that climaxed in the humiliating event dubbed the Tumu Incident, many of the imperial army's horses were lost in battle (see Object 29).

Devastating losses had an immediate impact on future military policy, and prompted methods that sought to replenish stocks swiftly. In the late Ming, thirteen 'horse–tea' markets along the border were authorised by the Board of War, but their continued operation was a sensitive issue subject to local conditions, as a document dated 1637 and kept in the National Museum of China evidences. It concerns the reopening of the Zhangjiakou market after a period of closure for an unspecified reason – much to the relief of various parties. 'Now that the market has reopened,' it reads, 'merchants have flocked here, goods and silver are as plentiful as stars in the sky. Officers and soldiers can mount fast steeds again, and local people too have benefitted from the trade. In less than one year the barrier [the Great Wall] has taken on a new look and worn out troops are energized . . .'

When analysing the various means of obtaining horses, one inevitably returns to the same old problem: unsustainability. This directs us towards finding the reasons for an apparent degeneration of horse quality. China is famous not only for its inventiveness, but also for copying. Nowadays, fakers obtain an 'original', make copies for a fiftieth of the price and sell them for a tenth of the price, by which time the domestic market no longer wants the overpriced genuine articles any more. So why, once China had obtained fast, strong horses from its nomadic neighbours, could they not let the mares and stallions do the rest? This becomes a more intriguing question in the late Ming, when horse–tea markets created a mechanism for importing more horses.

We get a hint about the mystery from the Jesuit missionary Matteo Ricci (1552–1610), when he wrote about 'the fertility and products of the Chinese Empire' in his journal. 'They [the Chinese] have countless horses in the service of the army,' he wrote, 'but these are so degenerate and lacking in martial spirit that they are put to rout even by the neighing of the Tartars steeds, and so they are useless as war horses.' Ricci added that 'the Chinese know little about the taming or training of horses'.

It seemed that once the horses had left their steppe motherland, they just weren't the same, an apparent fact that has never been convincingly explained. Was it disease or a deficiency that accounted for the lacklustre performance of breeding programs for 1500 years? Or might their languor be explained more simplistically by the change in the horse's habitat – by being too far removed from its homeland of cool temperatures, clear streams and lush grasslands?

The question of the inability of the Chinese to successfully and consistently breed quality war horses is an historical mystery, but one which, according to Professor Lev Gumilev (1912–1992), may have a possible biological-environmental explanation. The Russian historian and anthropologist theorised that a lack or excess of selenium in China's soil was the problem. This element is important to all animals for cellular functions, and each species has different demands and tolerances. Horses are known to be intolerant of both too little and too much selenium: they can only develop healthily and reproduce strong foals if the level is within this certain range.

Gumilev's theory certainly warrants further research. I do think, as observers across the ages have noted, that the problem of quality was not solely related to the horses, but also to their training and their riders' horsemanship. If you're to win a fight you must have a good sword, but you must also be capable of using it.

32.

Sixteenth Century Typos

Bluestone stele bearing construction records

When I worked as an editor at the Xinhua News Agency in central Beijing in the late 1990s, my role as a 'foreign expert' was to improve the standard of reporters' writing; the most important thing was to avoid printing any errors. Senior Chinese editors would often recall the dark years of the Cultural Revolution, when any mistake – factual, grammatical or typographical – was considered a serious political error, especially in any writing relating to Chairman Mao.

Things were clearly different 450 years earlier, in the Ming, when this small tablet was inscribed. The writer made two *cuobie zi* or faulted characters among the stone's total of fifty-eight, rather like our own spelling mistakes or incorrect usage of a homonym or homophone. Surprisingly, one of them is a botched version of His Imperial Majesty's reign name. The proverb 'Heaven is high and the Emperor is far away' might partly explain the reason for the sloppy writing, for this stone was made in Jiayuguan, almost the whole length of the Great Wall away from Beijing.

While the highlights of history always attract the most interest, it is sometimes the more utilitarian artefacts – or, in the case of this inscription, something hastily done in the lower ranks – that survive and challenge our understanding. Measuring just nine-teen by eleven centimetres, this thin bluestone slab is roughly the size of a page from a standard paperback, and is inscribed on both sides. Seeing it for the first time, I was struck by four things: its small size; the quite varied size of its characters; the freehand style of the writing; and the very odd 'layout'. It's more like a hast-ily written news brief than a carefully composed and designed official document. Yet this does not detract from its value; on the contrary. Its provenance and errors take us far away from the Mid-dle Kingdom's centre, the capital region where all was standard-ised, checked and perfect, to the far-flung western reaches of the Ming frontier. It allows us to see how things were done on the empire's rough edge.

What we have here at Jiayuguan is an apparently impromptu record of a bunch of workers who built a section of rammed-earth Wall. It's poorly written on a scrap of stone, cramped in layout, and contains either language mistakes due to low literacy or per-haps a form of shorthand, depending on whose opinion you prefer.

The fifty-eight-character text reads from right to left, top to bot-tom (I'll use capitals to denote the larger characters):

> [Front] THE FIRST WORK GROUP . . . [In the]
> nineteenth year of Jiajing [during the] seventh month
> [from the] first day [to the] tenth day . . .
>
> [Back] MEI STARTS CAI FINISHES . . . first section
> Li Qing's team starts [comma] second section Mei Xi's
> team [comma] third section Wang Yuan's team [com-
> ma] fourth section Hou Xun's team [comma] fifth sec-
> tion Wei Zong's section [comma] sixth section finishes.

When I look at this tablet, I'm pleasantly surprised to find that

I can actually read it. When I look at larger, longer, perfectly produced tablets in the Beijing region, I can read very little of them – most Chinese, too, struggle to comprehend their contents. The challenges are numerous. For one thing, there's no punctuation. Names come with attached military ranks and imperial titles, which are composed of rarely used characters which most people today don't recognise. The characters are all traditional (complex), while today's are simplified (with fewer strokes).

In contrast, the Jiayuguan tablet has brevity and simplicity: there's a limited range of characters, it repeats several common characters, and it avoids complex ones. It reminds me of the simple love letters that I wrote during my very early years of language-learning to my fianceé (now my wife). My very limited knowledge then meant that I could only choose words I could write. Anyone learning a language first masters the name of the person who's most important to them. For a baby, that's the names of its mother and father. For me at that time, it was my girlfriend's name. Then my own name. The next thing we learn is to count and write out those numbers.

Etched on the Jiayuguan tablet we find all these simplicities. Thirteen of the fifty-eight characters, for example, are simple-to-write numerals. Of the remaining forty-five characters, the simple three-stroke character 工 or *gong*, meaning 'work', is used eight times – it was a word the men knew well. Six of the next thirty-seven characters are *dui*, meaning 'team'. Fourteen of the remaining thirty-one are peoples' names. But while early learners quickly master proper names of importance to them, coming to terms with the names of occupations is a bigger challenge. That's why there are names but no ranks on this tablet. To compensate for this shortcoming, the names of the two most important officers are emphasised in a much larger script: regional military bigwigs surnamed Mei and Cai.

For me, the most intriguing 'blemish' on this stele is the incorrectly written (or is it a short form?) first half of the Emperor's reign name: Jiajing. In order to record the year, it was essential to inscribe this. The character used by our Jiayuguan writer for *jia* is actually the most commonly used of all the *jia* characters; it means 'plus', which would have become familiar to anyone who had learnt even basic arithmetic. But the *jia* character that forms part of His Imperial Majesty's reign name is less common, so it seems that, back then in 1540, our writer used the first character he knew that sounded right.

Yet the explanation may not be as clear-cut as that. Some researchers explain the 'mistake' as a deliberate abbreviation: the *jia* the writer used constitutes the lower part of the *jia* character he should have used. Is it possible that the writer took it upon himself to abbreviate the Emperor's name?

The second 'typo' concerns the character *di*, which is used as a character in context to denote an ordinal number. One of its homonyms, in the double form *didi*, means 'younger brother'. This seems certain to have been a mistake, with the writer using the name of a family member. Chinese people rarely call their siblings by given names. Mostly they use terms such as *didi*, explained above, *jiejie* for 'elder sister', *gege* for 'older brother' and so on, and these would have been among first the characters anyone learned.

But again there is an alternative explanation. Research has found that *tong jia zi*, or 'incorrectly transposed characters', were commonly accepted. So, the 'younger brother' form of *di* was widely used for the ordinal form of *di*, and this, some claim, makes it acceptable. In both Chinese and English today, of course, all kinds of grammatical 'rules' are broken: *u* is used for *you* in English, while 5 is used for *wo* (or 'I') in Chinese. If it sounds right

DESCRIPTION:	A small bluestone stele, nineteen centimetres by eleven centimetres, and two centimetres thick, dated and bearing a short inscription recording the names of contractors in charge of work groups building the rampart
SIGNIFICANCE:	A rare on-site record of the construction of a rammed-earth Wall

ORIGIN:	Inscribed circa August 1540; found in 1975 in the ruins of a rammed-earth Wall at Shiguanxia, near the Jiayuguan Fortress
LOCATION:	Jiayuguan Great Wall Museum, Gansu

and takes less time, it works.

Whatever the case, the Jiayuguan tablet shows us that a writer – probably the most literate officer available – decided to carve an inscription, and he used his very limited vocabulary to record the August 1540 event.

According to Yu Chunrong, curator of the Jiayuguan Great Wall Museum, researching in *Suzhen Huayizhi*, or 'Records of the Suzhen Military Border Region', it was during the previous year, the eighteenth of the Jiajing Emperor – that's 1539 – that Li Han, commander of the Suzhen Garrison (today's Jiuquan) received a directive from the Board of War ordering the construction of border defences on either side of the existing Jiayuguan fortress. Why, then, did he delay one year in carrying out the imperial order?

One explanation may have been the availability of the sub-commands' personnel whom Li Han assigned to oversee the construction work. The four large characters on the reverse of our tablet include Mei and Cai, surnames that appear in the 'Records of the Suzhen Military Border Region'. These two men were in charge of the very large Suzhen-Wei and the Liangzhou-Wei (today's Wuwei) subcommand regions, respectively, and the stele implies that they were onsite at the time of the construction work beside the Jiayuguan fortress.

While I don't imagine for one moment that these sub-commanders personally presided over the construction of hundreds of kilometres of the Wall throughout their regions, I can understand their superior's particular attention in sending his top field men to represent him at Jiayuguan at this time. The fortress had stood alone at the western extremity of the Ming Wall since the 1370s. Located in the middle of the narrowest part of the long Hexi Corridor, strategically it commanded land between the natural defences of a gorge carved by the Taolai River to the south and Mazhong Shan ('Horse Mane Mountain') to the north. The location merited a top-quality structure, and to ensure this Li Han sent his two best men.

The tablet also tells us that the work was done between the first and the tenth days of the seventh lunar month of 1540. This translates as between 12 August and 21 August of the Gregorian calendar – high summer. These are revealing details concerning duration and the working season.

First, the construction period was very brief: out west at Jiayuguan, the builders were making ramparts of rammed earth, which is much easier and faster than a defence made of quarried rock. Such 'soft' Walls were far easier to build than 'hard' Walls. Second, the work at Jiayuguan was done at the hottest time of the year. By contrast, construction-related steles found along the Wall's eastern sections – in the Beijing and Hebei regions, for example, which were built of rock and brick – show that the work there was carried out primarily in spring and autumn, when temperatures were not extreme. Why, then, was the Wall out west built in high summer? Answer: because at that time one of the essential building materials fell out of the sky.

Water was needed to wet the earth in order to tamp it down, and the planners preferred to let nature deliver it directly, rather than increase the risk of workers' discontent and exhaustion by having them transport the heavy commodity for several kilometres in searing summer temperatures (see Object 6). Jiayuguan receives its heaviest rainfall in July and August; thunderstorms form in the region when the Gobi's hot and unstable air is forced to rise rapidly by the 4000-metre-plus Qilian Shan range, which rims the southern edge of the Hexi Corridor. So there was no delay as such. The command just waited for the next building season to come around.

History gives us relatively few fragments of evidence that assist our understanding of the ordinary people – the workers – who participated in great events. What I like about this object is its ordinariness, its earthiness, and the crude way in which the low-ranking names are recorded beside their commanders. It tells us that six groups of builders in the charge of officers Li, Wang, Hou, Wei, Mei and Zhang (written in 'small font' characters) had their work overseen by regional sub-commanders Mei and Cai (big names indeed, and written in 'large font' characters) as they carried out the Emperor's building order.

This stele, with its distinctive ad hoc appearance, says: 'We did this.' It expresses the honour low-ranking officers felt at working with top men from HQ. It's a remarkable message from the Wall's north-western frontier, posted in 1540 and received in 1975, telling of resourcefulness, creativity and pride, and with a thought for posterity.

33.

STONE AGE WEAPONS

Gunpowder rock bombs

I've never been directly involved in a war. I suspect that few, if any, of my forebears can make such a fortunate claim. In childhood, though, I often heard World War II stories told at the dinner table. I particularly remember my mother's recollections of the night-time air raids on the port of Liverpool, when the city's main defences were hopes and prayers. I remember thinking that nothing could be as terrifying as that.

But perhaps it could: when death was planted, lurking silently in wait. The ground would suddenly heave up. Everything within a radius of several metres – earth, leaves, grass, bush, horse and man – would rise and fall in the supernatural eruption. When a landmine exploded, hell itself surfaced.

I found my first landmine quite by chance. It was 1996, and I was exploring the Wall in the Beijing region. I'd followed a path out from the village, hoping it would lead all the way up to the Wall, but it led only to the top fields. Beyond, I forged on cross-country, through the woods and along gullies. It was very slow going, and hazardous too. I spotted a rock that looked different from the others. It was natural but sculpted.

The rock was only lightly attached to the black earth, so I pulled it free. It was the size and shape of a large pineapple; it was grey but it glinted. It was a bright alien among dull commoners. I realised it had been hewn by hand: I could see chisel marks pocking its surface. Turning it around, I found a perfectly round opening at one end. I grabbed a twig to probe inside. Under a cobweb and a dried bug or two was hard-packed earth.

Once cleared, the cavity was about two-thirds of the rock's full length. Peering inside, I saw that it was of remarkably uniform diameter throughout, and it had a finely cut notch running down into its chamber from the lip. Near the base of the chamber was a small hole. Originally, the rock's chamber had held gunpowder. The notch and the hole were surely clues as to how it was detonated.

Later, I returned to the location to measure the distance from the Wall and observe the lie of the land. As I did, I found more mines, some whole, some broken into pieces. The gully was fifty metres or so in front of the Wall, and it appeared to have been a minefield.

The igneous rock used for the mines was crystalline and coarse-grained, dark-grey with a greenish tinge; once seen, it couldn't easily hide among the native limestone. My eyes became accustomed to its distinctiveness, and it soon reappeared, this time on the Wall itself, peeping out from the rubble of a watchtower. I scratched around it and freed it from the debris. It was a similar mine-type weapon.

Although this watchtower weapon had the same cylindrical shape and rock type as the landmine, there were two differences: it was much smaller, approximately half the size and weight, and it lacked any ignition hole. In the same ruined tower – in fact, within the same square metre – I discovered two more weapons, roughly the same size and shape. I'd found what remained of a watchtower's arsenal.

Both these 'off-Wall' and 'on-Wall' weapons were made of the

DESCRIPTION:	*Shipao* and *dilei*, or 'rock bombs' and 'landmines'; carved chunks of rock that were hollowed out to hold gunpowder; ranging in size from fifteen to thirty-two centimetres high, twelve to eighteen centimetres in diameter, and five to fifteen kilograms in weight
SIGNIFICANCE:	Purpose-made, either to be dropped as rock bombs from the Wall's ramparts or buried as landmines in front of the fortifications
ORIGIN:	Made in the 1570s in the Beijing region; discovered in Huairou District, Beijing, in the late twentieth century
LOCATION:	Author's collection, Beijing

same rock, not easily sourced, which had been shaped cylindrically and were strong enough to withstand the explosive forces created inside. They effectively functioned as stone cannon barrels that would explode at some distance from their operators. Although the weapons looked the same, their differences strongly suggested different methods of ignition. The larger examples, at eleven to fifteen kilograms, were too heavy, and were found too far from the ramparts, to have been thrown. They had been planted in front of the defences, in a gully through which any enemy had to pass: these were the *dilei*, or landmines.

The smaller pieces, weighing five to seven kilograms, were light enough to be pitched a few metres. The fact that they were found in watchtowers, which are known to have served as storage facilities for weapons, suggested that they were deployed either from that position or from the adjacent ramparts. They might have been tossed over the battlement or dropped out through its loopholes, and would explode just below the battlement. These were *shipao*, or rock bombs.

As a geographer-geologist by training, I was not only impressed but also somewhat mystified by the work that must have been expended to produce just one of these stone weapons, let alone thousands or tens of thousands. Each was hewn on the outside and hollowed on the inside. There was a high degree of uniformity in their cylindrical design. Did they need to be sculpted so precisely? More challenging by far was the task of hollowing out the gunpowder chamber, which had a remarkably smooth consistency. In sixteenth-century China, when these rock bombs were made, there were no drills capable of cutting granitic rocks. Masons had to rely on technology, not on the hardness or strength of their tools.

Rudolf Hommel, while travelling through China in the 1920s, noted the use of the 'bow drill' for boring into and cutting stone. The broken landmines I'd collected allowed me to examine the interior surface of the chambers. I found both vertical marks, indicating chiselling, and fairly smooth curved surfaces, suggesting drilling. An abrasive interface, such as quartz sand under a drill head, could have done the job, if the drill shaft was held stable by one person and rotated rapidly (in push and pull fashion) by two others. They would all be working for a long time.

The wonderful title of Hommel's book – *China at Work: An Illustrated Record of the Primitive Industries of China's Masses, Whose Life is Toil, and Thus an Account of Chinese Civilization* – discloses all the methods upon which the manufacture of these weapons must have depended: it was primitive toil, done by the masses. The book's expressive title also outlines a time-honoured approach that had been paraphrased in ancient times by the idiom *shui di shi chuan*: dripping water pierces stone. Recent experimentation by Egyptologist Denis Stocks has shown that a team of three persons – one pushing the tubular copper 'drill' head down, and two others pushing and pulling the bow drill shaft to generate its rotation on abrasive quartz sand – could achieve an impressive drill rate into granite of two centimetres per hour. Based on such a figure, we can suppose that it may have been feasible for a gunpowder chamber in a medium-sized rock bomb to be drilled in a single long day's work.

So much for the labour, but what about the technology behind its detonation? It is obvious that these two weapons – mines and bombs – would have utilised different methods of ignition, as indicated by the small fuse holes penetrating the mine casings and the neatly cut grooves running down into the chambers (possibly a backup detonation arrangement). The missing links in their operational mysteries can be found in the *Huolongjing*, an outstanding treatise on hot weapons compiled by Jiao Yu, who lived from the mid-fourteenth to the early fifteenth century. He was a military strategist who played a key role in the Han rebellion against Mongol rule that saw Zhu Yuanzhang found the Ming Dynasty and become its first emperor, in 1368.

One version of the book's complete name, 'Illustrated Fire Dragon Technology of Magically Efficacious Weapons', is no exaggeration. In this compendium of explosive weapons science we find descriptions and woodblock illustrations of a veritable storm of late-fourteenth-century killing technologies: 'sky thunder', 'water thunder', 'ground thunder' and 'human thunder', known to us as rockets, sea mines, landmines and handheld weapons.

Although six centuries have passed since it was compiled, the *Huolongjing* has a distinct science-fictional feel, but back then it was accurate scientific fact – and top secret. Jiao Yu believed the revolutionary arsenal he was describing had been decisive in the Han's ousting of the Mongols, and like many an author he felt the need to record his knowledge for posterity. 'Lest these weapon techniques might be lost during a long period of peace, I endeavour to illustrate them with diagrams and describe them in words,' he wrote in his preface, dated 1412.

Concerning *shicha pao*, or 'stone-cut explosive landmine', the *Huolongjing* says:

> This is a piece of rock carved into a spherical shape, and it can be of various sizes. Inside it is hollow, and contains explosive (formula) gunpowder which is packed in tight with a pestle to fill up nine-tenths of the space. A small section of bamboo is inserted for the fuse. The gunpowder is covered with a piece of paper, above which is placed some dried earth . . . for the defense of cities the landmine is buried and hidden underground, and this is what is used for ground thunder.

The *Huolongjing* does not specifically mention the use of *shicha pao* at border defences, but that is understandable: the technologies described in the treatise were used primarily during the period of insurgency to overthrow the Mongols, and in the pacification of the north that followed. By the early Wanli Period (1572–1620), soon after Qi Jiguang had taken command of the Ji Military Region, in the 1570s, we know he had purpose-made pavement-level openings called *shilei kong*, or 'rock bomb holes', built in the Wall's battlements, most famously at Jinshanling. These permitted the targeting of dead ground at the foot of the Wall, seven to nine metres below.

The weapon's base, being heavier than the hollowed-out section, helped the muzzle end of the bomb point upwards as it fell, for maximum impact. Clearly, precision timing was everything, and bombs would be lined up in readiness. The chamber's uniform diameter enabled efficient packing of gunpowder. Fuses would have had short ignition times – a matter of seconds. If it was too short, the operator would be decimated. If too long, the enemy would have time to escape the area, or perhaps even pick up the bomb and throw it back.

These weapons were probably used in fairly large numbers, thus creating a highly dangerous zone. The *Huolongjing* describes a variety of specialised gunpowders – of irritating, burning, poisonous and blinding types – and advises the use of shrapnel, all of which would have made being in a bomb's vicinity extremely hazardous. This chemical component would have made it extremely difficult for the enemy to throw back any rock bombs.

While a besieger might expect bombs to be launched or dropped from defensive ramparts, he was less likely to anticipate landmines. A number of mines are described in the *Huolongjing*, but their methods of detonation are kept mysterious. Of the *wu ti di lei pao*, a mine described as having a metal case, the book merely says that 'at a given signal the mines are exploded, emitting flames, fragments and a tremendous noise'. I agree with Joseph Needham's view in volume five, part seven of *Science and Civilisation in China*, dubbed 'The Gunpowder Epic': 'one has to suppose that a long fuse was ignited by hand from an ambush or some sort of concealment just at the right time. The speed of transmission along the fuse would have had to be nicely calculated.'

The fuse was likely to have been braided hemp, generously impregnated with gunpowder of the fast-burning (not explosive) formula. It's possible that wet-weather problems might have been solved by housing the match cord within a damp-proofed (oiled) bamboo tube, cleared of its septa and with air holes drilled.

While such a setup might appear complex and unreliable, it sounds much simpler than the *zifan pao* or 'self-tripped trespass mine', also described in the *Huolongjing*.

> It is made of iron or rock, or even porcelain or earthenware, with a cavity inside, very like the *shicha pao* or 'stone-cut explosive bomb' [mentioned above]. Outside, the fuse runs through a series of 'fire ducts' which connect together several of these devices installed at strategic points. When the enemy ventures on to ground containing one of these mines all the others are set to explode quickly one after another.

'Fire ducts', however, would merely have transmitted the fire. The question of how some kind of automatic ignition system might have worked is only vaguely referred to:

> The hollow, explosive mine has black powder rammed into it. A thin bamboo tube is inserted, which in turn houses a fuse, while outside the mine a long fuse leads through fire ducts. Pick a place where the enemy is

likely to pass through, dig pits and bury several such mines in the ground. All the mines are connected by fuses through the gunpowder fire ducts, and all originate from a steel wheel (*ganglun*) . . .

It was two centuries after the *Huolongjing's* reference to the origin of the spark – the *ganglun*, or steel wheel – that other military works finally explained how it worked. *Ping Lu*, or 'Military Arts', printed in the 1620s, describes it as consisting of jagged-edged steel discs and a drum affixed to an axle. Around the drum was a length of cord with a weight attached to its end, beneath which had been dug a deep pit. An enemy would unknowingly break a string or cause a pressure-sensitive pin to be released; the weight would fall down into the pit, rotating the axle, spinning the discs to grate on flint, and creating sparks that would ignite the gunpowder and explode the mines. Although it has been described and illustrated, this flint ignition system has never been discovered, and probably never will be.

I found stone mines to be very rough in appearance, and I discovered them to have been used in very specific locations. I came to appreciate that they relied on highly skilled operators, and perhaps on extremely complex ignition technologies as well. Stone they were, but stone-age? Definitely not.

A Bird's Eye View

Fired-clay roof guardian

I've taken an unconventionally broad and multidisciplinary approach to finding out all I can about the Great Wall, employing the fitness of an athlete, the guts of an adventurer, the mind of an historian, the hands of an archaeologist, the eyes of a photographer, the perspective of a geographer and the heart of a conservationist.

If I had to privilege one of these disciplines, though, it would be archaeology. There, the whole subject depends on finding a solid source, which more often than not is rendered incomplete by the vicissitudes of time. What's missing provides an opportunity for informed speculation, imagination. What could surpass the thrill of being the first person to hold an object for hundreds or thousands of years?

This little bird fits into that category, and in my hand. It's a figurine that was placed on auspicious guard duty on the roof of a watchtower: it's known as a roof guardian. Soon after I discovered it, bringing it back to the light for the first time in centuries, I took this photograph of it: a phoenix reborn.

I used my geographer's logic in naming it. As it was found near Wulonggou, or 'Black Dragon Gully', I dubbed it the 'Black Dragon Phoenix', a curious but fitting name. For one thing, it's actually made of grey brick, but it stood behind a dragon as a subordinate for much of its working life.

It's in two main parts and has a broken neck: whose wouldn't be, if one had fallen three metres onto the ground? Fortunately, the pieces fit together perfectly. Its features are detailed, though rough. You can see plumage flecked on its bulbous body, particularly on both wings and its plump chest. Its tail feathers are stubbed, and its short legs, which anchored it to a roof tile, are missing. The bird's long neck and head show a flowing mane, an upright crest, a curved beak and eyes deeply set in their sockets.

It's an odd bird – not natural but mythical. Rare, too, not being mass-produced at a kiln. It's fairly unique, and that makes it an object of crude beauty. It's made of the simplest and cheapest of materials: the same clay used in the Wall's brick battlements, and for the slabs on the Wall's pavement. Those were produced on a huge scale, and were standardised (see Object 6). That was production-line manufacture, but this phoenix was small-scale, handmade. It bears all the marks of its maker.

I can imagine him, having been assigned the job by his section foreman. His task? To make enough figurines to perch on the tops of two adjacent towers which were nearing completion at either end of an eighty-metre stretch of Wall.

At the valley kiln site, he took a lump of clay over to a flat boulder that functioned nicely as a table, sat down in front of it and started clawing away pieces with his fingers. The form of a creature began to appear. Now he used his fingernails and palette knife, and from his whittling a mythical bird began to take shape.

He wasn't a sculptor, not even an artist, just someone who had proved he could do a good job before. Other workers likely gathered around, watching him as he worked, entranced by seeing something rare: not just another brick for the Wall but the creation of an ornament. Some gave advice, encouragement, jovial

DESCRIPTION:	The Black Dragon Phoenix, a roof-guardian figurine; fired clay (brick), seventeen centimetres in height; made circa late-sixteenth century
SIGNIFICANCE:	An auspicious roof-tile ornament from the ruins of a watchtower sentry-post on the Ming Great Wall
ORIGIN:	Upper level of a watchtower, two kilometres west of Wulonggou, Laiyuan County, Hebei Province
LOCATION:	Author's collection, Beijing

criticism, for these were golden autumn days for most workers now, the first respite they'd had in more than ten weeks of relentless toil. The outstanding tasks were easy, minor, even pleasurable, compared with the earlier backbreaking toil of levering, lifting and winching quarried blocks, and carrying and laying thousands of bricks.

All that remained to be done now was wait for the figurines to come out of the kiln, nestle them in straw, pack them into baskets and carry them up the long mountain path to their places of duty.

Roof guardians were believed to keep the watchtowers safe, along with all the men to be garrisoned in them. Our man had created not only the organic from the inorganic, animal from mineral, but also objects of spiritual significance. But these scarecrows were never going to faze attackers. Their function was auspicious, to bring luck to those on duty: they gave them peace of mind, and perhaps a moral boost. The placement of roof guardians on any building in the Great Ming Empire branded it as official imperial rank.

Along with the dragon, the phoenix was one of up to nine semi-mythical, animal-like figurines that graced the roofs of buildings of imperial importance. One of the earliest references to roof-tile ornaments is found in an eleventh-century Song Dynasty construction manual, *Yingzao Fashi*, or 'Treatise on Architectural Methods and State Building Standards'. Compiled by Li Jie (1065–1110), the book covers every aspect of building work, from laying foundations to putting up roofs, from carpentry to stonework, from budgeting to ornamentation. However, the construction protocol guidelines began to take form from *Zhou Li*, or the 'Book of Rites of Zhou', one of the Confucian classics.

Roof guardians are rare exhibits in most museums, until the Ming. The oldest *in situ* specimens are only found on the best-preserved palatial buildings, most notably on the repaired roofs of Beijing's Imperial Palace. Visitors are intrigued when they spot rows of tiny figurines standing in a line along the hips of the golden-glaze tiled roofs. The creatures remain frustratingly mysterious for various reasons: their tiny size, inaccessible locations and auspicious meanings. The numbering guidelines, however, were reasonably straightforward.

Roof guardians (*jishou*) in procession are often, but not always, sandwiched between human figures riding a phoenix (*dunshou*) and a dragon (*chuishou*) and may be three, five, seven or nine in number. There's only one absolute national exception to this rule: on the roof of Taihedian ('Hall of Supreme Harmony'), which has nine plus one, the extra figure being an immortal man. Other buildings of premier imperial rank (with nine roof guardians) dominate the palace's central axis, such as Qianqinggong, the Emperor's evening palace. Separate 'palaces' of the Emperor's principal wife and sons (the princes) were accorded seven roof guardians. Five sit atop buildings occupied by the concubines. Old photographs reveal five guardians on the gates of Beijing's city wall, and three on the city's *pailou* gateways and libraries.

No perfectly preserved sentry-post structure on the Ming Wall has survived to indicate directly how many stars were accorded to the Emperor's border defences. However, because the procession of guardians had a set pecking order, from one to nine, based on circumstantial evidence researchers have been able to deduce that the Ming Wall's sentry posts (*pufang*) or its observation posts (*wangting*) had groupings of three roof guardians. Number four, the *tian ma* or 'sky horse', or five, the *hai ma*, or sea horse, have never been found in any sentry post's rubble.

According to Wu Menglin, the historian who oversaw the reconstruction of the Mutianyu Great Wall in the mid-1980s, the incorporation of roof guardian trios on Sanzuolou when it was reconstructed was based on this evidence. The first is the dragon (the Emperor and his imperial authority), the second is the phoenix (auspicious), and the third is the lion (bold and powerful, brave and fierce). Despite their good intentions, they are all a pretty crude and ugly lot, so I was fortunate to have found the most attractive of the trio, the phoenix.

So, if some of the Wall's component buildings had three guardians, what does that say about the defence's overall ranking? To see the number of guardians as equating solely to the importance of the building is perhaps overly naive. What were the criteria for assessing 'importance'? Were palaces for concubines really considered more important than border defences? My thoughts are that the ranking reflects not what is important, but who is important – or, more precisely, who is closest to the Emperor. He comes first, followed by his wife and sons, followed by his concubines, ministers and scholars, then by the masses living within the city wall, and then by the guards on the gates. Far away, over the northern skyline, come the soldiers on the Wall.

Yet surely no one worked harder in His Majesty's service than the labourers and the military families who built and manned his border defences. The laying of roof tiles and their ornamentation would therefore have been carried out with relief and ceremony.

Having seen rural farmhouse roofs being built and repaired in North China (my own farmhouse in a Wall-side village was one), I can imagine the scene. The apex roof framework, consisting of a main central beam and a purlin on each side, gave support to forty or fifty rafters. The space between was filled with a lattice of long, thin branches. Next, on the exterior, came a thick layer of sticky mud. On top of this, slightly overlapping tiles were laid, with the lowest ones bearing special decorative tile ends, typically featuring a monster effigy; these protected the gable rafters from rainwater.

Eight groups of the triads and perhaps a few spares made the journey up the mountain. A builder unpacked them, scaled a short ladder and, with dryish mud, stuck the roof-guardian tiles into position, paying attention to the pecking order. The process was repeated at the three other corners. Two rows looked towards the outside from opposite ends of the building, and two rows looked inwards.

If you looked for sentry posts now on the Ming Wall in the mountains, at least on the Wild Wall, you would have to walk a long, long way. A few fine examples can be found in Funing County, Hebei Province, but the vast majority of these lookouts, crow's nest buildings, lie in ruins. They were vitally important places, where guards were expected to remain alert, especially during the night, when the doors and window shutters down below would be closed, at least in winter.

As sentry posts were the highest parts of any tower, which themselves were often built on peaks along the Wall's line, they were in very dangerous locations when nature unleashed its wrath. Certainly they would have been exposed to gale-force winds the year round, but the probability of lightning strikes during summer thunderstorms was more alarming still. Given the frequency with which tourists have been struck dead by lightning whilst on the Wall in recent decades, it's obvious that sentries would have been greatly endangered. It wasn't only their altitude and exposure above almost everything else nearby, but also their widespread use of metal, in the form of swords, armour and helmets. All they could do was pray that the roof guardians did what they were supposed to do. Today, on the renovated Wall at Jinshanling, for example, science and superstition work in parallel, with roof guardians sitting beside copper lightning rods.

It's likely that the Black Dragon Phoenix fell from the roof during a thunderstorm at some time post-1644, when the Wall was abandoned. And because I found it myself, I can tender an archaeological brief. Its two pieces lay semi-buried amidst general brick and tile rubble, scantily overgrown with thin vegetation, on the top storey of a tower. Access to the upper floor was via a wide but high opening in the ceiling; it was extremely difficult to climb up, and even more difficult to come down.

This object was quite a find. I should say that I've never taken tools to excavate at the Wall; I've just kept my eyes peeled for anything that could tell me the Wall's story. Fortunately for me, it lay there, waiting. I picked it up, pieced it together and brought it home – perhaps saving it from captivity behind a glass case in a museum. I believe my decision to take it was justified. The Black Dragon Phoenix has a fascinating story to tell us – the story of its rise and fall, and of its place in the history of the Wall.

35.

History in Situ

Ink rubbing of a stele

Although it was only 'made' in 2002, I fear that this ink rubbing is on the verge of becoming an antiquity itself. It faithfully reproduces the contents of an inscribed tablet on the Wall, which is endangered. I first saw it in 1996, and each time I return I fear it will be gone, like other tablets before it.

The stone belongs to a genre of antiquities that any archaeologist or historian will tell you is the most revealing and hoped-for discovery they could wish for: an inscription *in situ*. That means it directly communicates information about an event: who did what, and when. By such objects, people from the past literally communicate with us. And for the residents of a village in the mountains north of Beijing, it's even more than that: it's a family message, with ancestors from twenty-five generations back telling their descendants what they did.

When it was carved, in 1578, such stone records were quite common. Typically, they were placed within a battlement at the end of a season to mark the completion of a length of the fortification. When this rubbing was produced, in 2002, the number of such stones remaining *in situ* had become much, much rarer. For millennia in China, rubbings have been a traditional and revered method of obtaining exact copies of stelae (see Object 13).

Involving the simplest of materials – paper, a water-glue solution, a brush, hand thumper and ink – the craft is as sustainable as any process can be. This rubbing, which took Mr Hou Ronggui about two hours to complete, including drying times between multiple coats of ink, is not immediately stunning. It's light-black overall, and any inscribed writing or design has stayed white. But look at its decorative edge, explore its cracks and blemishes, and read its characters. Both nature and man have shaped this rock, with weathering, masonry and writing. Even before we decipher its message, we can see how it represents a powerful link between the past and the present.

> In the autumn of the seventh year of the reign of Emperor Wanli, two sections of the border defence wall, 69 *zhang* in combined length, were constructed.
>
> One section, which snakes westward from Wong'eryu Gully to Duantouya ('Lose One's Head Cliff'), is 53 *zhang* long. The other starts at the Duantouya Cliff, extends westward and ends at the Right Army Barracks at Liangzhu. It is 16 *zhang* long.
>
> The following persons were put in charge of the project by Imperial Envoy Guan Xia:
>
> He Tianjue, commander of the Baoding Military Command and chief of staff of the Zhongshun Army Brigade;
>
> Li Xueshi, a staff member of the Imperial Army Headquarters and formally a staff member of the Shaanxi Provincial Military Command;
>
> Zhao Jiusi, a staff member of the Imperial Council of Supervision and formally a lieutenant at the Military

Recruitment Office; and

Wan Guo, representative of the Changzhen Government Office and formally a staff member of the Military Recruitment Office.

The following military officials oversaw the work on the spot:

Captain Wang Shizhong, also a civil official, in charge of 1000 households

Lieutenant Yang Zhou, also a civil official, in charge of 100 households

The following were project managers:

Li Shangzhi, Dong Guangxian and Zhang Xun, who are all military officers with the rank of battalion commander.

The tablet was erected on the most auspicious day of December, in the seventh year of the reign of Wanli Emperor.

The ancient *zhang* unit converts to 3.3 metres, so this inscription records the building of 227 metres of Wall, beginning at the start of autumn and finishing by winter – a period of approximately eighty days. The latter part of the text tells us who really did the work: Captain Wang and Lieutenant Yang, who were jointly in command of 1100 military families, which may have provided around 4000 workers.

After completing their task, they held a celebration, and on that auspicious winter day the stone, already inscribed, was set in its place. Of course, it wasn't the 4000 who were named but the officials who bore responsibility for the quality of the work; this is one of the fundamental reasons for the making of such records.

To appreciate how this stone survived four long centuries *in situ*, we need to go for a walk along the Wall in search of others.

We are at a section of the premier Great Wall in the Beijing region, in Huairou District. We walk one of the district's sixty-one kilometres of remaining Wall, through six or seven watchtowers, but we don't see a single inscribed tablet. The majority were placed within the fortification, the most favoured position being in a frame-like arrangement of bricks on the inside face of an exterior battlement – so we just need to look for those frames. We discover that not only have the tablets gone, but the removal operations proved to be very messy, and frames were even gouged away to get at them. At other locations, entire battlements were wrecked to loosen them.

The reason so few tablets were preserved in situ was their accessible position. They were purposely set in convenient locations so that people could read them. Dimensionally, they were slightly smaller than a broadsheet newspaper, and weighed between twenty and forty kilograms. Easy to reach and not too heavy, they've presented themselves as easy pickings. Qi Jiguang called the purpose-made openings in the battlement for releasing rock bombs *shi lei kong* (see Object 33). I refer to the places where tablets used to be as *shi bei kong*, or 'tablet gaps'.

Clearly, those tablets still in place at the Wall are endangered. That's what makes our rubbing increasingly precious – it's a copy of a rare *in situ* tablet, which only remains because it was placed in a very atypical position, on the outside face of the Wall's containing face (where nobody could read it), and five metres above the ground (where it was difficult to reach). To access it, read it, rub it or remove it, you'd either have to rappel two metres down from the battlement, or climb a ladder five metres up from the ground.

I was thrilled back in 1996 when I first spotted the tablet by chance. In 2002 I led Hou Ronggui there, a master rubber of tablets from Beijing's Temple of Confucius, to produce a rubbing for me. We borrowed a ladder from farmers in the nearest village, a

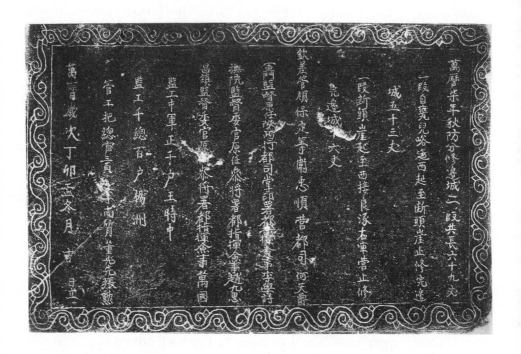

DESCRIPTION:	Ink rubbing on paper of an inscribed stone tablet; sixty-eight by forty-four centimetres, dated 1578 and extant in the stonework of the Ming Great Wall, Huairou District, Beijing
SIGNIFICANCE:	Records the names, ranks and productivity of men building a 227-metre section of the ramparts
ORIGIN:	Rubbing made September 2002
LOCATION:	Author's collection, Beijing

kilometre away. Our project was so successful that Mr Hou and I returned to the same village in 2010 to repeat the process for a TV documentary that I was presenting for the National Geographic Channel. The farmers in the village were adamant that the tablet had since been stolen; thankfully, they were wrong. But there's no smoke without fire, and it was apparent that the brick frame around the tablet had indeed been further gouged in an unsuccessful attempt to dislodge it. In this knowledge, the tablet takes on enhanced importance because of its endangered status.

From studies of the contents and positions of the relatively small number of tablets that have been preserved in museums or can still be found *in situ*, they fall into five main groups. They are tower tablets, above doorways, which showed a number – in other words, the tower's 'address'; inspection tablets, which commemorated the visits of high-ranking military officials checking up on the fortifications and those garrisoning it; boundary tablets, recording the military division involved in the building; tablets containing poems written by visiting military officials; and, most interestingly, tablets detailing the construction work, as ours does. Had we walked along our one-kilometre section in the early 1640s, we'd have seen examples of all the above tablet types.

What's gone missing is the real-time story of the Wall – its construction, its organisation (numbering of towers), the names of the army divisions involved, and its top brass visitors. This information was written on the spot, then and there, slab by slab, season by season, tower by tower, stage by stage, as building proceeded and was concluded, as operations progressed and as the Board of War sent its inspectors out from the capital. We're now left with what amounts to a book without most of its pages.

Based on the existence of tablet gaps on our one-kilometre section of Wild Wall in Huairou, it's estimated that there were originally (before the Wall's abandonment) approximately eighteen inscribed stones along its length, positioned at various places. That equates to 180 tablets every ten kilometres, or 1800 over 100 kilometres.

Given that the Ming Great Wall survey organised by the State Administration for Cultural Heritage found there to have originally been 388 kilometres of fortifications built within today's Beijing municipality, then we might have expected to see an astonishing 7000 inscribed slabs of various shapes, sizes, styles and purposes back in the 1640s – which illustrates the scale of what we have lost. Etched upon these tablets was the Great Wall's life story, its autobiography, written by the men who built, operated and inspected it.

Optimists estimate that around 100 tablets may still remain with the Beijing region, but I'd put the number at half of that. That's one from every seventy. Their survival depends on two criteria: weight and location. As we have seen, inaccessible tablets are relatively safe; large and heavy stones, too, have proved just too difficult to remove.

As for those carted off, I've seen them in the bushes below ramparts, used as doorsteps to farmhouses, under water butts, as stones for rubbing the washing upon, at the bottom of wells, in pigsty walls, and in some Great Wall museums. But the balance sheet does not add up. Conclusion: the whereabouts of many are still unknown, and their contents remain unanalysed. The pages of this ransacked book lie torn and scattered over villages and valleys below the Wall.

Unlike the biblioclasm of Qin Shihuang back in 213 BC, which involved great fires as records on wood were burned, the destruction of the Ming Great Wall's life story was neither sudden nor politically orchestrated. Rather, a slow, sustained scavenging has befallen the ramparts since their abandonment in 1644. It continues to this day, targeting the last remaining tablets. Since my last visit to the site of our tablet, in November 2010, photographs by other researchers suggest that further efforts to gouge it out have been made.

As of 2013, the tablet had remained there for 425 years, surviving earthquakes, floods, war and revolution. It seems inevitable that the epitaph to this tablet's longer-than-usual life story may soon be written, for surely not even its height will protect it for ever. And it's highly likely, and ironic, that the culprits, or at least collaborators, will be local, will be namesakes of those etched on the tablet – Wang, Li, Yang, Zhang and Zhao – but whose own ideas of ancestor worship falls short of preserving their extraordinary achievements.

36.

RELIC OF A GRAND COMMANDER

Qi Jiguang's steel sabre

The Wall's story is a war story, and in discovering it we have encountered weapons of increasing complexity and ferocity. Each of the five weapons we've met brought either a marginal or a major advantage to its user. The overall trend is one of resourcefulness, and of progress: the lamination of the bow, the mechanics of the crossbow's trigger mechanism, the blast of gunpowder, the control of cast guns, the shock of landmines. This weapon, however, is not the next advancement. It takes us back to basics. It's a sword – but it's a very special sword.

In the auction world, there's a category of objects termed 'celebrity memorabilia'. Such items may fetch very high prices or be museum pieces because they animate a famous person's life and times. This steel sabre belonged to an historic personage. We know that because it has ten characters etched into its blade, just under the pommel. The writing is in a style that's quite the opposite of cursive script – these are the same unusually angular characters that we saw on the barrel of our blunderbuss (see Object 30). It was difficult to write on this hard steel, so the etcher was unable to curve his strokes. Nevertheless, the inscription transforms this one-metre-long,

DESCRIPTION:	Steel sabre with a ten-character inscription
SIGNIFICANCE:	Personal weapon belonging to Commander Qi Jiguang (1528–1588)
ORIGIN:	Made at a foundry in Shandong in 1581
LOCATION:	National Museum of China, Beijing

430-year-old Ming Dynasty sword into a special weapon that hung from the belt of Qi Jiguang (1528–1588) sometime after 1581, the tenth year of the Wanli Emperor's reign, when it was cast.

Qi Jiguang's tenure as commander of the Jizhen Military Region, one of the nine military border regions (see Objects 37 and 38) spanned sixteen years, from 1567 to 1583, so it would seem that this was his trusty sword for the concluding two years of his service at the Wall. Geographically, his border defences stretched from the capital to Bohai Gulf. Although he was ousted in 1583 and sent south into exile, dying there in 1588, we shall discover that neither dismissal nor death could diminish what is without question a truly monumental legacy.

Qi Jiguang's career at the Wall began in 1567, but his calling originated in the autumn of 1550, when he was in Beijing and experienced at close quarters a vitally significant event. Virtually unopposed, 10 000 Tumed Mongols, led by Altan Khan, a seasoned raider of Chinese border towns since the 1530s, stormed through the Gubeikou Pass, just 120 kilometres north-east of the capital. Altan Khan's approaching cavalry sent the capital into siege mode behind its lofty city wall. Among the 700 000 inhabitants was the young Qi Jiguang, aged twenty-two, who was visiting from Shandong to undertake his written and martial military examinations.

The marauders plundered the countryside between the Great Wall and Beijing for two weeks, and then, to everyone's relief, turned north again. An army was called to cut them off. They'd come south through the Wall virtually unopposed, but could they get back through it with carts laden with booty? They succeeded.

The double debacle pitifully illustrated the Wall's malfunction, and had a profound influence on Qi Jiguang's military thinking. But it would be another seventeen years before he was called up for frontier duties. In Beijing's ministries, the young Qi Jiguang was still a nobody.

He returned south, charged with confronting a growing menace: Japanese pirates who not only made perilous the sea routes along China's coastline, but now were attacking coastal communities. They also made ever deeper forays inland, including one rampage as far as the 'southern capital', Nanjing. Although these pirates posed no direct threat to Ming sovereignty, the havoc they wrought was capable of triggering peasant discontent, civil unrest, poor harvests, empty granaries, reduced tax incomes – and thus rebellion. Accordingly, Qi Jiguang's task had real political importance.

He gained the upper hand in the fight against the so-called *Wo Kou*, or 'Dwarf Bandits', winning recognition in Beijing from the capable Grand Secretary, prime minister per se, Zhang Juzheng. Qi Jiguang's moment finally arrived in 1567, when the Jiajing Emperor, who had reigned since 1521, died. The installation of the new sovereign, the Longqing Emperor, provided the perfect opportunity for a changing of guard. With the prime minister's support, Qi Jiguang was summoned to Beijing.

New to the north, and new to fighting nomads, Qi Jiguang rode several thousand *li* to inspect the existing defences. He wished to understand where they were, who was manning them and how. Ultimately, he had to answer the question that had churned in his mind ever since 1550: how could the Wall be such a great failure?

When Qi Jiguang arrived, the Wall was infrequently dotted with small, blocky structures called 'battle platforms', whose shed-like sentry posts provided only very limited garrisoning and storage space to a handful of disgruntled, dispirited troops. He probed their psychology, tested their effectiveness and morale, and listened to them as they talked about their hardships.

Concluding that the Wall was seriously undermanned, Qi Jiguang proposed an entirely new design, and stressed that these new-era structures had to be close enough together to permit the guards in adjacent towers to defend the rampart between them.

He presented his vision in a 'memorial', or policy proposal, to the Longqing Emperor in 1569, advising the construction of 3100 new towers: the famous *kongxing dilou*.

Wherever his plans were carried out, the Wall was transformed into an imposing edifice that, with the passage of centuries, has matured into what today remains as environmental art. Architecturally speaking, this is the classic Dragon Wall, and it defines the 'Period of Grandeur'. Its signature structures are processions of *kongxing dilou*, literally 'towers with enclosed spaces', or chambers and aisles. They are perched foursquare at every peak, trough and turn, like guards on sentry duty. Along the vast section from the capital to the ocean, Jinshanling has the Ming Wall par excellence.

In this enclave of antiquity we can imagine ourselves back in time: we might see the servicing of the towers, the annual clearing of bush in front of the defence, the burial of landmines in the gullies, the scattering of caltrops, target practice, sword play, and wolf-smoke drills. Here Qi Jiguang achieved his vision of transforming a dormant shield, mere hardware, into a grand, imposing line of defence, invigorated by garrisons of well-trained soldiers brimming with self-belief, with twenty or more assigned to each tower.

Some of the towers have domed interiors which make me think of the magnificent curved span of St Paul's Cathedral in London. Beneath that, one finds a modest Latin inscription marking the resting place of its architect, Sir Christopher Wren: 'Reader, if you seek his monument, look around.' One has the same feeling at Jinshanling: 'Walker, if you seek his monument, continue east to the Yellow Sea.'

As we do, we see section after section of Wall that underwent the Qi Jiguang makeover. In scores of locations we find the field commander's name inscribed on tablets, recording his inspection visits. We see his statue in Wall-side towns. Yet his legacy is not only in the defences he built, but in the inspiration he generated.

Inland from Shanhaiguan, the village of Chengziyu, in Hebei's

Funing County, is nestled below the Wall. There, I met Zhang Heshan, who claims descent from a Wall-building family and talks of Commander Qi Jiguang as if he were not a distant historical character, but someone much closer. Zhang's ancestors were among the 4000-strong group of loyal fighters – dubbed Qi's Army – that originally accompanied him north to the Wall.

Zhang led me up to a section of Wall over which (by inheritance) he has assumed stewardship. We reached *Xifu Lou*, or 'The Women's Tower', just as dawn sunlight illuminated a rare, carved doorway adorned with flowers, vases and the Chinese characters *Zong Yi Bao Guo*, or 'Defend the Country Patriotically', said to be in the hand of Qi Jiguang.

Despite all this, we shouldn't assume that Qi Jiguang got everything he wanted. All the way, he faced logistical and financial hurdles, and eventually political problems that would lead to his exiled 'retirement'.

You only have to stand in one of Qi's towers to appreciate the scale and the challenges of his grand makeover proposal – and the sheer cost. Adding so many towers was simply an enormous undertaking. Building new towers and converting existing platforms required engineers and builders who could construct roofs and archways and understand spans and stress. Aside from the construction itself, kilns had to produce thousands upon thousands of bricks. All of this required a very large and sustained flow of money.

The Ming economy, however, was spiralling into recession in the aftermath of the so-called Jiajing Earthquake of 1556. This disaster – the most devastating earthquake in recorded history, in terms of immediate loss of life – caused 800 000 people to perish, and ruptured dykes along the lower reaches of the Yellow River, flooding farmland, reducing output, lowering tax incomes and causing granaries to be emptied.

With cash so hard to find, 'only' 1000 or so of Qi Jiguang's planned 3100 towers were built, mainly between 1569 and 1571. But as the funds for this 'hardware' investment dried up, Qi Jiguang managed to maintain the effective momentum of his makeover by improving the Wall's 'software' – its men and their fighting spirit. He wrote his theories and drills in *Lianbing Shiji*, or 'Records of Military Training', and organised a military show involving 100000 soldiers, with Prime Minister Zhang Juzheng in attendance. In the wake of this event, he led his men north of the Wall in 1573 to defeat the Duoyan tribe, and the Xiao Wang-zi tribe in 1579. For sixteen years under his authority, the Ming held the upper hand against their nomadic adversaries. Despite this dominance, Qi Jiguang lost favour after Zhang Juzheng died. Feared as being militarily too popular and strong, in 1583 he was posted to far-off Guangdong Province, never again to see the Wall he did so much to strengthen.

I began retracing Qi Jiguang's career at the Wall in the crowded National Museum of China, in Beijing. As I peered into the glass cabinet there, I wondered: how had this one man merited having his sword displayed here?

I found the answer in many places, but perhaps most evocatively in front of a large granite boulder in a lonely valley beside a river that weaves its course through Hebei's Funing County. The rock's flat face bears a poetic tribute to Qi Jiguang, composed by two of his officers, and marks the place where they prepared a field banquet to celebrate their commander's fifty-third birthday. 'May you outlive the mountains and rivers,' they wrote.

When I look up at his watchtowers, I understand why he is still the Ming Wall's most outstanding personality, the man who made the Wall work. He sharpened the Dragon's teeth. He modernised it. He reinvented the Wall.

37

VIEW FROM THE HIGH COMMAND

'Map of the Nine Border Regions'

When I confront the famous *Jiubian Tu*, or 'Map of the Nine Border Regions', I can't pretend it is immediately clear to me. Although the map is very large and richly coloured, it appears disorienting and confusing. It seems as much a painting as a map. For most of its length, the Wall is largely camouflaged within a green-brown, jungle-like landscape. Trying to follow its route is like tracking a snake wriggling away in the grass. First, then, let's explore the map's visual content – its shape, colours and symbols – and then we'll consider its textual content.

Almost without realising it, we intuitively try to position ourselves on any map by working out its geographical coverage. But whoever made this map didn't top it with a title, grand or otherwise. Nor did he tell us the map's length or breadth. As it lacks scale, we need to look out for distinct markers or shapes – the clearest of which are usually coastlines.

We pay attention to coastlines because they functioned as our umbilical cord when we first ventured out of the area we knew. I use 'we' in its original, general form, referring to our common ancestors in East Africa. Sixty thousand or so years ago, we followed coastlines on our journey on foot out of Africa and began to explore the world. Even six hundred years ago, maritime voyages of discovery preferred to stay within sight of the shoreline.

On the *Jiubian Tu* we find a stretch of coastline in the map's bottom-right corner – but it's neither long enough nor distinctively enough shaped to help us orient ourselves. It appears to be surrounded by land, so it must be some kind of inlet or gulf. Still, we can deduce that we're probably looking at a regional map, and that we are focused on an area of special interest.

The colours of the Earth's features – of landscapes and landforms – have often been replicated in maps. Yet, even allowing for this map's colour changes over the centuries – fading, damage by dampness and pigment breakdown – it seems that our cartographer didn't use his paint box to the full. One senses an impressionist approach in this map, rather than geographical, and our mapmaker has overdone his one and only in green. In doing so, he takes us to a mountainous jungle.

Inland from the coast, we find a number of shapes that command our attention: curved natural features and straight-edged manmade structures. The most frequently represented objects on this map are the green, pyramidal peaks (commonly shown in threes, like the Chinese character 山 or *shan*, meaning 'mountain'), which sometimes appear in chains or clusters.

Between and beyond them come the other dominant shapes: hundreds of blocky structures, of various sizes, with thick walls and symmetrical openings at the four cardinal points. A visual scan of the whole map tells me there are as many as 500, and fifteen or so of them are much larger than the others. Their distribution gives some parts of the landscape a suburban feel, and seems to show fairly heavily populated regions separated by empty countryside. This, however, is a distortion created by artistic representation. If drawn to scale, the structures – actually fortified military bases – would only merit being marked as tiny dots.

Next we should look at the elongated shapes and symbols. The most prominent is curvy, wide and dark-brown, and appears on the left-hand side from top to bottom. It turns out to be the map's key marker, a giveaway shape that should be recognised by any primary school student: the Yellow River.

Another linear feature is somewhat harder to follow. It's curvy in parts, straight in others, and it traverses the whole width of the map. It looks to be part natural, part manmade. Across the big bend of the Yellow River, it takes a straighter, more direct course. East of the river, it heads directly over mountaintops. It's not a single line, but divides and reconnects, and several offshoots can be identified. Along its entire length, at set intervals, are towers. Beneath this linear structure we find almost all the military bases; above it there are only a few. The route of this structure appears to be another primary focus of the map.

Although we know well the structure's identity, its characteristic features are worth noting again. It's been built, yet it follows – and utilises – natural features such as ridges and cliffs. It's not a single line but has a complex, network-type layout. There is uninhabited or sparsely habited land outside (or above) it, and populated land inside (or below) it. In length, it rivals the Yellow River – it's subcontinental in scale. It is becoming clear that we're looking at a swathe of territory in the order of 800 kilometres in depth, and twice that in length, inland from the Bohai Gulf.

My initial overwhelming impression of this map was its sheer size; one literally stands before it. One of mapping's great magic qualities is its power to shrink the world, making it more understandable, more manageable. We're used to maps that fill our computer screens, or perhaps wall maps that sit above desks in classrooms. When I move close to this map, it dwarfs me. It's six or seven paces long, and taller than I am even with my arm stretched upwards. I suspect that these unusual dimensions are important clues as to its purpose, and its possible place of use.

I've seen 'mega-maps' used in a few places and situations. There are examples in the Doge's Palace in Venice, and in the Gallery of Maps in the Vatican, both of great decorative and informative beauty. Other examples are in war movies. The Cabinet War Rooms in London – from where Churchill directed World War II – are an underground chain of rooms adorned with mega-maps that covered entire walls, showing the front line, the Allied territory and 'theirs', troop concentrations and movements and the like.

This was likely also the purpose of our map. It was made for the high command. It was large so it could be seen used by military top brass in some sort of war operations room.

It shows the Ming Great Wall, but in a way we've never seen it before. The last ancient map showing a Great Wall that we looked at was the *Huayi Tu* (see Object 13), drawn in the mid-Tang, circa AD 800, by Jia Dan. It showed a Wall sweeping arc-like across China's north. The position of the Wall was approximate and symbolic; it showed simply that a Wall was somewhere up there. Seven centuries brought no improvement in cartographic detail – even during the mid-Ming, the Wall was shown on national maps equally inaccurately. It was still just an arc. Hearsay and imagination have been the sources for marking the Wall.

The maker of this map put the Ming Great Wall, as well as the military bases in the area, at the top of his list of inclusions. They were the very reason for the map. He had experience in the region. He was an insider. He produced what was tantamount to the first specialised Great Wall map. And he produced his map for other insiders. It's what today might be in the *neibu kan* category of Chinese document – for internal use only, specifically by the military, and that means the Board of War.

Now it's time to actually read the map. The largest text block, fourteen lines of characters, is at the top left in panel number two, and turns out to be the author's foreword. From it we learn that Xu Lun produced this map in 1534, that it's called *Jiubian Tu*, or 'Map of the Nine Border Regions', and that it's based on his treatise *Bian Lun*, or 'Border Commentary'. Additionally, he makes various expected patriotic statements, hoping that his efforts will be of some strategic value, and unexpectedly tells us his age. He compiled the map at the age of forty-seven, when most men in the Ming period were retired, if not dead. Moreover, it transpires that the map didn't even mark the peak of Xu Lun's military achievements, but only the beginning.

Exploring the hinterland of Xu Lun's map, we discover that it's bilingual – in Chinese and Manchu, indicating that this example is a later edition, from as early as 1625, a period when there was great demand for border intelligence. Reading it, we can see border regions' place names, read various 'signposts' telling us how far it is to adjacent bases, and, in some locations, we can tell from the placement of 'boundary posts' where one region's administration ended and another's began.

Bases were ranked in order of scale – from the smallest, *guancheng*, through *pucheng*, *suocheng* and *weicheng*, to the largest, *zhencheng*, of which there are nine. From east to west, these *zhencheng*, or 'commandery towns', are Lioadong, Jizhen, Xuanfu, Datong, Taiyuan, Yansui, Ningxia, Guyuan and Gansu. While there are no marked regional boundaries between adjacent commanderies, there are, for example, labels indicating '*Jizhen bian xi jie Xuanfuzhen bian dong jie*', or 'The western boundary of Jizhen meets the eastern boundary of Xuanfu'.

Frustratingly, while the ultimate purpose of all the work was to defend the Emperor in Beijing, the map area around the imperial city has been completely obliterated – there is simply a black void on the North China Plain. To the north, the picture resumes, with Xu Lun noting the distances in *li* from one base to another:

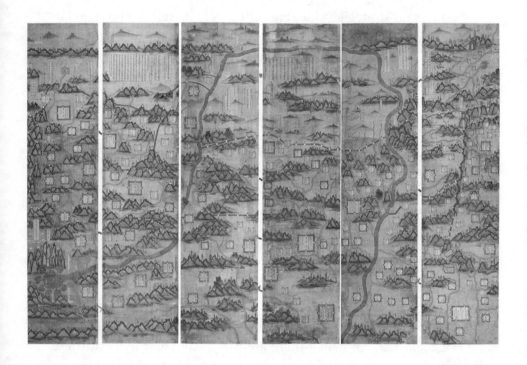

DESCRIPTION:	*Jiubian Tu*, or 'Map of the Nine Border Regions', composed of twelve vertical panels of painted silk, designed to form a screen; pieced together, the map measures 2.08 by 5.67 metres
SIGNIFICANCE:	The oldest extant Great Wall map

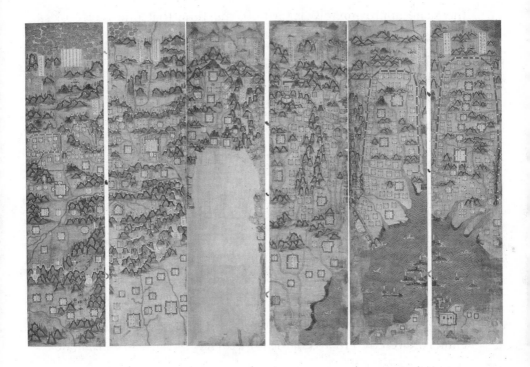

ORIGIN:	Drawn by Xu Lun in 1534, painted circa 1538; the original is lost, and 'amended' copies from the Qing are extant; this example dates from 1625
LOCATION:	Liaoning Provincial Museum, Shenyang

'Miyun to Shishaying, 100 *li* . . . Shishaying to Gubeikou, 150 *li*' and so on.

If we use these rough measurements to work out the map's scale, we can estimate that it covers about 600 kilometres from top to bottom and 1500 kilometres from right to left. This makes the scale approximately 1:250000, meaning that one metre of the map represents 250 kilometres of territory, and each of the map's twelve panels covers a band of land about 125 kilometres in width.

Xu Lun's map is clearly based on years of in-depth personal experience, but surely also benefited from those in more distant commanderies and from other cartographic works. The result is an advanced sketch map which shows military bases, the Great Wall, troop deployments and distances. As such, it's the first map to portray the Great Wall as a coherent defence system.

Venturing outside the Wall, we find snippets of military intelligence, especially concerning the locations of enemy encampments. Altan Khan's people, persistent adversaries, are shown 'nesting' north of Datong in their *chaoxue*, or 'lairs', while those nomadic tribes which have acknowledged the superiority of Ming China are referred to less derogatorily. They live in *jimi weisuo*, or 'won-over camps'.

Xu Lun's biography appears in *Mingshi*, or 'The Official History of the Ming Dynasty'. The third son of a vice-minister of war, he was born in 1487 in Lingbo, Henan Province. In 1526 he passed the *jinshi*, or highest-level imperial examinations, which permitted him to enter the Board of War at the age of thirty-nine. After producing his map, he served as military regional commander of the Xuanfu, Datong and Yansui commanderies. These were strung out along the soft underbelly of the Ming frontier. In 1558, at the remarkable age of sixty-eight, Xu Lun reached his pinnacle, becoming Minister of War. He died three years later – but that is not the end of the story as far as his map is concerned.

Xu Lun's original masterpiece had been placed before the Jiajing Emperor in 1537, meeting with his great approval. The Emperor ordered multiple copies to be reproduced and circulated to each of the nine commanderies. This bilingual Chinese–Manchu edition was discovered in 1949, during room clearance work at the Imperial Palace, Shenyang, home of the founding Manchu emperors of the Qing Dynasty (who ruled from there between 1625 and 1644). It is probably a descendent of the original Liaodong Commandery copy, which fell into the hands of the Manchus.

Ironically, therefore, sometime between 1625 and 1644 Xu Lun's map found itself in enemy territory. Captured, it was forced to speak Manchu, and it was turned upside down and used to show the Manchus the defence system they would have to overcome on the Ming's north-eastern frontier.

38.

A LONG STRIP OF WALL

'Plans of the Jizhen Commandery'

Before setting off on foot along the Ming Wall in 1987, I implemented every possible weight-saving trick, even down to territorial trimming. Unfolding my huge China map, I cut out a long corridor, approximately 200 kilometres wide, with the Wall's battlement running down its spine. My adapted map, although dog-legged, was now better suited to my needs. Focused and featherweight, it measured only one-twentieth of its original size and weight.

Anyone who has ever tackled a long-distance trail will appreciate the many advantages of a 'strip map'. It's an economic design, and it makes any long journey easier by dispensing with the need for large and unwieldy folding maps. These designs are descendants of much earlier milestones, such as the Peutinger itinerarium, a six-metre-plus series showing Roman roads circa AD 300, and a strip map showing a route for pilgrims from London via Rome to Jerusalem which prefaces Matthew Paris' work *Chronica Majora*, authored and drawn in 1250. The *Jizhen Tu*, or 'Plans of the Jizhen Commandery', coming 330 years later, may be regarded among these earliest strip maps, but it is truly superlative for its length and detail. When fully unfolded, it presented a panoramic view of the Wall in the Jizhen Commandery that was approximately 125 metres in length.

The folio was nearly lost on three occasions. Made around 1583, it was first rescued from an advancing army in 1621; then it was hidden away from marauding Red Guard hooligans at the beginning of the Cultural Revolution in around 1967, only to be forgotten about. Its re-emergence began with the dispatch of a large parcel from Jize County, in southern Hebei Province, addressed to the National Museum of China, Beijing. It had been packaged by Kang Junxiang of Macheng village, who explained in a note that he was a fourteenth-generation descendent of Kang Yingquan, a Ming scholar official of the early 1600s, who was responsible for military ordnance in Shandong and troop deployments on the Liaodong coast. In the course of those duties, in 1621 Kang was in Liaoyang just as the commandery seat was about to be attacked by Nurhachi (1559–1626), the unifier of the Jurchens as the Manchus, and the founder of the Qing in 1619. Fearing the consequences of the strategic map falling into enemy hands, Kang Yingquan took it home for safekeeping, and there it stayed as a family heirloom until the mid-1960s.

The villager explained that, at that time, his mother had hidden the folio in a willow basket, along other family treasures, such as ancient letters praising their ancestor's meritorious achievements, and the family genealogy. She was saving them from the rampaging red guards, who were campaigning to 'Smash the Four Olds', one of the rebellious anti-establishment whirlwinds unleashed by Chairman Mao Zedong on the nation's culture, customs, habits and ideas.

The contents of the package were studied in detail by Yang Wenhe, a senior research fellow at the museum. It contained a thick wad of pages – some loose, some attached, some rotted by dampness, some stuck together, others dried to dust – as well as

DESCRIPTION:	'Jizhen Changcheng Tu', or 'Plans of the Jizhen Commandery'; a painted and stamped accordion-form folio of 670 illustrated sheets, each measuring 33 x 19 cm
SIGNIFICANCE:	Detailed, comprehensive and complete field view of Jizhen defences, using innovative cartographic design layout of strip mapping and diagrammatic simplification

ORIGIN:	Produced c. 1580s
LOCATION:	National Museum of China, Beijing (not on public exhibition)

scores of loose labels that had once been attached to the sheets. Describing it as a 'ragged portfolio' and yet as an 'extraordinary acquisition', Yang set to work making sense of the plans. Following painstaking repairs, the folio was exhibited in 2006 at a joint exhibition in Sydney, Australia, curated by the National Museum of China and the Powerhouse Museum.

I obtained photographs of a number of consecutive sheets from the two different parts of the fragile folio, photocopied them, enlarged them and spliced them together. It was immediately clear that one of the plan types was not a map in the conventional sense, but a skyline view. The other type, again not a map as such, looked more like a diagram to which labels bearing text were affixed.

The skyline view plans employed two artistic approaches. Looking at the dark-grey mountain slopes, we see thick brushstrokes: these parts of the plan were painted in ink wash. Along the ridge we see the outer face of the battlements, built in 'tiger skin' style with roughly quarried rocks bound with mortar and topped with battlements, and towers positioned at various intervals. Visually, the towers are identical – tall and thin, and each topped by a *pufang* sentry post with a small flag – and were produced by a stamping technique. They were then coloured – bluish-grey if completed, or red if planned.

This part of the plan presents the actual view one would have seen if approaching the Wall from the outside. Facing it, we can clearly see that we are looking 'into the Walled Empire'; labels tell us that 'the distance to the next tower in the west is fifty-four *zhang* [178 metres]' and so on. The plan's unorthodox orientation immediately arouses one's curiosity. Why was the age-old convention of having north at the top of the map not observed by the plan's maker?

The reason surely related to the plan's users and the orientation of their workplace. Generals stationed 'inside' the Wall worked in offices that faced south. Compliant with cosmological practice, the rooms and furniture within them would also face south. A general seated at his desk and using this plan therefore only has to open the plan and it's oriented correctly. Additionally, the plans show the defences as the enemy might approach them. Using these plans, operators, administrators and inspectors could see the defences just as their enemies did.

While the skyline view plan features commonly used strip map simplification techniques, such as a relaxation of cardinal direction and scale, the second style of plans in the folio further simplifies the appearance of the defences. Towers are arranged equidistantly from one another. Large labels are attached above each tower noting the deployment of military personnel and any temporary assignments. This part of the plan functions as a noticeboard, recording who is on duty and where.

Both plan types employ presentation techniques used by virtually every city that has a subway system. Ever since Richard Beck's iconic London Underground Map of 1931, dubbed 'The Diagram', subway operators worldwide have abided by 'London Rules' in straightening out bends, showing stations as equidistantly apart and removing surrounding clutter, usually preferring a plain white background. The Jizhen plan did the same, 350 years earlier. Further, its maker decided against using a scroll display method – a long piece of paper between two wooden rollers – which was the traditional way to present large, long documents. Instead, he folded the pages like an accordion. Users would turn the folios to progress along the fortifications.

While the large *Huayi Tu* (Object 13) was made for imperial use, and the *Jiubian Tu* (Object 37) for ministerial hall or war rooms, this long strip map, cleverly conceived and compactly packaged, was designed for those working in the border defence's Jizhen Commandery.

Now, one can only wait in hope for a fourth rescue of the plans, taking them from the oblivion of museum storage and onto the web. Digital scanning would enable anyone worldwide to make a fascinating online tour of the Jizhen Commandery's circuits as they were in 1583, showcasing the final stages in the development of the Great Wall border defences.

39.

GLOBALISATION

Cornelis de Jode's 'new' world map

I think my search for this object began subconsciously during my first trip to the United States, back in 1980, soon after I purchased a beautiful illuminated globe from *National Geographic*'s headquarters in Washington D.C. When I switched it on, I saw that it showed the Great Wall. A future quest lay in store: to discover the Great Wall's debut on a map of the entire world.

Superficially, the place where I'd likely find the answer seemed obvious. Surely the journey would lead me to a map of the world of Chinese origin: not only is that where the Wall is, but it's also where the materials for making maps were invented: paper, the compass and printing.

Twenty-five years later, however, I would refined my search. I was still looking for the earliest world map to feature a Great Wall, but it had to show the world as we know it today. This narrowed the search area to Europe, the continent which excelled in geographical learning during the fifteenth and sixteenth centuries – the Age of Discovery. In the early sixteenth century, 'world' maps were based partly on superficial knowledge and largely on speculation and imagination – and they didn't show any Great Wall. Later sixteenth-century world maps were based mainly on navigation and detailed knowledge.

Research in the 1990s led me to elucidate the importance of Abraham Ortelius' *Theatre of the World*, the world's first internationally distributed atlas, and its significant inclusion in 1584 of a China map, showing the Wall (see Object 1). This discovery led me towards an answer to the global Great Wall question. It seemed logical that, soon after 1584, a designer of a world map, using the latest available country maps as his sources, might consider the Great Wall worthy of inclusion on account of its purported, vast length: 400 leagues (which equalled 1200 English miles, according to a Latin annotation on Ortelius' map).

In 2003, during the SARS epidemic, circumstances of self-confinement in our Beijing apartment created the perfect opportunity for a diversional desk project. I went online and spent several hundred pounds on the most expensive contemporary book that I've ever purchased: *The Mapping of the World: Early Printed World Maps, 1472–1700* by Rodney Shirley.

I embarked on searches in converging directions, from older to newer maps, and from newer to older. The search parties met in the Netherlands, above an extraordinary map in the collection of Utrecht University Library. Revealing itself under my magnifying glass, there in the grey murk, was a Wall in China. The map was thought to date to 1590. Older maps never showed the Wall, while younger ones almost always did. The Wall was now firmly on the map, in all senses of the phrase.

The astonishing accomplishment of this map – titled *Nova Totius Orbis Descriptio*, or 'A New Description of the Entire World' – by Cornelis de Jode of Antwerp can be understood if we declutter it a little. Let's remove the zephyrs from the margins, the medallions of illustrious explorers and the galleons they sailed, and the Latin title board, and then let's add some colour.

If we were to show the result to citizens around the world today, I'm confident that people from Beijing to Paris, from Pretoria to Panama, would describe it as a world map. Not an *ancient* world map, but a *world* map.

This map was printed four and a quarter centuries ago, in about 1590, or the nineteenth year of the Wanli Emperor's reign. I provide this date in the Gregorian and the Chinese calendars because we are talking about a threshold in West–East relations, a time when, in certain areas of knowledge, the tables are being turned. After being a world leader in virtually every discipline, China is standing still, while the West is advancing fast.

The geographical accuracy of Cornelis de Jode's world map is emphasised when we compare it to those being produced in China and the rest of Asia at that time. Showing any Chinese, Japanese or Korean 'world map' from the sixteenth or seventeenth century to a modern audience would, I'm confident, lead to widespread bewilderment. These so-called 'maps of the world' were merely maps of those lands, with little beyond. They showed 'the world' as a rounded landmass – a Pangea-type supercontinent – within a round border, at the centre of which lay the Middle Kingdom. Cornelis de Jode's map is so good that few people today, if given a pencil and large sheet, could draw such a world that they know so accurately. While the former lacks almost everywhere, the latter can only be bettered by the addition of Australia and New Zealand.

Rather cleverly, the design of *Nova Totius Orbis Descriptio* conveys the fact that although it is drawn on flat paper, the world it depicts is round, a true globe. For one thing, it features overlapping landmasses, offering two possible routes between Europe and China, one to the east, one to the west. Secondly, it shows a dotted line across the Atlantic, Indian and Pacific oceans – the route of Sir Francis Drake's circumnavigation in 1577–1580. Thirdly, if we focus on the Great Wall, we see a long section at

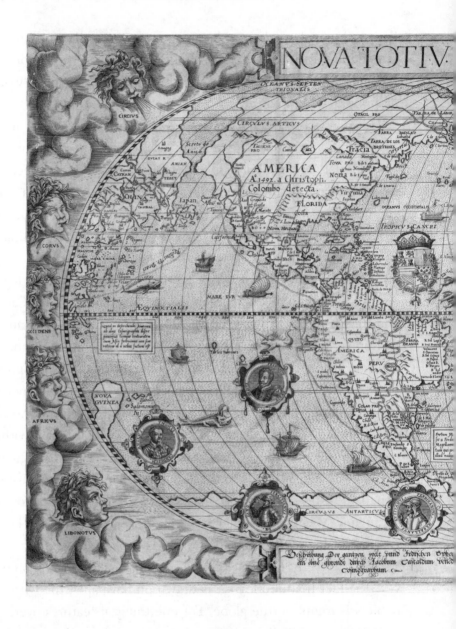

DESCRIPTION:	*Novo Totius Orbis Descripto*, or 'A New Description of the Entire World', a copper-plate printed world map measuring 48 x 81 cm
SIGNIFICANCE:	The earliest world map that looks like the world to show the Great Wall

ORIGIN:	Possibly Antwerp; based on a mid-16th century map by Venetian cartographer Giacomo Gastaldi, with printing plate amendments made c. 1590 A.D. by Cornelius de Jode in order to show the latest maritime discoveries
LOCATION:	Utrecht University Library rare maps collection, Netherlands

the far eastern edge of the map, and two shorter sections at the far western edge. This map is an advanced view of the world, the product of a multinational European cartographic community that was motivated to pioneer for profits. The Chinese map-making system, on the other hand, remained shackled to the political idea of Sinocentrism.

Our world map of the Wall is but part of a great European cartographic advance. For the first time in history people are seeing what the real world looks like, and what wonders it contains. Awareness of the Great Wall's existence in China was no longer limited to a small band of Jesuits and their society in Rome. Initially, atlases that displayed the Wall were so expensive that they would only be purchased by the powerful and wealthy. The Wall's existence – if it was noticed at all – was a privileged view only for those living in palaces, castles or mansions, or those studying in Europe's first universities.

During the seventeenth century, the widespread inclusion of the Great Wall on European maps certainly increased people's awareness of it, yet its significance seems to have gone unappreciated. I first realised this when I began to travel widely and see the world's other great ancient constructions. Naturally, I compared how they measured up to the Great Wall in size, antiquity, materials, location, function, symbolism, beauty, and of course the human effort required to build them. During these ponderings, I concluded that the inclusion of the Great Wall on world maps was a succinct statement of its greatness, as it highlighted an attribute that other leading wonders – such as the Great Pyramid of Giza, Petra, the Colosseum, the Taj Mahal or Machu Picchu – didn't have: a geography. It was cartographer Cornelis de Jode who had first depicted this for the world to see. It seems, however, that he gained neither recognition nor profit for his vision.

De Jode's updated map was made as he strove to keep his

family's map-making business alive. His father, Gerard de Jode (1501–1591), had been developing an atlas, the *Speculum Orbis Terrae*, or 'Mirror of the World', which was to rival Abraham Ortelius' *Theatrum Orbis Terrarum*, or 'Theatre of the World' (see Object 1). After Gerard's death, Cornelis struggled to make the business pay – the atlas' publication in 1593 proved disappointing.

Disillusioned, he sold the printing plates of the entire atlas to the powerful Antwerp printer V. B. Vrients, in the hope that he would distribute it more successfully. But Vrients also acquired the printing plates of Ortelius' atlas, and chose to streamline production and simplify distribution by publishing only one of the great atlases. He chose Ortelius' *Theatrum* as it had an established market presence. The plates of the de Jode family's *Speculum* would never be brushed with ink again.

Cornelis de Jode began to focus on niche cartographic projects, including the production of single-sheet maps that illustrated the very latest discoveries. They were simpler, cheaper and quicker to produce than high-investment master volumes. Our *Nova Totius Orbis Descriptio* – which we might even translate as 'An Updated Map of the Whole World' – is a prime example. Its zephyrs, medallions, galleons and title vividly announce that it relied on the recent discoveries of the explorers – Drake, Cavendish, Del Cano, Magellan, Columbus and Vespucci – who captained ships on voyages of discovery between the late fifteenth and late sixteenth centuries. But as we have only a single copy of the map – perhaps it's a proof copy – we can only speculate that it didn't advance to wider public sales.

The Great Wall remains the one and only individual building that graces world maps and globes to this day.

40.

MOVING TARGETS

Foreign-style 'Border Pacification Cannon'

With its heavy metal and hardness, length and thickness, it's difficult not to be impressed by this gun, although I'm more intrigued
by its boastful name: 'The Mighty, Golden, Victory, Blasting, En-
emy-Eliminating and Border Pacification Cannon'. There's also
a fascinating description hung around its neck which calls it a
hongyi pao, or 'foreign-style' cannon.

The Badaling Museum of the Great Wall has made a commend-
able effort to show this cannon in its context, placing it behind a
mock battlement, yet to many of its viewers it inevitably remains
lifeless, rather like a stuffed tiger. No longer able to roar or shake
the ground, it begs to be released from captivity. I take note of its
measurements in my notebook.

In order to put this cannon back *in situ*, I will review it from
the ramparts, where I can consider the surrounding field situation
and the enemy's nature, and thus work out if it might really have
brought victory, eliminated the enemy and pacified the border.
Put simply, I want to learn how significant this big gun was. Did
its performance match its status as the most advanced weapon
ever deployed on a Great Wall?

What is meant by 'a foreign-style cannon' is much more of a

DESCRIPTION:	Muzzle-loading 'foreign-type' cannon cast in two layers, iron interior and copper exterior, by the Board of War; called 'The Mighty, Golden, Victory, Blasting, Enemy-Eliminating and Border Pacification Cannon'; length 1.70 m, barrel diameter 22.3 cm, 8.5 cm calibre, weight 420 kg. Bears a 69-character inscription
SIGNIFICANCE:	Largest weapon-type used on the Great Wall at height of the Ming Empire; impressive yet ineffective
ORIGIN:	Dated 'Chongzhen Wuzhen Year', or 1628 A.D.
LOCATION:	Badaling Museum of the Great Wall, Yanqing, Beijing

conundrum, and requires a look much further afield to understand it. The pertinent question is this: if the Chinese invented gunpowder and designed the first guns, why were they styling their cannon on foreign designs? How did this world leader in hot weapons become a follower?

First, the easier leg of my investigation. I need to walk the ruins and find a string of *paotai*, or cannon platforms, which are brick table-like structures built up to the level of the battlement's embrasure. These will tell me precisely where the big guns were put into service. The cannon is dated *Chongzhen Wuzhennian*, or the first year of the Chongzhen Emperor's reign. Just sixteen years later he was driven to commit suicide, the Ming Dynasty fell and its Great Wall was abandoned and then looted.

A Ming officer, an Inspector General Xu, has left behind picturesque details of both the Wall and the mood of its soldiers. He composed a poem just a few years before the cannon was cast, sometime in the 1620s, during the reign of the former emperor, Tianqi (1620–27). The poem was then engraved on a tablet and placed in the Wall, close to the 'Nine Windows Tower' – like Badaling, also in Beijing's Yanqing District. The latter part of it reads:

> Banners and flags fluttering, our soldiers, in full armour, stand to attention
> Briskly we climb this precipitous mountain
> High above us circle eagles and vultures, lively as if in a painting
> Peace prevails, and it seems the watchtowers can be closed
> Shining brightly over the mountains are the sun and the moon
> Decorating the land of China are flowers so enchanting

Our mighty empire is safely nestled behind the all-
powerful Coiling Dragon
There's no need for us to retreat south for protection!

By this account, it appears that my visit is taking place as Ming China – the third-largest unified empire in the world, with a population of 100 million, ruled from the safety of Beijing's Forbidden City – stands tall and proud. The poem unfurls as a glowing report on the state of the Wall. The inspector coins an evocative term for it: 'the Coiling Dragon'. Watchtowers are no longer needed, he says, and he notes the disciplined men in shining armour – but he says nothing about cannons.

Archaeological clues such as the *paotai* ruins suggest that cannons were deployed only sparingly; perhaps they were limited to defence of particularly vulnerable locations. As I stand on the ramparts and imagine muzzle-loading such a cannon with two *jin* of gunpowder and two *jin* of lead shot, I realise that its target area would have been within a very narrow band. Tilting the 400-kilogram-plus barrel up or down, even with the right levers, would have been an effort. This monster was too big, slow and clumsy to have been an effective weapon against a swift-moving enemy.

Why, then, was this 'foreign-style' cannon deployed at all? I think the answer lies in its boastful name, which, alongside its looks, exists primarily to impress. It's a statement of imperial might. How it got there is a longer story, one that can only be answered much further away, way down south.

The stage is the Zhujiang, or Pearl River, in the environs of Guangzhou, where the Chinese first laid their hands on foreign guns and cannons in around 1519, seizing them from ships from the 'Land of Franks' – Portugal. A Dongguan customs officer, He Ru, boarded one of the ships and saw 'overseas Chinese' among the crew. Surnamed Yang and Dai, they lived among the foreigners at Melaka (today's Malacca), at the tip of the Malay Peninsula, a Chinese vassal state. Upon seeing the mobile Portuguese arsenal defending the ship, and learning that the Chinese had become acquainted with the Franks' methods of casting such guns and making gunpowder, He Ru offered them enticing rewards to defect. The *Mingshi Bingzhi*, or 'Ming History: Book of Weapons', suggests He Ru also managed to buy some guns there and then.

Soon after, with only tacit approval from local officials, the Portuguese landed at nearby Tunmen to trade, hastily constructing buildings and defences there. Their 'thunderous guns' and their rumoured wish to buy children to eat filled the local community with fear. At the death of the Zhengde Emperor (1505–1521), the Portuguese were ordered to leave, but they refused and fighting broke out. During these conflicts, more cannons were captured, soon to be copied.

Portugal was one of the most powerful maritime powers in Europe – along with France, England, Spain, the city state of Venice, Holland and Germany. These nations were often in conflict with one another, and their regular sea battles fuelled a European arms race, with many minor weapons improvements being made.

A month after I inspected Badaling's *hongyi pao*, which served on the land-locked frontier, I saw another cannon, one that had served on a maritime frontier and had been lifted from the seabed by marine archaeologists. These two frontiers were 8500 kilometres apart – one in northern China, the other the English Channel – but both cannons were huge, about the length of a tall man and approximately 400 kilograms in weight. Visually, they were virtually identical – in size, shape, length, design and colour. Only the inscriptions gave them away.

The one in Chinese we know. The other, in Latin, reads 'H I', which stands for *Henricus Invictissimus*, meaning 'Henry the Most Invincible'; it came from one of the gunships of King Henry

VIII, who reigned from 1509 to 1547. Thirty-one huge English cannons were recovered from the wreckage of the ill-fated *Mary Rose*, which sank in July 1545. Surprisingly, the Badaling cannon, excavated locally, was cast some eighty-two years later, in 1628.

These cannons are counterparts, and oddly so, because they were made and used continents and cultures apart. The fact that, feature by feature, the English cannon is more advanced than the Chinese signals what has happened. Although the Chinese invented gunpowder and designed the first guns and cannons, by the sixteenth century foreigners had adopted them, perfected the technology and forged ahead.

What does all this have to do with the Great Wall? The return of an upgraded product to its native shores, where it would be used against its original inventors, turned out to be a highly significant event. The Chinese conflict against the Portuguese at Guangzhou proved to be just the first of many Sino–European military interactions.

Historically, the Sino-nomadic relationship – largely fierce conflict – had been over products, access and trade. Denying nomads access to sought-after Chinese goods had sustained a protracted war along the northern frontier for 2000 years. Dutch and British embassies headed by diplomats would come to China in 1655 and 1793, respectively, only to have their requests to access the China market rebuffed. The denial of enough Chinese goods that home markets craved – for example, tea to the British – would lead to a real trade war. It would be fought and won by well-armed gunships, which annihilated the Chinese coastal fortifications and ships. As Henry VIII's cannon-laden *Mary Rose* shows from as early as 1545, European gunships boasted formidable and highly mobile firepower.

Eventually, ten foreign powers – eight European, as well as Japan and the United States – would come by ship to China on an international land grab that would open a new age of treaty ports along the coast and major rivers, and foreign concessions in cities. All were marks of Chinese humiliation – ironically, made possible by the spread of China's own technology. Inventing and then losing the lead in weapons development cost China dearly, and caused a dramatic shift in military focus: away from the traditionally volatile frontier zone of the north, and towards the east and the new enemies along the coast.

41.

THE LAST EMPEROR

Admonition decree from the Board of War

Most agree that it was Qin Shihuang back in the late third century
BC who was the mastermind of the Great Wall (see Object 11),
but few pause to consider the other end of the Wall's chronology.
Which emperor presided over its ultimate demise?

Chongzhen (1627–1644) was the last man to rule an empire
protected by a Great Wall. He was a central figure in a tumultu-
ous event that lies at the core of one of the most chaotic periods
of Chinese history – the end of the Ming. It's a well-known and
much studied period, so my challenge is to find an object that
provides some deeper insight.

Between early February and late May of 1644, a chain reaction of events changed China, transforming the Great Wall from a
military defence to a monument. On a 2014 calendar I circle the
key dates and places. The next steps in my quest are clear: I will
revisit the key locations in the four-month story, trusting that time
and place will bring me inspiration.

I begin at the Wall, one late winter afternoon. A pale-red sky
heralds the onset of dusk; shrieking ravens tell me I'm intruding.
That is what I came to do, after all – to think about the Wall's
twilight months in early 1644.

The Wall was barely functioning that March: towers were skel-etally manned, troops had long stopped training, but they hunted and collected firewood and listened – perhaps sceptically – to their commanding officers talking about the renovation work that had been postponed for several years already.

By April, rumours were rife. From the south-west came news that a rebel army was storming its way towards the capital. From the east, scouts returning from spying forays into Liaodong (a Manchurian region) reported that the Manchus were assembling a massive cavalry army.

May was unusual: there were none of the usual cartloads of food to relieve the bitter winter, no ministerial inspections, not even any messengers. The only normal thing was that there was no cash. The inactivity sparked immense speculation. It was said that northern China was starving, that the rebels had besieged or even taken Beijing, and killed the Emperor. Another report said the Manchu army had passed through the Wall at Shanhaiguan without having to fight at all.

That was the view from the frontier, but how about at the em-pire's heart, from the capital? The place to be was the largest hall in the Forbidden City, the date 8 February 1644. It was the dawn of the Year of the Monkey, the 276th year of the Zhu family's continuous rule over China. Chongzhen was the fifteenth family member to inherit the mandate of heaven, the god-given right to rule, and for two and a half centuries his ancestors marked the auspicious occasion by presiding over a grand ceremony in *Taihe-dian*, or 'The Hall of Supreme Harmony'.

Pillars of *nanmu*, the redwoods of China, held up the hall's high roof, while the pillars of Chongzhen's empire – men from the ministries and military – assembled below, mingling uncom-fortably among swarms of eunuchs, whom they despised for the overwhelming collective power they now wielded; such was government, late Ming style. News filtering through the state's administration predicted that it was going to be yet another very tough year. In the past twenty years, as many as 15 million out of China's 100 million population had perished – from starvation, disease or disaster.

Fate was closing in on the Emperor and all under heaven from several directions. Out of the sky and up from the ground, the forces of nature were conspiring against him. His reign witnessed the coldest period in the so-called mini ice age. Dry desert air from the north had kept the rains away for five years in succession. The Emperor's name was irrevocably linked with the disaster, which was dubbed the Chongzhen Great Drought. In the south, the lower reaches of the Yellow River, once a landscape of neat paddies, had never recovered the loss of its protective dykes, which had been ruptured in the Jiajing earthquake of 1556. More than 400 major floods and changes of course came in its aftermath. No longer filling the granaries and tax coffers, the rice bowl became wild and marshy, the home of wild ducks. People starved, populations dwindled, unrest stirred. Peasants believed the mayhem reflected imperial incompetence.

Also in February 1644, the rebel peasant Li Zicheng founded his Shun Dynasty in Xi'an, pronouncing himself king. His army headed for Beijing, aiming to overthrow the Ming from the inside. Just outside the Wall, in the north-east, the military muscle and statecraft of the Manchus, who had long eclipsed the fractured Mongols as the main danger to Ming sovereignty, threatened the same from the opposite direction. The two threats peaked at the same time, and both put the dynasty at risk.

Before the Lunar New Year celebrations had concluded, on the thirteenth day, the Chongzhen Emperor spoke to his Minister of War. Five days later, Zhao Kaixin, present at the recent ceremonial gathering, was ordered to write out stern words of warning to the

DESCRIPTION:	'Concerning "Goddamn" Outlaws Who Deceive the People', a handwritten scroll propagating imperial orders, written by Zhao Kaixin and dated the eighteenth day of the first lunar month of the seventeenth year of the Chongzhen Emperor's reign, or 25 February 1644; 157.5 centimetres by thirty-three centimetres
SIGNIFICANCE:	Last-ditch effort by the last Ming Emperor, Chongzhen, ordering that all government officials should resist Li Zicheng's rebellion

ORIGIN:	Board of War, Beijing
LOCATION:	National Museum of China, Beijing

government officials, as spoken by the Lord of Heaven. What the Emperor said, which we have reason to believe is as word-perfect as a recording, shows the gravity of the situation. Knowing full well that his provincial armies were refusing to fight for him, he resorted to waging war with words, warning officials of the grave consequences for anyone who dared to conspire with the 'god-damn' rebels.

It would take the rebels nine more weeks to reach Beijing, so we can regard this circular as being an early, long-distance shot. It was designed to be sent down a long chain of communication: from palace to ministry, from capital to provinces, and then to counties, prefectures and magistrates.

After such a journey, can you imagine how these words were received?

> The Emperor absolutely prohibits local officials according welcome to the outlaws . . . to forget the Great Ming that has fed and sustained you and your ancestors for 300 years, and to give support to bandits that suddenly approach is inexcusable . . . just compare the two sides, the Emperor, a benevolent father who's nurtured you, and outlaws, murderers, thieves, arsonists and rapists . . . you should to be loyal and listen to your father and the Great Ming . . . his imperial majesty orders that all outlaws, and anyone siding with them, will be beheaded and have their heads displayed publicly so to bring shame on their families . . .

Outrage, laughter, ridicule? One seriously doubts whether this circular was ever actually circulated. If it was, just how far beyond Beijing might it have reached? Perhaps its preservation is a sign that it was never actually transmitted. Although it didn't work, it's still highly relevant to our story as it helps us appreciate the final, climactic episodes.

On 25 April, just south of the Juyong Pass at Changping, Li Zicheng's army forced Tang Tong, commander of Beijing, to surrender; a statue of the rebel leader on horseback now marks the spot. That same day, the Chongzhen Emperor escaped the approaching rebels, heading to Jingshan, the artificial hill created by the excavation of the Imperial Palace's moat. There, one of his eunuchs assisted him to hang himself from a tree.

The rebels took Beijing soon after, and then headed towards the Ming's last great stronghold, the fortress town of Shanhaiguan, which marked the Wall's seaside terminus. There, General Wu Sanggui was trapped between the advancing rebels on the inside and the Manchus on the outside, so he struck an eleventh-hour deal with Prince Regent Dorgon of the Manchus, to join forces with them and intercept the rebel army's advance. The Fuyuan Gate was opened, permitting the passage of tens of thousands of Manchu horsemen and paving their way into the heartland of China.

The next day, 27 May, the battle of Shanhaiguan raged between the 'allies' and Li's rebels, resulting in a decisive victory for the former. The Manchus alone would add the postscript, founding the Qing Dynasty just months later, and occupying the Ming Imperial Palace.

Three key locations – Changping, a suburban district north of Beijing, Jingshan, a hillock overlooking the Forbidden City, and Fuyuanmen, a gate in Shanhaiguan's Great Wall – staged different events of the story, but all witnessed remarkably similar spineless responses from leading Ming figures: surrender, suicide and treason. All were cowardly actions in light of the circular sent by Chongzhen, who pinned his hopes on the loyalty of government officials to resist the rebels' pressure.

They didn't, of course. And although it is clear that Chongzhen's circular did little or nothing to save him and the Ming, the episode reveals how the endemic dereliction of duty – from magistrates to governors, from commanders to the Emperor himself – led to the Ming's, and the Great Wall's, final demise.

Part Five

RUINS

Objects from 1644 to 1987

The fate of the Wall was sealed by the Manchu Qing's vast territorial gains, which rendered it useless. Under the rule of Kangxi and Qianlong, Qing China reined in the steppelands; it was almost fifty per cent larger than China today.

Meanwhile, pressures from the West mounted. The roles and aims of the Jesuits became highly contentious. Foreign embassies were rebuffed. Gunships arrived in their wake, trade wars erupted and port-city enclaves were forcibly ceded to overseas powers.

Heralding its rediscovery, the Ming Wall was highlighted by a survey in 1708. Foreigners tried to explain it, while images showed mere specks of it. Breakthroughs occurred in 1907–08: Stein explored part of the Han Wall, and Geil traversed the Ming Wall. Both produced landmark field studies.

Revival, revolution and renewal followed in the twentieth century. The Wall became a line of resistance during the Sino–Japanese War. The Communists adopted it as a national symbol, then set about destroying it in the Great Leap Forward and the Cultural Revolution. Mao's anti-culture was opposed in 1984, as Deng Xiaoping urged China to love and rebuild the Great Wall. Once again it was the symbol of the nation, becoming a world heritage site and a major tourist attraction.

In 2008, an extensive survey revealed the Ming Wall's immensity as an outdoor museum of ruins. Surrounded by the world's fastest-growing economy, and newly accessible to an increasingly mobile society, what remains of the Wall stands in desperate need of visionary curatorial work and public guardianship.

42.

SCIENCE CONVERT

'The Jesuit Atlas of Kangxi's Realm'

Several of this atlas's thirty-five sheets are of enormous interest to me. As I arrange them in adjacency from east to west, they reveal the Great Wall's minutiae from end to end, showing its main lines, divisions, branches and loops. Tracing the battlement-like symbol, I see that more than 300 points along its length are named – a veritable procession of places ending in the characters *kou* ('pass'), *men* ('gate') and *shuimen* ('water gate'). Rolling a wheeled map measurer along the same route, I can 'recalculate' – perhaps as a curious mind did 300 years ago – a plausible figure for the Wall's total length: 6700 kilometres.

Remarkably, this charting of the Great Wall proved to be the opening stage of the first nationwide field survey in the history of cartography, and it was a team of foreigners, French Jesuit missionaries, which carried it out. After more than a decade of fieldwork the surveyors' maps were presented to the Kangxi Emperor (1661–1722) in 1718. The largest territorial China in history had become the most intensely and accurately mapped land in the world.

For the makers of the atlas this was no overnight, ten-year success story. Since the first Jesuits had arrived in China in the mid sixteenth century they were aware of the great uses and roles of maps, for themselves, their hosts, sponsors, and most importantly, for advancing towards their ultimate goal. This atlas shows just how far their mission got, by the early seventeenth century. They won the approval of the Emperor, mapped his empire, but failed in their main aim: conversion of China to Christianity. However, as our object's name – 'The Jesuit Atlas of Kangxi's Realm' – indicates, this work stands as an extraordinary testament to Jesuit diplomacy and perseverance, scientific and geographical endeavour, and to the vastness of the Emperor's domain. Among these elements, it was accurate surveying techniques that ensured the success and legacy of the great enterprise.

To appreciate the surveying achievement of these map-makers, consider what would be involved in making a map of your own immediate locality – say, within a radius of about five kilometres of your home. At your disposal is standard desktop stationary, a protractor, a compass and a few other essentials.

How might you approach the task? Would you bother to actually go out and survey the ground? Would you use the compass to take bearings, observe the sun's highest point to record an accurate local noon time for comparison with GMT (be sure to protect your eyes), and get up in the middle of a clear night to measure the angle to the North Star above the horizon (provided you are in the Northern Hemisphere)? Could you do the follow-up maths, to work out a scale and make a grid on the paper, and then make a real map covering your eighty square kilometres? Could you give the latitude and longitude of your home address?

If you were to do anything less, you'd merely be making a sketch map, and you wouldn't have met the challenge that the makers of our atlas first faced: to impress upon the Kangxi Emperor that their skills were unparalleled, and should be utilised.

Father Jean-Francis Gerbillion, Father Superior of the French mission, had interpreted for the Qing court at the Treaty of

Nerchinsk negotiations with the Russians in 1689. Having won the respect of the Emperor, Gerbillion used his influence to praise the French mission's map-making expertise. By 1705 he managed to receive Kangxi's permission to oversee the making of a demonstration map for imperial examination.

'Job seeking' had long been an essential part of Jesuit evangelising activity in China. Whatever knowledge and skills they imported – astronomy, timekeeping, mathematics, cartography – its sharing was directed at achieving a singular 'short-cut' result: the empire's adoption of Roman Catholicism. The Jesuits aimed to show that it was God alone who granted their outstanding abilities, and that their belief in Him gave them the best understanding of the Earth and its place in the universe of all things. And if they could convince the Emperor himself to convert to Christianity, most Chinese under his rule would follow.

The Jesuits were China's first foreign experts. Matteo Ricci (1552–1610) spearheaded the Roman Catholic Church's mission in Ming China, leading the order from the Portuguese enclave at Macao to Beijing in 1601, and then into the circle of the imperial court. Ricci was granted land to build a church, and upon his death a plot for a cemetery. Many outstanding Jesuit scientists followed in his footsteps. Formally the Fathers of the Society of Jesus, Jesuits were known as the most academically brilliant and practically capable group of their church. (The current Pope, Francis, is a Jesuit.) After religious studies in Rome, Jesuits trained in specialist skills and awaited the right mission.

For a group of French Jesuits specialising in the science and art of map-making, their chance came up in China during the late 1600s. With the recent rise of the Qing it seemed probable that scientific cartography might capture the imagination of China's new rulers, if they could be convinced of its accuracy by speakers in their own Manchu language.

King Louis XIV (1643–1715) sponsored the French Jesuit mission. His investment had multiple aims: to break the dominance of other European Jesuits in China, to obtain better knowledge of China and to gather astronomical data, particularly concerning the local timings of the regular eclipses of Jupiter's moons, for the astronomer Gian Domenico Cassino (1625–1712), who was compiling tables to enable easier calculation of longitude.

Cassino had been appointed the King's astronomer at the newly established Parisian Academy of Sciences, also known as the Paris Observatory, where Jesuit fathers had trained under his direct tutelage, focusing on mathematics, astronomy and cartography. It was also mandatory for Jesuit missionaries to become outstanding linguists in their destination countries, and in Kangxi's China that now meant learning Manchu as well as Mandarin. Typically, Jesuits went out on their mission, worked and died there.

I looked for the survey team at Zhalan cemetery, now in the grounds of the Beijing Communist Party Training College, and Wutasi, or the Five Pagodas Temple, where the headstones of Jesuit graves have been pieced together, rescued from the desecration they suffered during the Boxer Rebellion (1900). I found gravestones for the four 'fathers of the survey': Gerbillion (1654–1707), Jean-Baptiste Régis (1663–1738), Joaquim Bouvet (circa 1656–1732) and Pierre Jartoux (1669–1720); all bore crosses and dragons, and were written in Latin and Chinese.

Sometime in 1705, this group of fathers surveyed an area of flood-prone flatlands to the south-east of Beijing, between the capital and today's Tianjin. They followed their fieldwork with tabletop cartography, and after seventy days submitted their map for imperial examination. They gave instruction on how to use it, how to orient it, how to work out distances and how to appreciate the relative positions of its features. It was no decoration, but a tool. All we know is that the map pleased the Emperor.

Kangxi was becoming increasingly interested in having good maps for two reasons. First, he was directing territorial expansion like no other emperor before him, and he needed to record these accomplishments on authoritative maps. As they still do, maps then served as national land deeds, so Kangxi wanted to make known his borders to the rest of the world.

Second, accurate maps would provide valuable strategic intelligence for future military campaigns, especially in the lesser-known border regions. A number of nomadic tribes inhabiting the fringes of 'Chinese Tartary', or that part of greater China north of the Great Wall, especially the Zunghars, continued to threaten, and Kangxi was aware that his empire was most fragile at its distant edges.

Geographical knowledge of a potential theatre of conflict along these new frontiers was considered basic knowledge in the art of war, and Kangxi knew well of the perils that lay in wait for the logistically unprepared. He scorned the attitude of past and recent Han Chinese officials, saying they were ignorant of the geography of these outer regions. In 1697 he had found bodies of his own 'Green Battalion' troops who had died of hunger the year before while pursuing the Zunghars.

Next, for an inexplicable reason, but very much to our advantage, in 1707 Kangxi gave an ailing Father Gerbillion the go-ahead to ready Jartoux, Régis and Bouvet to prepare to survey 'the country surrounding the Great Wall'. They began the project in June 1708, but why the Wall? No one really knows. Perhaps the legendary defence, built to keep out Kangxi's ancestors and their likes, had somehow ignited a special fascination within the mind of the ruling Manchu as he sat enthroned in Beijing's Imperial Palace.

According to Father Jean-Baptiste Du Halde, the French order's historian in Paris, who compiled the observations of twenty-eight French brothers active in China in *Description de la Chine*,

'A Description of China', by January 1709 the fathers had returned to Beijing . They presented Kangxi with a map, measuring 4.5 metres in length, which showed the Great Wall from Shanhaiguan to Jiayuguan. Unfortunately, this original map has been lost, but an intriguing question arises: did any of the Jesuit priests individually travel the entire distance between the Wall's two main terminal points, perhaps recording an historical first? We know that Father Bouvet retired ill after two months, but we cannot be sure whether the team divided its labour to cover the ground, as was their approach later in the China survey.

Although the foreign map-makers had taken this second examination, it seemed they were still 'on probation'. According to Du Halde, they faced their key test at the end of 1709 when asked to produce a map of Peichilli, the province around the capital, which Kangxi knew very well. It was their excellent work here that did the trick. Oddly, when Jesuits first arrived in China they were banned from learning Chinese and prohibited from travelling. Now they were about to embark on the longest of journeys, mapping the whole empire. Kangxi explained his decision:

> . . . because the existing maps for the land and cities of
> China were sketchy, and had distances that were inac-
> curately calculated, I sent the Westerners to map the
> empire from the far south to Russia and from the east
> to Tibet, using their methods of calculating the degrees
> in the heavens to obtain precise distances on earth.

The long survey began. It was a crippling workload in the harshest conditions, and several fathers perished. To obtain faster results the team divided up its labour. They also utilised previously determined astronomical observations made at established

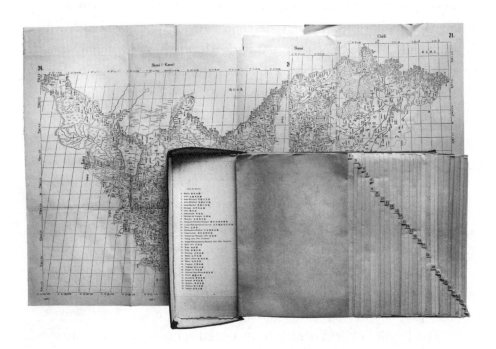

DESCRIPTION:	'Jesuit Atlas of Kangxi's Realm', a boxed set of 35 maps (atlas)
SIGNIFICANCE:	Contains the first accurate geography of the Ming Great Wall, gained by scientific surveying techniques carried out 1707–08
ORIGIN:	Opening phase of Jesuit-led imperial survey commissioned by Kangxi Emperor from 1707–17. Led to production of sheet maps, bound and boxed atlases in various editions, languages and locations between 1718 and 1941. This edition is a facsimile of a 1721 woodcut-printed edition, published Beijing , 1941
LOCATION:	Author's collection, Beijing

mission stations across the empire. Building on this existing grid of information, the Jesuit surveyors recorded latitudes in darkness, using 'astrolabes' to measure the angle of the North Star above the horizon. Forefathers had previously measured local time and its difference from the Paris Meridian, an imaginary line passing through the Cassini Room of the Paris Observatory, but for the Kangxi survey they made calculations of longitude by either observing the eclipse timings of Jupiter's moon or with reference to the Peking Meridian.

Eventually, the Jesuits recorded the precise locations of 641 points to form a grid. They then used triangulated compass bearings and simple geometry to work out the intermediate positions and distances apart of many other places, as well as the shape and courses of various geographical and historical features. Thirteen years after making their demo map of just one small region, they returned to Beijing to work on the final presentation titled 'A Comprehensive Map of the Great Qing Empire'.

The Jesuit fathers covertly transmitted accounts of their survey back to France, their sponsor, where an equally talented and dedicated team processed and published the materials. Along with Jean-Baptiste Du Halde's 'A Description of China', which contained many maps, the King's geographer, Jean Baptiste Bourguignon d'Anville published *Nouvel atlas de la Chine, de la Tartarie Chinoise et du Thibet* ('A New Atlas of China, Chinese Tartary and Tibet') in 1738. Maps therein also served as demonstration maps: a new era of cartography had dawned.

Although the French had swiftly published and circulated their survey results, the Kangxi Emperor and his successors restricted the circulation of the maps. Qing cartography remained largely sketchy and decorative, and most Chinese were ignorant of the benefits offered by scientific geography. Kangxi's maps, it seems, were admired mainly because they showed off his conquests. The Emperor himself played down the accomplishments of the foreigners:

> I was careful not to refer to these Westerners – whom I had dispatched to make a map . . . – as 'Great Officials', and I corrected Governor Liu when he referred to the Jesuits Regis and Fredilli as if they were honoured imperial commissioners . . . For even though some of the Western methods are different from our own, and many even an improvement, there is little about them that is new. The principles of mathematics all derive from the 'Book of Changes' and the Western methods are Chinese in origin . . .

Qing China remained traditional, resisting change, looking inwards and backwards, resting on the laurels of its early inventions. By contrast, Europe relished the Enlightenment, pioneering new knowledge, forging a global view, spreading education, looking outwards and forwards.

It would be almost 200 years before Kangxi's maps were 'declassified' to reach a wide viewership. In 1929, after the discovery of copper printing plates in the Manchu Imperial Palace, Shenyang, a reprint was published under a title that referred to the map's secret history: *Qing Neifu Yitong Yudi Mitu*, 'A Confidential Map of the Qing Empire'. Even then, some of its maps remained the best available.

This map of the Great Wall in 'The Jesuit Atlas of Kangxi's Realm' represents its zenith, and nothing better follows. It would be 300 years exactly before the next survey was conducted, in 2007–08 by the State Administration of Cultural Heritage. It used GPS technology, and would prove very different to the Jesuit survey in one major respect. In 1708 the surveyors set out to learn what was there; in 2008 they discovered what had gone.

43.

IN GREAT DETAIL

Captain Parish's technical drawings

The qualities of these Great Wall images are best understood when you take them from the British Library in central London back to the foot of Crouching Tiger Mountain at Gubeikou, 120 kilometres north-east of Beijing. Doing so allows you to appreciate the journey made by their artist in 1793, and to examine the skill of his hand, the accuracy of his measurements and the discipline of his pen.

With scans of pages 158, 159 and 160 of Captain William Parish's field notebook in hand, I set off from the library. A three-stage journey brings me to the Wall at Gubeikou: the Tube to Heathrow Airport, a direct flight to Beijing Capital Airport, and a drive up the Beijing-Chengde expressway and along the G101 trunk road, which passes right through the Wall in the centre of Gubeikou town.

With the Crouching Tiger to my west, I walk 100 metres to the edge of the Chao River. I take off my shoes, roll up my trousers and wade across to stand in front of the newly rebuilt 'Sister Towers', a unique arrangement of two watchtowers side by side. I turn away from them to the north, passing the hamlet of Xishuimen, and ascend a path that leads up to the section of Wall that lies parallel to the river. I pass through the first tower and continue to the next. I retrieve the scans from my backpack and read Captain Parish's 'remarks', written in fountain pen, and then (eventually with the help of a ladder) I explore the three levels of 'Tower No. 2' with his cross-sections as my guide. Only seventeen hours have passed since I strode out of the British Library. In as many seconds, people all around the world will see the photographs I am taking of the tower.

Parish's images originate from the late eighteenth century, a slower-paced time. He set sail on the HMS *Lion* in September 1792 as part of a British Embassy delegation to China, led by Earl George Macartney (1737–1806). The next summer they made North China landfall at Dagu (Taku) on the Bohai coast (near Qinhuangdao), then proceeded upriver to Tongzhou, in Beijing's eastern suburbs, where they were accommodated near Yuanming Yuan (the Old Summer Palace). The British were not planning a cultural tour of the Great Wall; this was a serious business trip.

The British East India Company, which held a British government monopoly to trade with China, was frustrated by the restrictions imposed upon it (and on all foreign traders) by the 'Cohung' system, a monopolistic guild of merchants at the one and only trading port of Canton (Guangzhou). While British trade was booming worldwide, it had remained stagnant with China. Macartney's mission was to negotiate a relaxation of the restrictive regulations.

The British arrived in Beijing in late summer, when the Qianlong Emperor was still residing at his mountain resort of Chengde, 250 kilometres north of the imperial capital. After stressing that an important aim of the mission was to convey birthday congratulations from King George III to the Qianlong Emperor, the embassy was granted permission to travel north in the last days of

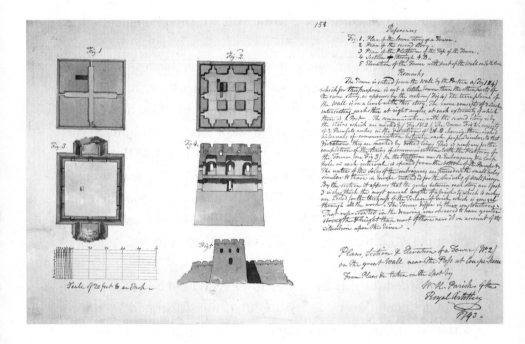

DESCRIPTION:	Technical drawings of the Great Wall at Gubeikou by Captain William Parish of the Royal Artillery, a member of the British Embassy to China, 1793
SIGNIFICANCE:	The earliest technical drawings and accurate landscape painting of the Wall

ORIGIN:	Made in September 1793 at the foot of Wohu Shan, or Crouching Tiger Mountain, Gubeikou, Hebei–Beijing border
LOCATION:	British Library, London (WD 961 158, WD 961 159)

Beijing's August heat. Two days out from the capital, the British had a chance encounter with the Great Wall at the fortifications at Gubeikou.

A guard of honour, composed of an estimated 1200 soldiers – divided into companies, flying five banners and accompanied by trumpets and music – made the British feel welcome, and very important. Soon after, this first international tour group clambered over the nearby ramparts. Sir George Staunton, the embassy secretary, who would author the official account of the mission, conveyed the great scale of the Wall to his readership, estimating that if the entire Great Wall was dismantled and rebuilt at the equator at a standard three feet high and wide, it would circle the globe two and a half times. While 'all the embassy went to visit it,' Staunton wrote, 'Captain Parish was particularly attentive to its construction and dimensions.'

Parish was an officer of the Royal Artillery, an architect and skilled draftsman. He used pencils, ruler, watercolours, ink pen and tape measure – and considerable time – to record meticulously the details of what he saw in front of him. The unique aspect of his work lay in the plans, cross-sections, elevations and views of the walled landscape of Crouching Tiger Mountain. Parish ignored what was purported to lie beyond, which was said to be so extensive that its volume was estimated to exceed that constituting Great Britain's buildings; he decided instead to examine and record its fascinating minutiae.

It would be a further three years before Parish could share his work with the British public. On his return to London it was rearranged and presented as a series of copperplate engravings printed in a large-format supplementary volume to *An Authentic Account of an Embassy from the King of Great Britain to the Emperor of China*, written by Staunton and published in 1796. Parish's view of the Wall snaking up the mountain at Gubeikou became the most widely published Great Wall image worldwide, and remained so for the next seventy years, until pioneering photographers began to show the diversity of the structure.

The British proceeded north to Chengde. Despite the failure of fifteen previous diplomatic trading missions to China – from Portugal, the Netherlands and Russia – the British were confident. Although King George III (1738–1820) reigned over a population of just 8 million British subjects, compared to the 330 million Chinese who lived in the Qianlong Emperor's Great Qing Empire, Britain was the first industrial power to come knocking on China's door. By the time of the Macartney Embassy, the British had already colonised land on all the world's continents, and were set to add most of Australasia within decades. Now they were determined to monopolise trade with China, shutting out any opposition.

The meetings between the British and Chinese took place during the mid-autumn of 1793, in Manchurian yurts set up at Wanshou Yuan, or 'Garden of 10000 Trees'. Earl Macartney presented Great Britain's requests: an envoy stationed in Beijing, the abolition of import and export duties, the opening of more ports to trade, and freedom for missionary work. Not only were these demands rejected, but Macartney was told that the Great Qing had no need at all for any British manufactures. Eventually, the British were deported. All in all, the encounter was an epic collision of cultural, diplomatic, economic and psychological sensitivities.

While the twilight years of Qianlong's long reign marked the zenith of the so-called 'High Qing' period, a much larger empire was starting to emerge beyond its borders. When the Qing fell, in 1912, its Emperor ruled the largest ever China, at 14.7 million square kilometres. At the same time, the British controlled some 33 million square kilometres, giving rise to the saying that 'the sun never sets on the British Empire'.

In contrast to China's traditional strength – centralisation around an ancient core – the British relied on the worldwide reach of their empire. Colonies produced raw materials, which were shipped to Britain's factories via a web of new shipping routes. In this way Britain produced a variety of goods for expanding urban markets.

For 2000 years Chinese refusals to trade on the northern frontier had aggravated the nomads of north-east Asia, leading them to attack and seize a share of China's material wealth by force, undeterred by distance or difficulty. Nor did the great distances and the bolted trade door put off the British. Their heavily armed gunships would soon be a new form of cavalry on the seaboard horizon of south-eastern China, just as mobile, manoeuvrable and unstoppable as the Xiongnu horsemen had been 2000 years earlier.

Although it drew a blank, the Macartney Embassy may be seen as the opening shot of a war to break out on a new frontier. And while these peoples, their eras, their homelands, their transport and their weapons technologies were vastly different, the core issue remained the same: access to trade.

Oddly, it was quite by chance that the British, in travelling across the globe for trade talks with the Chinese Emperor, chanced upon the Great Wall. There, a certain Captain Parish took his unexpected opportunity to walk on the ruins, draw and measure, and give the world a detailed preview of its appearance. Ultimately, the reception the British received from the Emperor convinced them that although the Wall had been abandoned, a new wall stood strongly in his mind, and its purpose was to keep foreigners out.

44.

NEW CONVOYS

Photo of the Beijing to Paris inaugural car rally

From the distant origins of the Great Wall's story to the latest media reports mentioning it, there is one ever-present issue: mobility. Without the robust Mongolian horse, northern nomads could not have crossed hundreds of kilometres of hostile terrain to China, in search of their material gains (see Object 25). And without the car, hundreds of thousands of Beijingers would lack the personal mobility that lets them escape the city's foul air and seek respite in the municipality's northern mountain suburbs.

After the grimmest of Beijing springs, which was plagued by weeks of dense smog, car owners in the capital made a mass exodus on the May Day state holiday in 2014, participating in what one local media source described as an 'epic 55-kilometre-long tailback'. The jam clogged the Badaling Expressway, leading from the northern edge of Beijing to the most-visited section of tourist Great Wall.

'Participate' is a key word here. On 31 January 1907, *Le Matin*, a leading Parisian newspaper, solicited the participation of both car makers and adventurous motorists in an automobile 'raid', or expedition. 'What needs to be proved today is that as long as a man has a car, he can do anything and go anywhere,' the editors wrote. 'Is there anyone who will undertake to travel this summer from Paris to Peking by automobile?' they asked. Eleven men in five cars took up the challenge that summer, although they eventually drove in the opposite direction to exploit better weather.

At eight-thirty a.m. on 10 June, the participants assembled outside the gates of the Caserne Voyrun Barracks, the new French Legation in Beijing, hoping to drive all the way to Paris. The favourite among the starters was an Italian aristocrat, Prince Scorpione Borghese, driving his Turin-made Itala. He had arrived weeks in advance of his car in order to reconnoitre on horseback the initial section of the route through the mountains leading out of Beijing. Using a bamboo pole cut to the width of his car, he was out to ensure that his Itala could pass through some of the valleys' narrowest defiles – and if it couldn't, he hired workers to widen the track.

The legation's arched entrance and protective walls were decorated with the French tricolour flag. A banner was draped across the street wishing the drivers 'Bon Voyage', while a military band trumpeted the French national anthem. Firecrackers were set off, the cars engines started, and, as one of several photogravures in *L'Illustration* shows, the vehicles disappeared under plumes of exhaust smoke.

At the dawn of the twentieth century, automobiles were relatively new, very dirty, mechanically unreliable and a largely untested means of long-distance transportation. They were uncommon, too, having only been used for twenty years or so, and their purchase was still largely the preserve of the wealthy. Ford, the first mass producer of motorcars to the American public, had only been founded in 1903. The world largest cities were seeking solutions to a transport pollution problem that was unimaginable to smaller town dwellers at the time: horse dung.

In China, roads were – and still are – called *malu*, or 'horse roads', for good reason. Horses (or anyone on foot, for that matter) made their way by picking a path step by step. This selective

DE PÉKING A PARIS EN AUTOMOBILE. — La troisième étape (12 juin) : vue prise un kilomètre après le passage de la Grande Muraille.

DESCRIPTION:	A photogravure print depicting cars and coolies in the lee of the Great Wall at Badaling, on the third day of the inaugural Peking to Paris 'Expedition' of 1907
SIGNIFICANCE:	The first motorcars at the Great Wall; this mode of transport led to the transformation of the Chinese landscape in the late twentieth and early twenty-first centuries, and had an increasing impact on the remotest sections of Walls
ORIGIN:	Double-page spread in a four-page report in the French magazine L'Illustration, published in Paris on 13 July 1907
LOCATION:	Author's collection, Beijing

action makes part of the way, the chosen way, smoother, while those places perpetually avoided remained rougher. Wheels, on the other hand, have to maintain continuous contact with the ground and so wear down a more consistent surface. An image in *L'Illustration* shows the advantages that the traditional held over the new – camels and horses are seen overtaking cars that have been stopped on the track by potholes, stones or boulders. Automobiles were encumbered also by their need for gasoline, which, ironically, had to be carried in advance by camels along most of the rally's Asian route.

Soon after leaving Nankou, on the second day, the motorists left the pan-flat North China Plain and entered the narrow Juyong-guan, a nineteen-kilometre long valley which threads its way between steep mountains up to the Wall at Badaling. This 'horse road' proved completely impassable to the cars, as our object, a double-page photogravure in *L'Illustration*, reveals. Not only does it show the first motorcars at the Wall, but also the Wall's first traffic jam. The caption read: 'Cars in difficulties after passing the Great Wall of China. The road was a road only by courtesy and resembled rather a very rocky beach. Petrol was no longer any use: ropes were attached to the cars, and with these they were dragged along by teams of coolies.'

Remarkably, after sixty-one days and more than 14 000 kilometres, Prince Borghese rumbled into Paris more than a week ahead of the three other vehicles that remained. But had he really proved that cars could take anyone anywhere?

One hundred and eight years later, roads are smooth, flat and wide, and cars are no longer only toys for the wealthy. In Beijing, they have become common possessions for *laobai xing*, or 'ordinary folk'. In 1907 there were only seven motorcars in Beijing; by 2014 there were an estimated 7 million.

Since 2000, the Chinese government has rolled out an unprecedented distance of top-quality roads, paving the way for this rocketing level of car ownership. Yet despite a century's advancements in automobile engineering and roadbuilding, the epic May Day traffic jam showed what the promise of personal mobility to millions has actually provided: hundreds of thousands of vehicles lurching at a snail's pace from the city to the Great Wall.

The situation illustrates what Canadian environmentalist Professor Ronald Wright terms a 'progress trap' – a situation that arises when technological innovation, often coupled with mass production, create conditions or problems that society is unable to foresee, or unwilling to solve. Traffic congestion in Beijing is now a daily event; a mass quest for personal mobility has led to mass immobility.

Would smoother, wider roads help, or faster cars? No, of course not. The real problem was the widespread belief that cars could provide a socially acceptable form of transport to the population of a mega-city like Beijing, which is thought to be approximately 20 million. Air-quality issues aside, another obvious alarming message of May Day 2014 was 'roadspace'. As Bill Ford, the fifth-generation family boss of Ford, the world's fifth-largest carmaker, acknowledges, countries with large urban populations will always suffer chronic gridlock when a lot of people take to the road at the same time, aiming to get to the same place.

The motorcar has left battle scars in many places along the route of the Wall, markers of neglect, ignorance and mismanagement. Before legislation was enacted to protect the Great Wall in 2007, hundreds of openings were punched through its ruins. Some widened already existing tracks of yesteryear, while others were new openings made by new government road-building programs . Rather conspicuously in 2005, the Ministry of Transport didn't enter into consensus with other ministries and administrations pledging to make unified and more vigorous efforts to protect the Great Wall.

Decades in which the smashing of old structures was condoned in the name of revolution – which was rife from the late 1950s to the mid-1970s – created a culture of widespread acceptance. The ruins of the Ming Wall, fragmented yet stunning, an extensive outdoor museum that stretched across nine provincial administrative regions of North China, were particularly vulnerable. Especially where it appeared less spectacular than the grander, more famous sections near and around Beijing, it was seen as an old and useless relic standing in the way of modern progress.

What the Scottish environmental philosopher John Muir said about those who felled trees is equally applicable to those who knocked down the Great Wall: 'Any fool can cut down trees; they can't run away.' In fact, I would argue that their foolhardiness was even greater, since the authenticity of the Great Wall's ruins can never be recovered. At the time, an oft-quoted development maxim promoted the need for 'more roads to pave the way to prosperity': the present and the future were more important than the past.

Whether on the road to the Great Wall, beside it or even through it, cars have caused it widespread damage. To accommodate peak numbers of cars on holidays, the development corporation at Badaling used land directly beside the ancient structure to build the largest car parks next to the Wall. The proximity of these seas of vehicles leaves another intrusive scar on the Great Wall landscape.

One year after Prince Borghese's achievement, Ford began mass production of its Model T, and man's twentieth-century love affair with the motorcar began. The Beijing–Paris event was revived in 1997; at the time of writing, the next event is planned for 2016.

45.

A MILESTONE JOURNEY

The Great Wall of China *by William Edgar Geil*

'There is a Great Wall of China. So much the geographies tell everybody; but they do not make it clear whether it is built of china, or why it is, or how long it is, or how long it has been.' So read the opening lines of the first book – in any language, anywhere – with the title *The Great Wall of China*.

With pertinent and witty questions, some with double meanings, William Geil summarised the outstanding mysteries of a structure made semi-legendary by maps, and announced his intention to go out and find the answers. It was 1908, and while the Chinese Wall was considered to be the largest edifice ever raised by human endeavour, its purported magnitude was counterbalanced by a void in knowledge that was beginning to engage the curiosity of daring human minds. The previous year, the British archaeologist Aurel Stein (1862–1943) had explored remnants of the Han Wall (see Object 14). But the Great Wall, as we see and know it today, being the Ming Wall whose remains were marked on contemporary maps, was the world's most famous building and yet the least known. It still lay waiting to be discovered in total.

The author didn't come from where one might first expect:

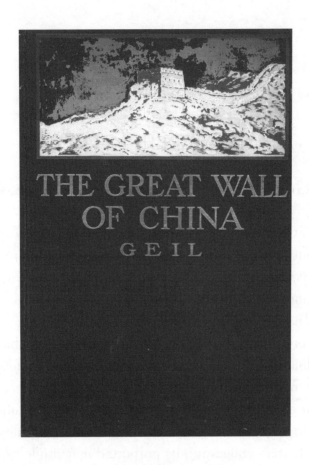

DESCRIPTION:	*The Great Wall of China*, illustrated book by Dr William Edgar Geil
SIGNIFICANCE:	The first book about the Great Wall in any language; contains field observations, history, legends, myths and photographs obtained during the author's milestone journey between Shanhaiguan and Jiayuguan in 1908
ORIGIN:	Published simultaneously by Sturgis & Walton, New York, and John Murray, London, November 1909
LOCATION:	Author's collection, Beijing

a Wall-side town such as Jiayuguan or Shanhaiguan, or an ancient centre of Chinese learning such as Xi'an, Luoyang or Hangzhou. No, he set out to become the first explorer of the Wall from end to end by taking a railroad across America, from Doylestown to Philadelphia to San Francisco. He then boarded a steamer across the Pacific, via Hawaii and Yokohama, disembarking at Taku, near today's Tianjin – an odyssey of thirty-nine days – before he reached China's distant shores and the Old Dragon's Head, the seaside terminus of the Ming Wall.

For generations, the Chinese had built the Wall, manned it, quarried it away and lived beside it. They made it, used it and then abused it. It was in their past and their present, and they assumed it would always be there. Its name – *Wanli Changcheng* – told them its length. They thought they knew it because it was there and theirs. It wasn't special because it was common. Familiarity led to oversight, even contempt.

Merely reading its evocative name, seeing it from afar, a barrier so long, so continuous, was enough to convince Geil of its greatness, that it was worthy of exploration from one end to the other. What a structure to be marked on a map! What a magical name! Earlier, Geil had noted 'how the West knew Greece and Rome well enough, and now was the time to go East, to China for a change'. His first odyssey there had been down the 'Long River' – the Changjiang, or Yangzi – in 1904, and in 1908 he returned to experience the Long Wall.

During the last few days of May 1908, a 'local' fixer, Luther Newton-Hayes, an 'old China hand' born in Suzhou to American missionary parents, sought men and mules for Geil's expedition at Shanhaiguan's 'West Side' market, a rigmarole described in the first of Geil's typewritten sheets headed 'The Great Wall Letters'. This was one of several documentation methods that he employed, along with hastily scrawled (and very amusing) diary notes, and comprehensive photography that would show, for the first time, the Great Wall's varied architectural elements and its diverse host landscapes.

Geil's hand scrawls were brief, often made on the go – perhaps akin to today's Tweets. 'From the saddle I can count 32 watchtowers' (Funing County, Hebei). 'Must send a photograph to this very *hospitable* gentleman – Mr. Zhou Chongwen, Zhuangdaokou Village, Huairou County, Beijing' (the Zhous are still there). Another mentions staying in the 'Lin' family village, whose surname Geil directly translated as 'Woods'; then the village was Chi'ligou, now it's called Xizhazi Yidui, and the Lins are still there, too. Further west, Geil tells us how he observed a true 'Sunday': sitting in the cool, shady chambers of a derelict Shaanbei watchtower, to avoid travelling on the Sabbath and under a blistering July sun.

Geil was a man of contrasting characteristics: Baptist missionary, gutsy explorer and inquisitive scholar. Standing a lofty 1.93 metres in height, he planted himself on the ground with size fourteen boots. He wore a dark suit and cleric's collar in Doylestown, but added a Stetson, a cloak and a Colt revolver along the Wall. He rode horses in China, while he drove a Model-T Ford in Doylestown and Philly.

His writing was also high-tech, when he had the time. He describes building a makeshift table of blue-grey Wall bricks below the Horizontal Ridge Pass (Huairou's Xidachang), so he could type out one of his 'Great Wall Letters'. His Blickensderfer No. 6 portable typewriter and carbon paper attracted audiences en route as he 'blogged' his progress, sending letters by mail when the opportunity arose; thankfully, he kept reference copies. He summarised his route by listing the places he passed through, recording their names in both handwritten Chinese characters and typed transliterations. He also noted the distances in *li* between them, as well as the dates he arrived and departed.

Eighty-one days after leaving the stele overlooking the Yellow Sea which bears characters that translate as 'Heaven Made the Seas and Mountains', Geil passed through the portals of the Jiayuguan Fortress, taking a photograph of the 'opposite' stele, inscribed 'The Martial Barrier Under Heaven'. It was 21 August 1908, and mandarins of the Yamen held a celebratory banquet in his honour. With amusement, Geil recorded the nineteen dishes they served, which included sea cucumber despite their distance from the ocean. He made no mention of any sentiments expressed by his hosts over his accomplishment. It appears the mandarins honoured him as a foreigner who had come from afar, from *Meiguo*, 'the Beautiful Country', not for how or why he had come.

The next morning Geil and company rode horses to 'the real end of the Wall', following the rammed-earth Wall through a line of several watchtowers and collecting a brick from one of the encased towers en route. Seven *li* from the fortress stood the very last watchtower, a cliff-edge perch above the Qilian Gorge. Here, it was calculated, the Shanhaiguan stele stood a distance of 1145 miles, as the crow flew, from the Jiayuguan stele, while the actual length of the 'Great Barrier' between the two stones twisted and turned along loops and spurs for 2550 miles.

Standing against the last tower, Geil posed for a photograph, his American flag unfurled and with his brick in his hands. After the photo he ceremoniously dropped it into the river below. It was not an issue of weight but of conservation. As a memento he collected a maroon and white stone for a paperweight.

This was not the end of Geil's journey, but merely a turning point. He returned to the fortress and then headed back east, along the Hexi Corridor. One of his most profound diary entries reads: 'No end to the G.W. No end to it in the East, or the West. The name is not correct which says 10,000 *li* . . . it has no end.'

His outbound journey had been through the inferno of northern China's summer, and on his return leg he travelled through chilly autumn and brutal winter conditions, bringing him down with pneumonia. He followed strands of the Great Wall in Qinghai, along the 'Lanzhou loop' in south-east Gansu and up the inside line into Hebei's Laiyuan. The final weeks of his journey were through a chaotic Empire that was mourning the death of the Guangxu Emperor and the Dowager Empress Cixi.

In April 1909, one year after leaving Doylestown, Geil arrived back in the United States, with his photographs, papers and paperweight packed in cases. He was whisked to the White House in Washington D.C., where he briefed President William H. Taft on his discoveries. By November he had published his book.

Some of the objects in this series are from my own collection, and from that group it's William Geil's book that I treasure the most. An inscription I made on its inside board explains what Geil's legacy meant to me:

> Presented to me in 1991 by Mrs Marjorie Hessel-Tiltman, this book inspired a second exploration of the Great Wall for both William Geil and I, best described as 'The Wall of Two Williams'. I used Dr Geil's photographs herein to see and show how the same locations looked almost one century later. This work resulted in the publication of a 'joint work', entitled 'The Great Wall Revisited', which I dedicated to William Geil as the First Explorer of the Great Wall. This too is the book that was exhibited at the national exhibition 'The Great Wall Revisited', staged at the Capital Museum, Beijing in 2007 and the Imperial Academy, Beijing in 2008. That year, 2008, marked the centenary of Dr Geil's historic journey, an event I commemorated by

travelling to his hometown of Doylestown, Pennsylvania. I carried this book on that occasion, quoted from it and rested it – momentarily – on his grave.

'Our' work together in the decade up to 2008 elevated William Geil's profile from unknown foreigner to an intimate *Lao Weilian* or 'Old William'. He is widely recognised in China now as being the first Great Wall explorer, and the first to write a book on the subject. My rephotography of his 1908 Wall views, which reveal a century of change, have influenced a better future for the monument and helped stir a desire in China to make the next century a better one for the Wall. Geil's photographs proved that the universal Chinese assumption that the Wall would always be there was quite wrong. His photos showed a Wall that, in mine, is often no longer there.

In the United States, however, Geil made the opposite journey, from fame to oblivion. He died of pneumonia in Venice in 1925, whereupon his bereaved wife, Constance, locked up his study, including his expedition records and belongings. Decades passed and his Wall achievement was forgotten. His body, transported back to Doylestown, was laid to rest in the family plot, which is marked by a large granite cube standing proudly in the town's cemetery.

In June 2008 I visited him there. His headstone inscription recorded his life in name and dates:

William Edgar Geil
Oct. 1, 1865–Apr. 11, 1925

To honour the man who showed us what the Great Wall looked like in the past, when it was a little greater, I had commissioned the design of a bronze plaque on behalf of the International Friends of the Great Wall. On it was a map of China marked with the Great

Wall, and I placed it beside his headstone during a ceremony on 16 June 2008.

On Geil's grave I rested my copy of his book, which had inspired a second Great Wall journey for us both. It was a collaboration that also led to a Chinese translation, which has guided many others since to follow in our footsteps.

I took off my cap to him and said: 'William Geil, you were the first man to travel all along the Great Wall, turning over a new page in its long history. Study and appreciation of the Great Wall began with your journey, book and photographs, and your complete panorama of the Great Wall, which have taught us a great deal. You are the first international friend of the Great Wall.'

46.

BUILDING FICTION

Kafka's Great Wall short story

Author Franz Kafka (1883–1924) never saw the Great Wall; he never even visited China. It was said that he only once set foot outside his native city, Prague, travelling to Berlin to live with a woman. But in his imagination he ventured to a place at the Great Wall where no one had been for more than 300 years. Yet it was a place seen in the present tense: a construction site at the building of the Great Wall.

Kafka was lured to the Great Wall as a setting for his story because of its relentless consumption of time and the repetitive work endured by the builders, which allowed him to explore the psychological toll it took on them. He probed the Wall's alter ego in this way by writing *Beim Bau der Chinesischen Mauer* ('At the Building of the Great Wall').

It's literature, not history – a story, not a source. It's plain, not eloquent. It's dreary, bewildering and disillusioning, not uplifting. Fiction, not fact. Kafka wrote it for himself, not for us. During his life, he burned ninety per cent of his manuscripts, and relatively few existed unpublished when he died in 1929. His last instruction to Max Brod – a fellow Czech, a fellow Jew, and a lifelong friend, writer and confidant – was to burn all his remaining papers unread. Brod couldn't, and didn't. Had he complied, he would have destroyed a rare piece of the Great Wall's story, among other works.

Brod's defiant act of preservation makes Kafka's Great Wall reachable today, and all the more important. It prompts us to think outside the box for a change – to consider the Wall in a different light, not as a spot-lit wonder but as an absurdity.

The Wall had been dubbed the world's longest cemetery, and clearly had drained the labours of untold millions. Legend had it that men were torn away from their families and worked to death at the Wall, their corpses becoming its fill. Writers of limited imaginations might have written of the physical brutality of the enslaved, of gulag conditions on the frontier, but that was too straightforward and simple for Franz Kafka.

The English writer Somerset Maugham was one of the first to touch on the Wall's double-sided character, publishing a postcard-length piece in 1923 which began and concluded with the same line: 'There in the mist, enormous, majestic, silent and terrible stood the Great Wall of China.' Several years earlier, Kafka had already started focusing on the subtler conflict between the controllers and the controlled, the 'Builders' and the 'builders', showing their adeptness, shrewd politics and propaganda on the one hand, and their obedience, confusion, frustration, scepticism and mental anguish on the other.

Kafka's dominant motif is the Great Wall's absurdity in the eyes of his narrator, perhaps a middle-ranking builder. He's far from his home and, as he's a southerner, the Wall seems irrelevant to him; he even doubts the piecemeal fashion in which it is being erected. He is dubious about its purpose but feels trapped between his need to do a good job and his sympathies for his subordinates, who simply work for their pay, always moving towards an unreachable finishing line. He says that the Wall is planned to be so long that it can never be completed, not even if one lived for 500 years.

As I read 'At the Building of the Great Wall' (Kafka's title is often translated simply as 'The Great Wall of China'), I hear a strange echo. What I saw just yesterday, last week, last month, last year, in hundreds of locations for the last fifteen years comes to mind. During this time, the city of Beijing, my adopted home, has become a patchwork of countless construction sites, with a sky full of cranes. But under this mechanical-age exterior I have observed the down-to-earth efforts of masses of workers – largely manual labourers – as they moved mounds of materials, churned up dust and made incessant noise. Each observation can be captioned with a line from Kafka: 'months or even years laying stone upon stone' and 'hundreds of miles from their homes'.

The anonymity, scale and conformity of what I have seen makes everything seem more 'Kafkaesque'. The workers are dwarfed by what they're making. Resembling red ants or yellow insects – depending on which hardhats are worn at the site – armies of men create order from chaos. They speak southern dialects and have distant homes, so they have few diversions or downtime, which makes for fast progress. They've built skyscrapers, housing complexes, ring roads, expressways, stadiums, stations, airport terminals and office blocks. They've changed Beijing, tripling its size, transforming its skylines, making the star on the map (which is always used on Chinese maps to mark the capital) an exploding one.

These modern China scenes can be plausibly transposed across the centuries back to Ming China, the time of Kafka's story. Temporal and spatial divides, factual evidence and fictional views blur easily. I had a notion that Kafka's fiction was partly fact, and that some of the Great Wall facts that we have come to trust might just be fictional. The parallels between Kafka and now were quite extraordinary; they no longer appeared to be comparisons between

DESCRIPTION:	*Beim Bau der Chinesischen Mauer* ('At the Building of the Great Wall'), short story by Franz Kafka
SIGNIFICANCE:	Fictional insight into the thoughts of the Great Wall's builders

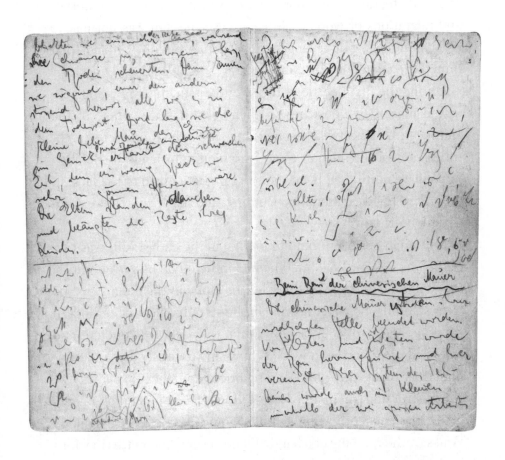

ORIGIN:	Written in 1917, published posthumously in 1931
LOCATION:	Author's collection, Beijing; the manuscript is held at the Bodleian Library, Oxford (MS Kafka 21, 3v 4r,)

past and present, but were more like recurring cycles, history repeating itself. Both building sites were of unprecedented scale, and both featured the enormous consumption of raw materials and migrations of workers; in each case the aim was not just to erect buildings, but to engage in a nation-building project that united the people in one cause.

During the first decade of the twenty-first century, Beijing generated more new construction each year than the whole of the European Union's twenty-something states. Four and a half centuries previously, the Yan Shan, the mountain range to Beijing's immediate north, had been the lynchpin in a chain of the largest, most sustained, material-consuming and labour-intensive construction drive in history.

A Russian envoy en route to Beijing in the early 1700s was told of the impact that Wall building had inflicted on its surroundings. 'The building of the Wall there left no stone in the mountains, no trees standing, no water flowing in the streams,' he wrote. Modern news reports have told of how Beijing's orders for concrete and steel had producers worldwide scrambling to satisfy demand, running their plants 24/7 and sending prices spiralling upward.

Construction then and now induced environmental blights without precedent. Ming China's grand makeover of Beijing's Wall saw the ravaging of a band of land several kilometres in width for its raw materials. Industrial landscapes intruded upon pristine ones. Forests were razed to obtain the timber that was needed to fuel brick and lime kilns. Fires belched acrid smoke, mixing with particulate rock dust from hundreds of quarries, creating a frontier-wide chain of devastation. Modern China's Beijing makeover triggered a similar but nationwide quest for raw materials: coal, aggregates, cement, steel and glass. Kafka wrote of 'forests being felled for scaffolding' and 'mountains being broken up into rocks'; the same is true today.

Kafka's Wall had been built piecemeal, section by section. After year five, builders were marched off home, passing other work in progress as they went, which enabled them to appreciate how their tiny effort was part of a grander, more important plan. They were treated heroically for a month or two, rejuvenated by home comforts, before returning to get on with the job – their jobs for life. In this way they changed the mountains, crowning them with battlements and towers, closing up the Wall's gaps, multiplying its length, transforming skylines, making the battlement-like symbol on the map (which marks the Great Wall) longer and longer.

Modern migrants, too, were watching the calendar. Kafka wrote of 'armies of labour streaming up from the depths of the provinces'. At week fifty they downed their tools and packed up, for it was time to travel home for the Lunar New Year celebrations, taking with them their wads of cash, and much pride. They saw that their efforts were not only lauded locally on hoardings around the construction site. Distant from Beijing, en route and in their hometowns, they saw billboards exhorting the same messages as they alighted from buses and trains. In 2005 it was 'New Beijing, Great Olympics'. In 2014 it is 'My China Dream'. After a few weeks' respite, their time was up.

Of his workers' return, Kafka wrote:

> The quiet life of home, where they spent some time, reinvigorated them. The high regard which all those doing the building enjoyed, the devout humility with which people listened to their reports, the trust which simple quiet citizens had that the wall would be completed someday—all this tuned the strings of their souls. Then, like eternally hopeful children, they took leave of their home. The enthusiasm for labouring once again at the people's work became irresistible.

They set out from their houses earlier than necessary, and half the village accompanied them for a long way. On all the roads there were groups of people, pennants, banners—they had never seen how great and rich and beautiful and endearing their country was. Every countryman was a brother for whom they were building a protective wall and who would thank him with everything he had and was for all his life. Unity! Unity! Shoulder to shoulder, a coordinated movement of the people, their blood no longer confined in the limited circulation of the body but rolling sweetly and yet still returning through the infinite extent of China.

Max Brod's overruling of his dear friend's dying wish made Kafka, too, part of humanity's bloodstream, a giant of twentieth-century Western literature. His works were put in a genre of their own, and the author was immortalised with the creation of an adjective to specifically describe his unique style: Kafkaesque.

It might also describe the section of Great Wall which we go to in our minds when we read 'At the Building of the Great Wall'. That place is called 'Kafka's Great Wall'.

47.

Back to the Wall

Press photo from the Sino-Japanese War

In the early summer of 1644, the ramparts of the Ming Great Wall became increasingly quiet, and they soon fell silent except for occasional thunderstorms and gales. The Wall's watchtowers, former shelters, storerooms and signalling stations for old soldiers, were particularly eerie, as they are to this day, devoid of men, empty of water, food and weapons, looted of their wooden doors and window shutters, stripped of the engraved stone tablets that sat above their doorways. Yet in spite of these losses and departures, the buildings weren't derelict in their duty. Most continued standing, as unarmed guards, their dark windows – *yan*, or 'eyes', as the Chinese call them – fixed on the north, as if doubtful that the last invaders had been and gone.

Immediately upon its dynastic transfer from the Ming to the Qing, the Great Wall was abandoned. Then a slower transformation of ownership ensued: from order back to chaos.

The prevailing attacks on the Wall came, as usual, from the north, but they weren't overland as before, but airborne. Trillions of the finest particles of sediment, small and light enough to be lifted by desert winds, came down every spring, smearing a veneer of loess on the Wall's surfaces. At first it was negligible, but over a century it amounted to an inch.

Seeds also came by wind, or landing from above inside pods of fertiliser – bird droppings. Rainfall brought germination, sprouting and sustained growth, colonising all bare surfaces, every nook and cranny. First came lower grasses and simple plants; as the soil deepened, bushes and trees began to grow.

Other processes, some faster, some sudden, contributed to Mother Nature's and Father Time's takeover. Summer storms brought deluges that made the fill sponge-like. Come winter, the moisture within froze and then expanded, prising out foundation blocks and triggering collapses. Occasional earthquakes rumbled, and lightning struck high points, especially the tops of towers. Bricks and mortar weathered, making the nearby soil alkaline. By the early twentieth century the Wall had become a walled garden, a unique wilderness. In autumn 1994 I coined the term 'Wild Wall' (a short form of 'Wilderness Wall') to describe the transition it had undergone.

Except for village folk using it as a ridge pathway, or a special plant-hunting ground to collect lime-tolerant *materia medica* for traditional concoctions, the Wild Wall of the 1700s, 1800s and the early 1900s saw few people. Surreal and sublime, serene and sacred, it was unimaginable that this memorial garden would be violently awoken from its silence. Then, in 1933, history repeated. Chinese soldiers returned to the Wall, in many thousands, and it was drafted back into national service.

A familiar story was about to unfold. In antiquity, Qidans, Jurchens and Mongols had first used the northern border regions of China as stepping stones on their way south to China's heartland. The new invaders appeared to be following a similar plan, having annexed Manchuria in late 1931 with minimal opposition. Predictably, they too were China's neighbours, but they were not descendants of the Huns, Mongols or Manchus. It was the Japanese, threatening China's territoriality not for the first time.

This anachronistic photograph of modern soldiers on the ancient Great Wall is one of many showing the armed conflict between Chinese and Japanese forces, and from it two important questions arise. The first asks how the occupation of a Ming Dynasty military defence, built 400 years earlier to stop cavalry and archers, could be of any use in the twentieth century against an army with machine guns, bazookas and motorised vehicles. The second, less obvious question is why the photograph was taken at all. Apart from simply recording the event, what purpose did it serve?

Scrutiny of the photograph can only tell us part of its story. To learn more, we need to know exactly where it was taken and when, for it has neither caption nor date. I purchased it on eBay from a seller in the United States, which perhaps suggests that it was taken by a foreign news correspondent. Fortunately, I half-recognised the location. I scanned and reprinted it, and took it to Luowenyu (Zunhua County, Hebei Province) in 2010 to check. I was right – it was there. But it's no wonder I only half-recognised it, for three-quarters of the Wall in this location had gone.

Records show that major fighting took place at Luowenyu on 17–18 March 1933. Battles also raged along the adjacent sections of the Wall during the first five months of that year, across a wide front from Gubeikou in the west to Luowenyu, Xifengkou, Dongjiakou, Yiyuankou and Shanhaiguan in the east. Consequently, the campaign became known as *Changcheng Kangzhan*, or 'The Defence of the Great Wall'. It aimed to halt the advance of Emperor Hirohito's Japanese army from its Manchurian foothold.

Standing where the first gunner had stooped behind sandbags, I could look down into the deep, twisting valley to the east – Luowenyu. It was clear that this perch presented its occupants with two military advantages: a bird's eye view and clear firing lines down to the valley below. If the Japanese plan for a successful southerly thrust was to make headway, they needed to win control of this and the adjacent strategic passes from the defending forces. Sun Tzu's ancient stratagem from *The Art of War* remained timelessly relevant: 'occupy the high ground and wait for the enemy to approach'. The Wall also offered other logistical benefits. Its towers were purpose-made barracks, which just needed a little patching up. And of course, the Wall was a mountain-top military road for moving troops to where they were needed and sending supplies. For these various reasons the Wall was reused.

A less obvious but equally vital stratagem lay behind the production and distribution of this photograph, one that was set to become an essential feature of twentieth-century warfare – using the power of the press to win political support and help the allies. It went far beyond the basics of informing viewers about a world event. It spoke much louder. Widely distributed, it made a convincing appeal to the civilised world. Had I seen it back then, this photograph would have told me that 'China was standing its ground, defending its Great Wall, in the face of outrageous Japanese aggression'. Seeing it would have made me take a side, and I would have stood against the belligerent. If we might paraphrase Sun Tzu's stratagem, the purpose of the photograph was to 'grab the headlines and wait for allies to approach'. Alliances, both established and new, would have major impacts in the Sino-Japanese War that was about to escalate and in the Asia-Pacific theatre of World War II, of which it was a major part.

Japanese presence sparked sudden (some say premeditated) 'incidents', which led to battles, the annexation of territory and a broader campaign along the line of the Great Wall in Eastern Hebei. A sustained war seemed inevitable.

Japan annexed north-east China in the wake of the 'September

DESCRIPTION:	A silver gelatin print of Chinese soldiers at Luowenyu, Zunhua County, Hebei Province, preparing to repel a Japanese attack during the 'Defence of the Great Wall' military campaign, January–May 1933
SIGNIFICANCE:	The ancient Great Wall rejuvenated as national defence line
ORIGIN:	Photo taken in the spring of 1933, around early March
LOCATION:	Author's collection, Beijing

18 Incident' of 1931 at Mukden (today's Shenyang). Lacking a national defence focus, the Kuomintang (Nationalist) government led by Chiang Kai-shek saw 'the Japanese as a disease of the skin, the Communists a disease of the heart'. With little opposition, the Japanese seized the entire north-eastern region of China, pronouncing the foundation of 'Manchukuo'. They enticed the last Qing emperor, the deposed Puyi, to return to his ancestral homeland and reside in a modern 'palace', and to be the 'emperor' again. The Sino-Japanese War of 1931–1945 was underway.

After Mukden, the next flare-up was the 'Shanhaiguan Incident' of January 1933, which developed into the *Changcheng Kangzhan*, or 'Defence of the Great Wall Campaign'. Within days, Japan's propaganda machine released photographs showing its troops waving the Rising Sun flag on the Great Wall at Shanhaiguan, hoping to hoodwink the world into believing they had conquered China. The campaign lasted just five months and resulted in temporary submission, but it did enable China to issue an international emergency call, and it circulated its own photographs of Chinese soldiers standing their ground on the Wall. At home, these images caused public outrage in the politically divided nation. The Chinese people were forced to ask themselves: are we Nationalists, Communists or Chinese?

The *Changcheng Kangzhan* ended in a Japanese victory, and in its annexation of a second piece of the Chinese provincial jigsaw map, Jehol, the now-defunct province partly composed of today's Hebei, Liaoning and Inner Mongolia. By signing the Tanggu Truce, Generalissimo Chiang Kai-shek ceded control of the Great Wall to the Japanese and recognised the existence of the Manchukuo state, before turning his attention inwards again.

Chiang set his forces against the Workers' and Peasants' Army, which was led by Mao Zedong and Zhu De, encircling their 'Soviet Republic of China', a revolutionary enclave straggling the

Hunan–Jiangxi provincial border. The Long March, a break-out and escape, ensued in 1934 and 1935, giving the Japanese war machine time to ready its army and air force for their next moves. In December 1936 China's civil war was put on hold as a United Front Pact was signed between Nationalists and Communists: the nation's forces would now confront the Japanese, not each other.

Reportage on the war and the Republic's lack of focus on the Japanese had helped bring about a temporary halt to domestic hostilities. Internationally, allies were catalysed into joining forces against a common enemy, but the allies and the Chinese were fighting a losing battle against the well-prepared Japanese. Month by month, more and more of China fell to the invaders.

Seven centuries earlier, as the Mongols advanced south, defeating the Southern Song, they killed 15 million Chinese with unprecedented barbarism and brutality. By the middle of 1945, the Japanese had killed an estimated 14 million Chinese in battle, by torture and through mass genocide. The dropping of atom bombs on Japan brought a rapid end to the Sino-Japanese War in China and World War II in Asia.

Part two of the Chinese Civil War began forthwith, and by mid-1949 most of Chiang's Republic of China had fallen under Communist control, prompting him to seek refuge on the island of Taiwan. Mao Zedong entered Beijing in late September and prepared for a ceremony at the city's heart.

Although fighting from the summit of the Great Wall in 1933 did little to deflect the Japanese advance, the participation of the reactivated fortifications was widely seen and always remembered as China's determined stance, its resistance. Thereafter, the Chinese drew spiritual inspiration from it, and continued to occupy the moral high ground as brave defenders, looking down on barbaric belligerents.

Sixteen years after the brief Defence of the Great Wall Campaign, the indomitable spirit of the ancient Wall was enshrined in the lyrics of a new national anthem. As Mao stood upon the rostrum of the Gate of Heavenly Peace on 1 October, 'March of the Volunteers' was sung to open the victory ceremony:

Arise, we who refuse to be slaves
With our very flesh and blood
Let us build our new Great Wall . . .

48.

PROP ART

1960s poster of peace and friendship

Years before Mao Zedong chose the PRC's new national anthem, with its self-sacrificial pledge by the people, he had recognised and used the Wall's innate power to inspire. During his leadership of the Long March, the cat-and-mouse pursuit campaign between the Nationalists and Communists that ranged across the breadth and length of China from south-east to north-west from late 1934 to 1935, he wrote the poem 'Liupanshan' ('Mount Liupan'). In demanding an extra effort from his men to carry on he wrote one of his most famous poetic lines: '*Bu dao Changcheng fei haohan*,' or 'Who are we if we cannot reach the Great Wall?'

The spur worked. The Long Marchers continued, established their new base area just south of the legendary Wall, and four-teen years later had won the right to rule China. In doing so the Communists became only the second Han regime since the tenth century to rule a China that was free of both northern nomadic polities and foreign enclaves (the first was the Ming). Unlike the Manchu Qing, who physically and politically abandoned the Wall they inherited, branding it a useless defence and a barrier to eth-nic harmony, the People's Republic rebuilt parts of it – not as a defence but as a national monument.

As the new Communist government readied itself to lead an old country down a new road, its leadership was conscious of the need to establish its legitimacy. Claiming links with the imperial past was dangerous, but the Great Wall, having been built by the masses, made it more acceptable. It stood as an example of what the Chinese people could achieve through unity. Propaganda chiefs set about re-creating the Wall's new role within the state's internal and external policies: it would be used to promote New China's national harmony and peaceful international intentions.

This poster illustrates the Wall's new lease of life as ambassador for peace. A quarter of a million copies were printed in 1960, and would reach approximately 600 million Chinese, ninety-six per cent of them Han, and the remainder ethnic minorities. Seven characters in red along the top of the poster – its title – are small; only twenty-five per cent of people at the time could read, so the text was not the primary focus. *Youyi Changcheng*, or 'The Friendship of the Great Wall', it pronounces, is *Wanli Chang*, 'Endless'.

Because so few could read this, the poster's message is carried primarily by the image. In the foreground it shows an ethnically diverse group, the multinational Chinese family; in the background the Chinese host visiting foreign friends. The montaged scene presents the ideal of New China's geopolitical relations during its first decade.

A woman from the ethnic Han majority, wearing a red dress embroidered with the national flower, the peony, stands with her hand raised aloft. Representing the heartland of China, she's surrounded by people of eleven ethnic minorities, mainly from the country's geographical peripheries. They're distinguishable by their brown, wavy hair, their national dress or their distinctive footwear: among them are a Korean, a Mongol, a Uyghur and a Kazakh.

Nationalities from the edges gathering around a woman from the centre, and all of them standing on the majestic Great Wall:

this is what is promoted as the embodiment of New China. The people are strong but friendly, a united nation of ethnic diversity living harmoniously and cultivating friendships with foreigners from afar. This ideal contrasts starkly with the Wall's historical role as a military defence. It counters the misguided view that the Great Wall cordoned off a hermit culture, one closed to the world.

Touches of modernity appear. One man clutches a camera, ready to record the joy of friendship in a group photograph, while another plays an accordion, making music, the perfect cross-cultural dialect. The moment captured by the artist shows the group releasing of a flock of doves, international symbols of peace.

'The Friendship of the Great Wall is Endless' was painted in 1960 by Liu Danzhai (1931–2011), a graduate of the China College of Art, Shanghai, during Communist China's age of 'prop art'. The genre began in the revolutionary years at Yan'an, during the mid-1930s, and began to wane after posters promoted the drive to achieve 'the Four Modernisations', a campaign of the early reform period of the 1980s.

Despite sabre-rattling by the main powers at the end of World War II, none really wanted or could afford more war. A costly Cold War did ensue, however, between the Western Allies and the Soviet Bloc, while a much warmer and cheaper propaganda offensive was launched in China, aimed at gaining wider international recognition. China's relations with Western countries were generally strained, and by the late 1950s the Sino-Soviet Non-Aggression Pact was under great ideological strain. After the split in 1960, China was left with only a limited number of working relationships – with some Eastern European and 'developing world' states. The second group on the Wall, in the background of our poster, are mainly Africans, enjoying the friendship experience provided by their Chinese hosts.

There are few earlier images that illustrate the Great Wall's

DESCRIPTION:	*Youyi Changcheng Wanli Chang* ('The Friendship of the Great Wall is Endless'), colour poster, 110 centimetres by eighty centimetres, 1960
SIGNIFICANCE:	Marks the Great Wall's emergence as a symbol of ethnic friendship and international peace
ORIGIN:	Painted by Liu Danzhai, Shanghai; 250 000 copies were printed and distributed nationwide via Xinhua bookstores
LOCATION:	Author's collection, Beijing

adoption as a national icon, a sign of peace and a must-see destination for foreign friends. This portrayal on the poster looks ahead to something that was already under construction: a designated Great Wall site for foreign guests visiting the PRC (a theme we will explore with our next object). While the location featured on the poster is imaginary, its character is definitely 'Badaling-esque'.

Conveniently located on Beijing's doorstep, eighty kilometres outside the city, Badaling, with its magnificent vistas and paramount building quality, was a natural choice as the most favoured Wall-viewing spot. Its forbidding valley approach was experienced by only the most adventurous visitors, among them the Scotsman John Thompson, who in 1871 endured a four-day round trip to get there and back for his prize – the first professional images of the battlements. In 1909 construction of the Beijing–Kalgan (Zhangjiakou) railway line made an away-day from the city to the Wall quite manageable. Prime Minister Jawaharlal Nehru of India was the first foreign head of state to officially visit the Wall, in October 1954, hosted by Premier Zhou Enlai.

Photographers to record future diplomatic visits only arrived from 1958. The earliest such photo shows a rather grumpy-looking Soviet defence minister Kliment Voroshilov, his expression indicative of the prevalent chill between Mao and Khrushchev – and perhaps also of the roughness of the conditions, for the climb up the ramparts appears unrestored. Later images show the battlements made safer for the increasingly frequent diplomatic processions. The Wall was firmly installed as a standard part of diplomatic protocol, an obligatory 'off-site' for each visiting head of state, regardless of the weather. Many foreigners donned headgear offered by their thoughtful Chinese hosts: large fur hats with earflaps in winter, or wide-brimmed straw hats in summer.

As of June 2014, some 490 heads of state – kings, queens, presidents, ayatollahs, chairmen, archbishops and governors –

had walked the Great Wall at Badaling. China's Foreign Affairs Minister through most of the 1990s, Qian Qichen, referred to it as a monument recording new China diplomatic relations. In fact, over six decades it has in fact contributed to China's 'soft power' offensive in its own right, providing millions of foreign tourists with their most endearing memories of a once unassailable land.

The Great Wall has taken on its new role with surprising ease and grace. Few visitors seem particularly conscious or concerned with its bloody and terrible past; they seem positively seduced by its scale, overawed by its majesty, impressed by its beauty. Her Majesty Queen Elizabeth II, visiting in 1987, reportedly said: 'It's one of the most beautiful places that I have ever visited.'

49.

'LOVE OUR CHINA, REBUILD OUR GREAT WALL'

Painting depicting Deng Xiaoping at the Great Wall

One of the more unusual books in my Great Wall library is *Changcheng Jushou*, or 'Gathering of Heads of State on the Great Wall', an illustrated who's who in New China's diplomatic relations between 1958 and 2004. You can learn a lot by flicking through its pages: about state visits, slack periods, busy periods, milestones. There was a diplomatic chill from spring 1966 to spring 1972, with Nixon breaking the ice in February. In summer 1973 the President of Mali visited. Traffic peaked between May 1983 and May 1989; that spring there were seventy-two visits.

These dates, periods and personages provide a useful political background check as we try to understand this unusual object, a modern painting produced to advocate defence of the defences on cultural rather than military grounds. It portrays a stately and besuited Deng Xiaoping (1904–1997) surveying the Great Wall as it snakes its way across mountains and through a sea of clouds. This is the same man who, as vice-premier, escorted the Mali delegation on 22 June 1973: a significant date in the Wall's modern history, when the right man first became aligned to a rightful cause.

Five years later, having survived demotion and demonisation by the Gang of Four, Deng bounced back. In 1978 he became China's paramount leader, and in 1984 he returned to the Great Wall.

A visionary, Deng reformed everything. The self-appointed architect of restructuring and rehabilitation, he set about changing China: from closed to open, from rural to urban, from wholly agricultural to partly industrial, from entirely poor to partly rich, from overly political to more pragmatic, from overpowering to understanding. Taking a calligraphy brush in hand on 20 September 1984, he wrote 'Ai wo Zhonghua, xiu wo Changcheng', or 'Love our China, rebuild our Great Wall'.

Strictly speaking, the brush was put in his hand, and the words were put into his mouth. A Beijing journalist had asked Vice-Premier Xi Zhongxun (father of the current Chinese leader, Xi Jinping) to support Badaling's efforts to fund an extension of its rebuilt ramparts by asking for the paramount leader to promote the idea in a project slogan. Aware of Badaling's importance for diplomatic 'walk and talks', Deng agreed. The scheme not only paid off, bringing in funds for the work, it also created a banner that was hoisted elsewhere to finance similar repair work.

However, the composition did more than transform a few sections of Wild Wall into 'Tourist Wall'. The leader's magic touch transformed a slogan composed for one project in one place into the central tenet of a much wider and spiritually deeper cause: the Great Wall's protection, and the rehabilitation of a self-wounded nation, with Deng as its patron saint. In the painting titled 'Spring Wind from the East', Deng's calligraphic call has been transformed into allegorical art, showing the man who brought an end to the Great Wall's, and metaphorically China's, dark winter by ushering in of a new season of rebuilding and hope.

From seven pencilled characters and the date on its reverse – '1994.09' – we know that the artist produced the painting to mark

DESCRIPTION:	*Dongfeng Chuilai Manyan Chun*, ('Spring Wind from the East'), a watercolour painting of Chinese leader Deng Xiaoping surveying a Great Wall vista; seventy-eight centimetres by forty-seven centimetres
SIGNIFICANCE:	A picturesque interpretation of Deng's influential call '*Ai wo Zhonghua, xiu wo Changcheng*', ('Love our China, rebuild our Great Wall'), written in 1984, which inspired reconstruction projects and ushered in the concept of Great Wall protection
ORIGIN:	Painted in September 1994, on the tenth Anniversary of Deng Xiaoping's call for action
LOCATION:	Author's collection, Beijing

the tenth anniversary of Deng's act. Any Chinese above the age of twenty would see the connection immediately. The lack of a signature on the painting is typical of the cautious self-preservation by artists when their subjects were state leaders – in case their work might be seen as a political slight.

The eight characters of Deng's chosen phrase are in classic *duizhang*, or couplet style, being numerically and phonetically balanced four-character clusters. While the composition obviously encourages patriotic love by rebuilding the Great Wall, it also alludes to recent episodes of destruction – of the Wall in particular, and of China's cultural heritage in general. *Wo* is used as an abbreviated form of *women*, meaning 'our', thus making the four character clusters possible, and stressing the need for 'us' to undergo a spiritual healing, for many people had participated in acts of wanton vandalism.

Just as Deng improved the Wall's health in the 1980s through his writing, Mao had damaged it during his rule by his speech. He orchestrated public campaigns, in which participation was mandatory. The mobilisation of a workforce of a few hundred million out of the population of 600 million in 1960, hyped by revolutionary propaganda, could have produced good or bad results. 'Correct' policies brought national pride – for example, in the construction of the mighty Nanjing Bridge across the Yangzi River. 'Incorrect' policies brought unmitigated disasters, to people, places and everything. The Great Leap Forward and the Cultural Revolution unleashed forces that would lead to the destruction of a great deal of China's national heritage, including the Great Wall. Both were later condemned by Deng Xiaoping when he was party leader. During what was the frankest political interview in New China's history, with Italian journalist Oriana Fallaci in 1980, Deng described the campaigns as 'Comrade Mao Zedong's errors'.

The Great Leap Forward induced 'three difficult years' from 1958 to 1961 as a result of Mao's foolhardy attempts to accelerate economic performance. His infamous policies ranged from bird-killing hunts – part of an effort to boost crop production – to advocating the use of backyard smelters to enable China to surpass Great Britain's iron and steel output. In construction, the people were encouraged to 'Let the past serve the present' – in other words, to use old building materials. Yet this was minor when compared to the rampage inspired by the 'Smash the Four Olds' campaign. Launched in August 1966, just months after the start of the Cultural Revolution, the Chinese people were ordered to destroy old culture, customs, habits and ideas.

Mao died ten years later, in September of 1976, and so did his Cultural Revolution – at least in name. I arrived in China less than ten years later, and from this point in our Great Wall story I've actually been present to witness the changes the structure underwent. I saw many Deng-inspired reconstruction sites, and I saw quite a few instances of destruction.

In 1999 I saw a farmer using a *gao* (a farming tool) to knock bricks loose from a watchtower turret; he was putting them in his basket and carrying them down to his Wall-side farmhouse. Passing through his hamlet five minutes later, I saw that all the buildings there were made of Great Wall bricks. Work making use of newly collected bricks was continuing; the past was still serving the present.

In 2000 I saw, for what turned out to be the last time, a perfectly preserved engraved tablet, dated 1570, at Huanghuacheng. It weighed perhaps 250 kilograms, but a farmer moved it to an inaccessible location a couple of months later. He was charging two *yuan* to use a ladder to go down and see the tablet, which had fractured in the process of moving.

In more recent years, at Jiankou's Zhengbeilou, I saw a mortared brick stairway – which, since the tower's construction in around 1618, had served as an entrance to its high doorway – gradually become lower and lower. Course by course it was demolished by a local farmer, making it necessary for walkers to use a ladder – for a fee, of course.

The first of these three examples differs from the other two. It's almost condonable as a means of survival, and it's a problem that has largely been overcome by education. But in the latter examples the perpetrators weighed up the risk against the potential gain. Considering it unlikely that they'd be reported, investigated or punished, they destroyed the Wall in order to profit.

Pondering these cases leads me to two conclusions. First, it's apparent that the culture of destruction created by Mao didn't die with him. Second, although Deng launched Great Wall conservation by writing the campaign banner, even his widely respected authority wasn't strong enough, nor his vision far-sighted enough, for 'Love our China, Rebuild our Great Wall' to be a panacea. It opened up a new era, brought the hope of every spring. At the same time, the side-effects of China's successful economic reform would soon conspire to impact on the Wall.

Several factors prevented more mileage from being squeezed from Deng's slogan. While Chinese society and lifestyles changed, one attitude remained exactly the same: turning a blind eye to damage. During Mao's time, destruction targeted sections of Wall that were most easily reached, while most Wild Wall sections stayed intact. Increasing social mobility since 2000, enabled by Deng's legacy and economic reform theories, has given large numbers of people the means and the opportunity to reach Wall that was previously preserved by its remoteness. In the past, damage to the Wall was caused by revolution or poverty; now, the problems are caused by the wealthier class: littering, graffiti and encroaching developments.

In September 1984 Deng became the first leader of China in more than 350 years to lead a campaign to 'maintain' the Great Wall, and the first to do so not for war but for peace. His brushwork ushered in the era of Great Wall protection. In 1985 he was named 'Man of the Year' by *Time* magazine for instituting 'sweeping economic reforms that have challenged Marxist orthodoxies'.

In 1987 the Great Wall was listed by UNESCO as a World Heritage Site. Fifteen years later, in 2002, and then again in 2004, the Great Wall landscape around Beijing was placed on the World Monuments Fund's list of the World's 100 Most Endangered Sites.

50.

A GIFT TO CHINA

Pair of photos of Luowenyu, 80 years apart

From the outset, my meeting with this Great Wall expert promised to be quite different from any other. For one thing, he was dead. Secondly, he was a 'foreigner' like me, and thirdly, I met him in a book that was gifted to me. *The Great Wall of China* by William Edgar Geil was swathed in bubble-wrap, a sensible precaution given it was eighty years old. When I opened the book, I felt like I was greeting the author with a hearty handshake.

I turned its foxed pages carefully, soon realising from its illustrations that the author had made my journey seventy-nine years earlier. I wasn't William the Conqueror – I was William the Second. Our respective sets of photographs showed the diverse appearance and architecture that we had each seen, and the varied landscapes we had crossed as we followed the Wall. He rode and walked west, while I went entirely on foot, heading east. Our journeys were parallel, often adjacent, sometimes intersecting.

One special point of convergence became clear when I saw Geil's photograph of 'Mule Horse Pass': I'd included the same view in my book *Alone on the Great Wall*. My caption had been 'Luowenyu', but there was another major point of difference. The

1908 black-and-white photo showed Geil sitting in front of a watchtower, while my colour photo in 1987, taken in self-timer mode, showed me walking in front of a mound – the watchtower had gone. What had happened?

'Perhaps the book is too late to be of use,' Mrs Marjorie Hessel-Tiltman had written as she mailed her copy of Geil's book to me. In fact, her timing was perfect.

In 1908 Geil had captured a full-length view of the Wall before a series of damaging events unfolded that made China a hostile environment for man and monument alike. By the late 1970s, a great many changes had occurred, and many components of the Wall were no longer there, as I would discover.

The next significant date in this story was 31 December 1999. Never before had so many people awaited a new millennium, and with such eagerness and trepidation,. I set off for the Wall from my farmhouse in the hamlet of Xizhazi shortly before midnight. The approaching moment, the antiquity of place and a face-numbing minus 23 degrees Celsius made for an emotional but silent atmosphere among my companions and me. It was a solemn moment in time for all of us.

I was particularly conscious of how tremendously impactful humankind's last-minute appearance on our ancient planet has been. If the whole existence of our planet took place over twenty-four hours, we modern humans have only been active for the last few minutes. We began to become 'civilised' just moments ago, and since then, we have unleashed changes that seem to threaten to destroy us altogether. If we lose the wisdom of our history teachers, how will we be aware of what we have done wrong?

As I neared the Wall, I pondered how its watchful towers, each dotted with eye-like windows, had seen the arrival of the years 1600, 1700, 1800 and 1900, and what each had brought with it. I wondered what they might witness post-2000. More tragedies,

DESCRIPTION:	A 'then and now' pair of Great Wall photographs of the same location, east of Luowenyu, taken by Dr William Geil and William Lindesay in 1908 and 1987, respectively
SIGNIFICANCE:	Images that inspired a project to revisit the Wall and show how much it had changed, using the technique of 'rephotography'

| ORIGIN: | Luowenyu, Hebei, 1908 and 1987 |
| LOCATION: | Author's collection, Beijing |

I feared, and I felt pretty helpless – until I remembered my old Wall photographs.

Since receiving William Geil's book, I'd collected others containing Great Wall photos, as well as single prints from various sources around the world. I had more than 400 vintage Great Wall photographs in my collection, which I believed might be the largest such archive held by anyone, or any institution. Inspired by that millennium moment, I decided how to use 'rephotography' as a tool of Great Wall advocacy and protection.

It's said that a good photograph is worth a thousand words; two photographs of the same place, with a time lag in between, will therefore say a lot more. They will strike up a conversation between the past and the present – with a message for the future. This is the technique known as rephotography. It arouses interest, stirs debate and is a means of protest.

Both Geil and I had made historic journeys of our own along the Wall. Each was a first in its own way, each in a different era. Now we prepared to return there. Our aim: to put together a visual state of the Wall report. We would travel in the past and the present, creating a dual view of the Wall. The physical adjacency of past and present would, we hoped, pose a question mark in viewers' minds about the future of the location, and of the Wall as a whole.

From 2003 to 2009 we covered more than 100 sites, documenting the century-spanning changes, including a joint visit back to where it all began: Luowenyu. This time, we asked 'how' it came about that what I insisted should be known as Geil's Tower had fallen. From afar, I had theorised that Luowenyu villagers may have helped themselves to the tower's bricks, but our site visit suggested otherwise. We saw that another tower, just out of our 1908 and 1987 photographs, stood strongly, making the demolition of a tower further away from the village (the place where bricks were reused) seem illogical.

Locals sometimes provided answers as to when and why certain negative changes had occurred, but in many instances such awkward questions remained unanswered. It seemed that most people adopted a *c'est la vie* attitude even when it came to the Great Wall, or they just never thought about it. Individuals pointed to the masses, blaming them. As for Geil's Tower, then? One possible cause of its downfall may have been the fighting between Chinese and Japanese forces that took place here in 1933 (see Object 47). Another very plausible explanation was the random destruction caused by the powerful Tangshan earthquake of July 1976, whose epicentre was just seventy-five kilometres away. Had Geil's Tower not fallen, the difference between the two photos would not have been striking at all. I think it's true to say that Geil and I met there for a variety of reasons: through an act of God, destiny, historical arrangement and generosity.

This fiftieth object – our final one – is different from all the rest. The two photos are not especially rare: each book had a print run in the thousands. The pictures have minimal monetary value, but as resources they possess the power to influence the future. How?

This pair of Luowenyu photographs, and the other 'then' and 'now' collaborative works that Geil and I created, have inspired some others who have seen them to go out and rephotograph things they care about, things they want their children and their grandchildren to see. Using improving devices and technologies, they are circulating their photos more widely than William Geil ever could. More people than ever before are participating in the protest against the disappearance of our history, of China's Great Wall.

It's a little more than ten years since I first revisited the Wall with William Geil. He used film cameras, as did I – in the main, at least. By the time our project of rephotography concluded, in 2008, we'd entered the digital age. Now, smartphones have empowered us even more. We generate mountains of data daily, including multitudes of images which we share on social networks. If harnessed, this speed and resource might well usher in a new age of protection for our great world monuments.

The Wall was built by unknown masses and manned by their descendants, and although much of it has now gone, what remains would still require an army to monitor it. But a motivated public might be mobilised to provide true guardianship. The technology they carry permits the anonymous masses to police the destructive actions of individuals, providing authorities with the evidence to bring them to book, and leaving them with no excuses. Only publicity and prosecution will reduce the frequency of damage.

William Geil's illustrated Great Wall book was a gift for China. The time is now right for a new gift: a full-length image of every remaining section of every dynastic Wall, in real-time, with 360-degree vision. It would be a new 'map' of the Great Wall, rich in cartographic details added by crowdsourcing. People will become the new army protecting the Wall, and social media will be their 'wolf smoke', sounding the alert whenever dangers approach.

I began this series of fifty Great Wall objects by exploring the Ortelius map of China, published in a sixteenth-century atlas. It made the Great Wall the most famous building in the world, albeit the least known. Now, fifty objects wiser, I conclude with an expression of hope, a wish for a ground-breaking new object existing in cyberspace, at everyone's fingertips. It will rebuild the Great Wall, remaking it as the most famous and the best appreciated of all the world's wonders.

EPILOGUE

'Get back to us for further details when needed.' That is what various objects had said to me during my Great Wall studies. When the time was right, I took up the offer, contacted them and set off, aiming to detail a story of the Wall from its foundations, to its apogee, to its fall into ruins and then to its rediscovery. My target was a nice neat fifty, but just as a plan to bake a dozen always seems to make thirteen, they grew. This epilogue is several things – part nostalgia, part overview, part behind the scenes, part postscript. It's also a fitting way to include the best of the leftovers: a 'lost and found' map that, in the end, could not be wasted. Its presence here confirms the star quality of the maps throughout the series.

Starting with a map is a tradition of mine. A standard-issue Oxford School Atlas featuring the Great Wall set me off on a journey – at first in mind and eventually on foot. I chose another atlas map of China to embark on this stage of my ongoing journey, although there was nothing standard about its issue. It was the first world atlas, the first internationally distributed atlas and the most expensive 'retailed' book of the sixteenth century. Ortelius' *Theatrum Orbis Terrarum*, or 'Theatre of the World', gave European viewers their first glimpse of 'a wall of 400 leagues' – an experience that I had the privilege of experiencing with the atlas on my study table. This is not the kind of book, of course, that one borrows from the local library: a Beijing-based Dutch friend, Maarten Buitelaar, an avid collector of China maps, had acquired a magnificent 1587 edition, and he generously lent it to me.

As I time-travelled over Europe and across Asia towards our destination, slowly turning the book's thick, rippled pages, I imagined what questions might have arisen in the mind of the atlas' first owner on reaching folio 169, *Chinae*, and seeing the Wall. His curiosity must have been uncontainable! Sadly, the likelihood of him learning much else about the Wall was slim. But for us it was the first of nine maps among fifty more objects, some of which are still making, or concealing, history.

The *Huayi Tu*, or 'Map of China and the Barbarian Lands' (Object 13), drawn circa AD 801, was copied onto a stone in 1135. For some reason, however, nobody in modern times appears ever to have seen the stone version. Scholars have been content to study rubbings of it, and, in their traditional way, have kicked back and forth what others had previously written about the map, perhaps adding their own spin. I approached the *Huayi Tu* by focusing on the significance of its belated inclusion of a symbol representing a 900-year-old Great Wall; I pronounced it to be the oldest extant image of a Great Wall. I had been intrigued by the map ever since I saw a rubbing of it at the National Library of China, Beijing. But the root object was the inscribed stone itself, and I wanted to see it.

I went to Beilin, or the Forest of Steles Museum, in Xi'an, to look for the 'stone map'. A forest is an apt metaphor for this museum: its pavilions and courtyards are crowded with more than 3000 tall, dark stones, standing in groves, inscribed with the periodic history of China. Courtyard by courtyard, I roamed the forest in search of what many geographers and historians had dubbed the earliest extant map of China. After much wandering around, though, I had failed to locate it. For such a supposedly important stone, its absence seemed conspicuous.

Lost in the forest, as it were, my next move was to request help at the curator's office through a very good connection, a university classmate who had also studied history at one of Xi'an's universities. 'It should be no problem,' was the optimistic response from the curator. 'Leave it with me for a day or two,' he said. 'I'll ask my team to look into it.'

A few days later came a most unexpected and frank answer: 'Nobody – no Chinese, and certainly no foreigner – is allowed to see that stone. It presents political problems.'

That was the end of that. But in seeking the object, I had at least discovered that, for some reason, the stone could not be seen. Its confinement – perhaps even its destruction? – turned out to hold an important lesson in political geography.

Huayi Tu – literally, the 'China–Barbarians Map' – has traditionally been regarded as a 'map of China' and thus vaunted as a 'national map'. Its original ninth-century AD perception was straightforward and apolitical. From the time of the map's creation until the end of the Ming in the mid-seventeenth century, the size and basic shape of 'China' had changed only marginally. It had expanded slightly, around what we may regard as a core region, while making some periodic westward extensions, notably during the Han and Tang.

By the Qing, however, the respected *Huayi Tu* had become seriously out of date. There were two main reasons. First, the area it showed as being China was now much larger, and second, the people of that land were not only Han but of many ethnic groups which historically had been described as 'barbarian'. Manchu expansion in all directions beyond the traditional Han heartland of China had seen the largest ever 'New China' extended to incorporate Tibet, Turkestan, 'Outer' Mongolia and Taiwan, a territorial zenith of 14.7 million square kilometres. The New China also redefined the meaning of 'Chinese' people via its *zhongwai yijia* ethnic philosophy of unity: 'inside and outside united as one family'.

After 1911, the successors of the Qing Empire founded the modern Chinese state: first the Republic (1911–1949), which was followed by today's People's Republic of China. Naturally, the land they inherited – what the Qing had redefined as 'China' – formed the territorial basis of these republics, the main exception being 'Outer Mongolia', which had made a bid for independence.

All this brings us to the *Huayi Tu*'s 'political problem'. To accommodate even today's China, which has been scaled back to less than 10 million square kilometres, the *Huayi Tu* is too geographically small, too politically incorrect and too ethnically embarrassing. China's own view is of a unified land, territorially, politically and ethnically. To most observers, it's a case of one country and two eras, with 1200 years of differences. To some Chinese, it's a political problem they'd prefer to avoid. Even the image of the *Huayi Tu* that I provided to illustrate my story in *National Geographic* was cropped to remove any possible grounds for conjecture.

While the *Huayi Tu* stone remains a political prisoner because it shows China as it was in the Tang, one of the maps based on the imperially commissioned survey of 1708–1718 by the French Jesuits (see Object 42), which boasted an unprecedented level of detail and accuracy, was coincidentally making headlines just as I was researching and writing about its Great Wall significance.

This event occurred when President Xi Jinping of China visited Germany in March 2014. Chancellor Angela Merkel presented him with a copy of a 1735 'China' map that was based on the Jesuits' endeavours. Although the Manchu rulers of the Qing, particularly Kangxi, had increased the area under their rule, such that they had the largest territory of any imperial dynasty, European interpretations of the imperial survey by d'Anville, King Louis XIVs geographer, and Du Halde, the French Jesuits' historian, propagated the notion that Han China was 'China proper', while the newly conquered, assimilated or annexed dominions on its peripheries formed 'Greater China'. Since the PRC teaches a seamless view of its geography, and works hard to promote its own modern version of the Qing's ethnic unity, Merkel's presentation caused much chagrin among the delegation, and much annoyance among Chinese netizens. The action was seen either as diplomatic clumsiness or as foreign interference in China's political geography.

These map episodes effectively highlight one of the great advantages of objects – beyond their pleasing tangibility, demonstrative value and aesthetic qualities. 'History' is, strictly speaking, a written account of past events, while 'solid sources' of various kinds, whether unearthed archeologically or collected and handed down, offer us material or visual evidence.

Writing can be changed more readily – by altering or obliterating text, by ripping out pages, by issuing a new edition. Solid objects, although they are no more than a snapshot of a past event, can sometimes preserve an authentic picture of what has been forgotten, or of what people want to forget. Imagine if the *Huayi Tu* had never been copied onto a stone in 1135. Only the transferral of the map onto a stone block preserved it for us today. I hope it survived the iconoclasm of the Cultural Revolution's fanatics, but we will only know when the powers that be decide that it's time to release it from captivity, and let it be seen for what it is: a national treasure of China's historical geography, and the earliest known image of the Great Wall.

The only genre of objects outnumbering maps in this book is weapons, of which there are ten. This isn't surprising; it reiterates that the Great Wall existed in a theatre of conflict. But the appearance of what stand as milestones in the history of global weapons development speaks loudly about the protraction of the conflict – over 2000 years. The same peoples, from the same sides, fought in the same theatre for largely the same reasons, and they stuck with what they did best: attacking on horses and defending from walls. But the weapons they fought with did change, as more complex technologies promised victory.

Wood and horn were joined by metal. Bows relying on elasticity and strength and skill were matched, even outmatched, by cross-bows with mechanical metal triggers, which required instruction and maintenance. Brute strength was joined by chemical ener-gy with the arrival of 'hot' weapons. Mines could even be preset though an ingenious automatic 'switch'.

The third group of note contains objects that have an equine connection – again, this is hardly surprising, given that I have précised the story as a conflict of horsemen versus Wall. There are six horsey objects. We have seen the horse as cavalry, as transport, as tribute and more. We have seen the regular reap-pearance of the horse as a bargaining chip; from the nomads' side, this never lost its appeal, nor did horses their value by be-coming overly plentiful. Why did the nomads keep giving the Chinese horses as tribute, and why at the same time could the Chinese not build a successful breeding program of war hors-es? Our concluding horse story – on the fascinating mystery of whether it was selenium deficiency or toxicity that was the root cause – is a prompt for further research.

In my interactions with students I always focus on the valuable lessons that the past has for the present. As Winston Churchill said, 'The further you look into the past, the more able you are to see into the future.' Ten of the fifty objects contain strong conser-vation messages. I've suggested, for instance, that the little-known version of the Meng Jiangnü legend, in which she discovers her husband's name inscribed on a brick marking his entombment, should be used in the campaign to prevent the Great Wall from becoming a graffiti Wall.

The most poignant conservation messages came from my enquiries into 'wolf smoke'. However wolf smoke had been made
originally, the term, preserved within the Chinese language, sig-
nalled a grave warning about the destruction of the habitat of
the wolves' main prey, gazelles, whose dwindling numbers now
graze on an ever-diminishing core of one of north-east Asia's major remaining ecosystems, the Great Eastern Steppe. Sourcing a
photograph of the Mongolian wolf in the wild proved to be a most
difficult task.

Contacting the majority of these objects took me out of my study
in Beijing – my own Great Wall museum, which contains a minor-
ity of chosen objects – and led me to museums along the Wall:
at Jiayuguan in the west, Shanhaiguan in the east, and Badaling
to the north of Beijing. In Mongolia I found fascinating objects,
which I was privileged to handle and study at close quarters at
the National Museum of Mongolia and the Museum of the Great
Hunnu Empire. In the United States I found objects and details
in the Smithsonian's Freer Gallery and at Doylestown Historical
Society. In my other home, Britain, my research took me back
to several familiar institutions: the Royal Geographical Society,
the British Library, the Victoria and Albert Museum and Oxford's
Bodleian Library. The most unlikely and difficult hunting ground
was at the Vatican Museum.

For years I was aware of the existence, somewhere there, of 'a
map of the Great Wall' of considerable length. I first saw a rather
murky photocopied image, credited 'Collection of the Lateran
Museum, Rome'. Following up, I located the one and only paper written about the map, authored by M. J. Meijer in 1956. In
his introduction he noted that in 1952 the map had been seen
by Leo Bagrow, founder of the cartography journal *Imago Mundi*;
according to him, the map had been 'taken to the Vatican for photographing and attempts to locate it since have failed'. The Lateran

Museum was dissolved in 1970, its contents absorbed by the Vatican Galleries and Museums, one part of which was the Missionary Ethnography Museum.

After my enquiries had failed to prompt any response, I took a shot in the dark and visited Rome. This, I felt, was the only way to make headway in the longstanding mystery over the map's whereabouts. However, my visit could not have been more badly timed: it was on loan to a museum in California, as part of the first ever group of Vatican antiquities to travel overseas. I salvaged what I could from my visit, managing a brief meeting with a curator, the aptly named Father Mapelli (which I thought surely must augur well). He did warn, however, that 'doing things in the Vatican is very difficult, very complicated and very slow'.

I returned to Beijing, and the map eventually returned to Rome. But I failed to get any response to my follow-up enquiries, addressed to the museum's director and to its principal researcher in Chinese antiquities. My last remaining working contact was the manager of the photo archive at the Vatican, and she provided around twenty low-resolution images of the map, allowing me to at least engage in some 'closer' distance learning. Stunned by the map's colour and its charming details, I was inspired to return to Meijer's paper.

This time I focused on the photostats of the map, included as an appendix to the paper. With the aid of a magnifying glass I studied the disordered strips. There were some long overlaps, and I slowly worked out which sections could be cut out and how a reproduction of the whole map might be spliced together. My work succeeded, and I now had a near-perfect scaled-down research copy of the original seven-metre-plus map. From end to end on the table of my Beijing study, my reproduction measured 1.62 metres. I could bring the 'Borgia Great Wall Scroll' back home.

In October 2014, as I was tidying up this book's manuscript and preparing to submit it to my editor, I had to decide what to do about this problematic leftover. Thinking of a possible winter break in Rome, a finale to wrap up the project, I searched online to check that the map was back on public display. The top find was new, and pointed me towards the 'Patrons of the Arts at the Vatican Museum' website, a portal which promotes the endeavours of this organisation to financially assist the Vatican Museum in the restoration of its antiquities. Listed among the projects requiring support in 2015 was none other than the Borgia Great Wall Scroll. It required cleaning, repairing and photographing, and the patrons were seeking approximately US$25 000 to fund the work.

I saw a chance for International Friends of the Great Wall to get involved and fund the restoration, so I contacted the patrons to make a proposal. I had established International Friends to organise contributions to the conservation of the Great Wall. The society had pioneered and sustained the campaign against garbage on the Wall, had the Great Wall landscape listed by the World Monuments Fund as an endangered site, and created and curated the influential conservation-research project that used rephotography to evidence changes that had befallen the Wall. Funding the map's repair would be a new kind of Great Wall 'conservation' work, and presented a special opportunity for a cultural connection between two states. I pitched the opportunity to a philanthropic Chinese friend and Great Wall advocate, and a few days later he confirmed the willingness of a select group of friends to donate, which would enable International Friends of the Great Wall to fund the restoration.

I contacted the patrons with the good news, and a few hours later received their response: an international patrons chapter had, just a few hours earlier, already pledged their support! We had been pipped at the post. The perfect conclusion had eluded me, and a chance to establish a shared interest in the Great Wall between Chinese people and the Vatican had been lost.

But our failure also means that my journey is not over. It reminds me that the best journeys never reach a definite end, and I will continue, with ears and eyes open, to search for more insights into the Great Wall story.

In the meantime, as an encore to *The Great Wall in 50 Objects*, I am thrilled to present what I have learned about this object, studied through what may be described as intelligence sources: a homemade, scaled-down edition of the map which presents a rarely seen panorama of the Great Wall in the most surprising, and inaccessible, of places.

51.

ITALIAN JOURNEY

The Borgia Great Wall scroll

To appreciate how distinguished this panoramic pictorial map really is, one needs to proceed along its whole length. As a scroll, it might be unrolled and rolled to reveal a series of overlapping views, but it's better still to unfurl it and slowly reveal it from end to end. My copy measures 1.62 metres.

Although it bears no title, no chop, no date, no preface and no author's name, this map seems to identify itself readily: along its whole length we see a continuous linear fortification. Strung out beside it are some prominent geographical features – mountains and rivers. These seem vaguely familiar yet strangely disorienting, until one spots a tiny character 北, or north, at the map's bottom edge. This immediately clears the confusion: the map is an upside down view looking south, not north. It's now apparent that the Hexi Corridor occupies the map's far right (west), that the Yellow River arcs through its central area, and that the Shanxi region is on the left (east). This coverage reinforces that the spinal-cord structure throughout is the Ming Great Wall – or at least three-quarters of it. And it seems to follow that the map is of Ming age.

This map really takes you there – panoramically, lengthwise – while the twenty or so images provide magnified snapshots of its colourful detail. Its narrowness contrasts with its length, further emphasising its focus. Most maps show us a view of the ground seen from above, and this one does too. The panorama we see has an aerial feel, as if we are flying across North China's predominantly arid, ochre-yellow lands following this remarkable landmark. Whenever we look down we can see the Wall.

For presentation purposes, the map's maker has simplified our flightpath, straightening out the Wall's twists and turns. To do so, he's broken some cartographic rules. The map's scale is irregular, and it's most inaccurate east of the Yellow River. What we have is a unique strip map of the Great Wall, a special geographical product with pros and cons, made by science and artistic licence, compressed and stretched and straightened, 'sketchy' in style.

Just like a conventional map, though, it has room for all kinds of information – whatever was of interest to its maker. Inside the Wall we see a procession of rectangular military installations – forts. On the outside, tiny drawings painted in bright colours provide glimpses of life there: nomads ride between tented camps, horses and camels graze, carcasses of meat dry in the wind, and the positions of wells for watering livestock are marked. In one place we see men sitting on rugs, at another women are dancing. These scenes are a far cry from the stereotyped, derogatory and Sinocentric views of the border region that we have seen previously. This is a two-sided perspective, showing not so much a cultural collision, but an interface. It conveys a change in tone.

On earlier Great Wall maps the nomads received short shrift, labelled *yi* ('barbarians') on the milestone *Huayi Tu*, or 'Map of China and the Barbarian Lands', of the ninth century (Object 13). On the sixteenth century *Jiubian Tu*, or 'Map of the Nine Border Regions' (Object 37), they were described as living like animals in 'nests' or *chaoxue* ('lairs'). This map's language and pictures are more objective, more informative, showing a tentative peace.

Hierarchies of officers are deployed to command sizable garrisons of troops at the forts, which are clearly ready for action if needed.

On the other side we can see some new-style encampments, where *gers*, or felt-walled tents, are pitched alongside, sometimes even inside, walled enclosures. The arrangement suggests that some nomadic tribes have not only benefited materially from frontier trade, but have also started to live a new life, part-nomadic and part-settled. The drawings make me think of the world's largest camp, composed of tens of thousands of white *gers* which, for better or worse, have been pitched by herders migrating to cluster around the built-up city-centre of today's Ulaanbaatar, capital of Mongolia. Back on our map, we can regard the lifestyle change as a new chapter of the Great Wall's story, a new phase of regional relations.

As well as its pictorial details, the map appears to bear large numbers of labels. They are rather like Post-it notes, not part of the map proper but made of paper and attached by users. This method would have been useful for recording information that was subject to change, such as the populations of barracks or the latest news concerning the shifting camp grounds of nomadic tribes. In Su-chou (modern name Jiuquan), for example, a label tells us that 3000 troops are deployed there under the command of a brigadier, several majors, captains and other officers. Throughout the Hexi Corridor, the figures on the labels add up to show that this is the most heavily fortified area on the entire map, with about 25000 men deployed in forts located in the lee of the Wall.

Outside the Wall there's one very revealing annotation: 'Outside the pass of Poluokou are the Tianba barbarians, who are under Galdan Khan's control.' It's this name – Galdan Borshigt Khan – that gives us a definite date range for the age of the map. Born in 1644, Galdan Khan in 1670 became ruler of the

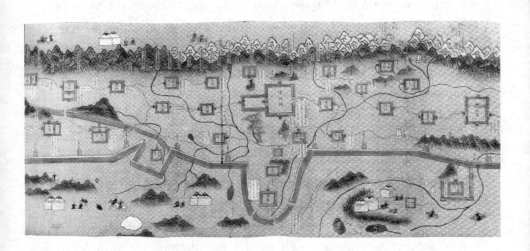

DESCRIPTION:	The Borgia Great Wall scroll, a painted silk strip map measuring 7.75 metres by thirty-eight centimetres and showing the Great Wall from Jiayuguan to Datong
SIGNIFICANCE:	The most extensive elongate map of the Great Wall
ORIGIN:	Qing Kangxi period, circa 1695; it was acquired by Jesuits post-1700, taken to Rome and eventually collected by Cardinal Stefano Borgia in his house-museum at Velletri
LOCATION:	Vatican Ethnological Museum, Vatican Museums and Galleries

Zunghars (or Western Mongols), who occupied land to the west of Qing China, roughly the area of today's Xinjiang region; they controlled it until 1697.

What purported to be a military map of the Great Wall, showing the fortification's relationship with forts in its immediate hinterland, now reveals itself to have been made during the overlordship of Galdan Borshigt Khan, in the last quarter of the seventeenth century – half a century or so after the fall of the Ming. The Kangxi Emperor (1654–1722) had by then abandoned any idea of maintaining the inherited Ming Wall. What, then, was the status of the Great Wall depicted on this map at that time, circa 1670 to 1697? What was its purpose, and who might have used it?

Referring to a petition delivered in 1691 to the Ministry of Works requesting funds for repair work on the Wall at Gubeikou, the Kangxi Emperor dismissed the structure as historically ineffective. Passing through the very location en route to his summer resort at Chengde, he made known his preferred policy of border security: 'by conferring favours on the Khalkha [Northern] Mongols, our dynasty prevailed on those tribes to take over the defence of the northern border [in the far north-east, against the Russians], and they are more impregnable than the Great Wall.'

In light of the reference to Galdan Khan (which is repeated elsewhere on the map), we must acknowledge that this cannot be a map of the Great Wall per se. Rather, it's a map that incorporates the Great Wall as a landscape feature in an area where the Qing thought it prudent to monitor Galdan Khan's activities. The Wall's towers were long empty of guards, and the ramparts were crumbling; it was now a 'ghost Wall', abandoned yet still very visible. But it also surely functioned as a road to follow, a highway leading westward.

Covering the interior three-quarters of the complete west–east extent of the Ming Wall, this map focuses on that part of the old frontier that was least known to the new Manchu rulers. They were accustomed to Manchuria's forests, valleys, mountains and plains, while the Yellow Earth plateau and desert terrain of China's north-west were alien to them. The coverage of this map, and its increasing accuracy westwards, points to its usefulness as a guide to logistics and defence planning in the region.

Surprisingly, though, it bears no Manchu script, which until the late Qing was the sole national script for imperial documents. One explanation may be that as most Qing banner strength was preoccupied in defeating the so-called 'Revolts of the Three Feudatories', which raged across the southern provinces between 1673 and 1681, the task of north-western defence remained largely the responsibility of the standing Chinese army there, part of the so-called 'Green Battalion' of ethnic Hans. We can assume that because the map is only in Chinese script, it was used by officers of that battalion, or by Chinese officials in the Board of War.

Galdan's Zungharia, the last steppe empire, stretched across Central Asia's steppe, mountain and desert lands, covering a huge expanse of territory between the western end of the Great Wall and today's Kazakhstan. Eager for resources, Galdan attempted to expand east and annex the Mongolian Steppe, a move which threatened Qing alliances in the region. In 1696 Kangxi personally led the campaign against the Zunghars, with the decisive battle being fought at Zuunmod, east of Ulaanbaatar. This determined Qing offensive, which drove Galdan to suicide the following year, is considered to have been Kangxi's finest military achievement. The victory checked the Zunghar expansion and brought much of today's Mongolia and some of Zungharia as far west as Hami into Kangxi's expanding empire.

The Ming Wall, once a frontier, now lay within a much larger Qing China, making it redundant. In the meantime, this nameless map, which conceals the Qing's adept political gaming across a cultural interface, was set to be involved in a different meeting of cultures. In due course it would in fact be given a foreign name.

Visually, this map is one of the most fascinating in our series. In the sub-category of maps, it has charismatic qualities of not only being large and long, but informative and surprising. With its misleading focus – and its extreme rarity, as one of only a handful of relevant Great Wall maps – I found it to be the least researched and known, having been studied previously only by cartography expert M. J. Meijer in 1956. And certainly it resides in a most unexpected place: Vatican City, whose tiny 0.44 square kilometres in the centre of Rome hosts the Vatican Museum and Galleries, and which therefore boasts the highest density of antiquities and artworks anywhere in the world.

The map is now known as the Borgia Great Wall Scroll, after its owner, Cardinal Stefano Borgia (1731–1804), whose fascination for antiquities was inspired by the Roman Emperor Octavian (63 BC–AD 14), who 'adorned his residences with things most precious for their antiquity and rarity'. The cardinal's collecting passion transformed his ancestral Palazzo Borgia in the hill town of Velletri into 'a house that contained the world's treasures'. The contents of its rooms were said to succinctly testify to a universal and encyclopedic culture, and he eagerly opened his doors to scholars of all creeds and nationalities. The Palazzo Borgia had few peers in Europe in its time. Among the prominent visitors was the German poet Goethe, who mentioned the collection in his classic diary compilation *Italian Journey*.

The scroll, too, had made an Italian journey of note. The Vatican was bequeathed most of Cardinal Borgia's collection after his death in 1804. But how had he acquired it? Borgia was well connected, as a renowned collector-curator, and well placed as secretary of the Sacra Congregatio de Propaganda Fide, the papal office responsible for acquiring antiquities brought back to Rome by the order's missionaries. It is likely that a Jesuit had acquired the map, for they alone cultivated high-level imperial government relations in China, and it must have been after a kind of declassification, following Galdan Khan's death in 1697. In 1708 Kangxi commissioned a Jesuit team to map the Great Wall region (see Object 43), an event that probably post-dates the acquisition of the Borgia Scroll. This means the most likely time the map travelled to Italy was around 1705, which was within a decade or so of its creation.

In the Vatican, on the other side of the world, the scroll would enjoy a fitting finale, exhibited under the same roof, in the same museum, and just a short stroll from the divine paintings and sculptures by Michelangelo, Raphael and Leonardo da Vinci. They and their works contrast poignantly with this painting and its creators, a cartographic representation of the world's largest construction, made by masses of unknown artisans.

CHRONOLOGY OF DYNASTIES

The Three Dynasties

Xia	circa 21st–16th century BC
Shang	circa 1600–1045 BC
Zhou	1045–256 BC
Western Zhou	1045–771 BC
Eastern Zhou	770–256 BC
Spring and Autumn Period	770–476 BC
Warring States Period	475–221 BC

The Imperial Dynasties

Qin	221–206 BC
Han	206 BC–AD 220
Western Han	206 BC–AD 23
Xin	AD 9–23
Eastern Han	AD 25–220
Three Kingdoms Period	AD 220–280
Jin	AD 265–420
Western Jin	AD 265–316
Eastern Jin	AD 317–420
Northern and Southern Dynasties	AD 420–589
Northern (est. by Xianbei)	AD 386–581
Northern Wei (est. by Tuoba Xianbei)	AD 386–534

Eastern Wei... AD 534–550

Western Wei.. AD 535–556

Northern Qi .... AD 550–577

Northern Zhou .... AD 557–581

Sui .... AD 581–618

Tang .... AD 618–907

The Five Dynasties & Ten Kingdoms

Five Dynasties (of North China) .... AD 907–960

Ten Kingdoms (of South China) .... AD 902–979

Song

Northern Song .... AD 960–1127

Southern Song 1127–1279

Liao (established by Qidans) .... AD 916–1125

Jin (established by Jurchens) 1115–1224

Western Xia (established by Tanguts) 1038–1227

Yuan (established by Mongols) 1279–1368

Ming 1368–1644

Qing (established by Manchus) 1644–1911

Note: At certain times dynasties coexisted.

Chronology of Ming Emperors

Hongwu 1368–1398

Jianwen...1398–1402

Yongle 1402–1424

Hongxi 1424–1425

Xuande..1425–1435

Zhengtong...1435–1449

Jingtai 1449–1457

Tianshun..1457–1464

Chenghua 1464–1487

Hongzhi 1487–1505

Zhengde...1505–1521

BIBLIOGRAPHY

Wall History

Cheng Dalin, *The Great Wall of China,* South China Morning Post and New China News Ltd, Beijing, 1984.

Idema, Wilt & Lee, Haiyan, *Meng Jiangnü Brings Down the Great Wall, Ten Versions of a Chinese Legend,* University of Washington Press, Seattle, 2008.

Lindesay, William, *Images of Asia: The Great Wall*, Oxford University Press, Hong Kong, 2003.

Lindesay, William, *The Great Wall Revisited: From the Jade Gate to Old Dragon's Head,* Harvard University Press, Harvard, 2009.

Lindesay, William, *The Great Wall Explained*, China Intercontinental Press, Beijing, 2012.

Luo Zhewen et al., *The Great Wall,* Michael Joseph, London, 1981.

Roberts, Claire, & Barmé, Geremie, *The Great Wall of China* (exhibition catalogue), Powerhouse Publishing, Sydney, 2006.

Waldron, Arthur, *The Great Wall of China: From History to Myth,* Cambridge University Press, Cambridge, MA, 1990.

Wimsatt, Genevieve & Chen, Geoffrey, *The Lady of the Long Wall,* Columbia University Press, New York, 1934.

Zhang Heshan, *Great Wall Folktales: Whispers from the Wall,*

China Intercontinental Press, Beijing, 2009.

Unspecified authors, *Gathering of Heads on the Great Wall*, Democracy and Construction Press (民主与建设出版社), Beijing, 2005.

Nomadic Cultures

Baarar, *History of Mongolia*, Cambridge University Press, Cambridge, 1999.

Baasan, Tudevin, *What is the Chinghis Wall?*, Unspecified publisher, Ulaanbaatar, 2006.

Barfield, Thomas, *The Perilous Frontier: Nomadic Empires and China, 221 BC to 1757*, Blackwell, Cambridge, 1989.

Di Cosmo, Nicola, *Ancient China and Its Enemies: The Rise of Nomadic Power in East Asian History*, Cambridge University Press, Cambridge, 2002.

Elliot, Mark, *The Manchu Way, The Eight Banners and Ethnic Identity in Late Imperial China*, Stanford University Press, Stanford, 2001.

Erdenechuluun, Purevjav, *The Sword of Heaven: Culture of Bronze Artifacts of the Bronze Age and Hunnu Empire*, Unspecified publisher, Ulaanbaatar, 2011.

Eregzen, G. (ed), *Treasures of the Xiongnu*, National Museum of Mongolia, Ulaanbaatar, 2011.

Hartog, Leo de, *Genghis Khan, Conqueror of the World*, Tauris, London, 1999.

Jiang Rong, *Wolf Totem: A Novel*, Penguin Press, New York, 2008.

Robinson, Carl, *Mongolia, Nomad Empire of Eternal Blue Sky*, Odyssey Books, Hong Kong, 2010.

Saruulbuyan, J., *National Museum of Mongolia*, Unspecified publisher, Ulaanbaatar, 2009.

Urengenge, Onan, *The Secret History of the Mongols*, Routledge,

London, 2001.

Weatherford, Jack, *Genghis Khan and the Making of the Modern World*, Crown, New York, 2004.

Weatherford, Jack, *The Secret History of the Mongol Queens: How the Daughters of Genghis Khan Rescued His Empire*, Crown, New York, 2010.

Cartography

Bazargur, Damnbyn & Enkhbayar, Damnbyn, *Chinngis Khan Atlas*, State Administration of Geodesy and Cartography, Ulaanbaatar, 1997.

Brotton, Jerry, *A History of the World in Twelve Maps*, Allen Lane, London, 2012.

Brotton, Jerry, *Great Maps*, Dorling Kindersley, London, 2014.

D'Anville, Jean Baptiste Bourguignon & Du Halde, J.B., *Nouvel atlas de la Chine, de la Tartarie chinoise, et du Thibet*, Paris, 1737.

Du Halde, Jean-Baptiste, *The General History of China* (etc), John Watts, London, 1739.

Fuchs, Walter, *Der Jesuiten Atlas Der Kanghsi Zeit* ('The Jesuit Atlas of Kangxi's Realm'), Katholischen Universitaet / Monumenta Serica, Beijing, 1941.

Harley, J. B., *The History of Cartography, Volume 2, Book 2: Cartography in the Traditional East and Southeast Asian Societies*, University of Chicago Press, Chicago, 1995.

Martini, Martino, *Imperii Sinarum Nova Descriptio* ('New Description of the Chinese Empire'), Johannes Bleau, Amsterdam, 1655.

Nebenzahl, Kenneth, *Mapping the Silk Road and Beyond*, Phaidon, London, 2004.

Ortelius, Abraham, *Theatrum Orbis Terrarum* ('Theatre of the Whole World'), Antwerp, 1587.

Ribeiro, Roberto & O'Malley, John. *Jesuit Mapmaking in China: D'Anville's Nouvelle Atlas De La Chine* (1737), Saint Joseph's University Press, Philadelphia, 2014.

Ronan, Charles & Oh, Bonnie, *East Meets West: The Jesuits in China, 1582–1773, Loyola University Press, Chicago*, 1988.

Shirley, Rodney W., *The Mapping of the Whole World: Early Printed World Maps 1472–1700*, Early World Press, Riverside, 2001.

Van den Broecke, Marcel P. R., *Ortelius Atlas Maps: An Illustrated Guide*, Hes Publishers, Netherlands, 1998.

Military & Weapons

Chase, Kenneth, *Firearms: A Global History to 1700*, Cambridge University Press, New York, 2003.

Kierman, Frank & Fairbank, John (eds), *Chinese Ways in Warfare*, Harvard University Press, Cambridge, MA, 1974.

Loades, Mike, *Swords and Swordsmen*, Pen & Sword Military, Barnsley, 2010.

Needham, Joseph et al., *Science & Civilisation in China, Volume 5, Part 6: Military Technology: Missiles and Sieges*, Cambridge University Press, Cambridge, 1996.

Sawyer, Ralph, *Ancient Chinese Warfare*, Basic Books, New York, 2011.

Sun Tzu (translated by Ralph Sawyer), *The Complete Art of War*, Westview Press, Boulder, 1996.

Werner, E. T. C., *Chinese Weapons*, The Royal Asiatic Society, North China Branch, Shanghai, 1932.

Yang Hong, *Weapons in Ancient China*, Science Press (科学出版社), Beijing, 1992.

Exploration & Eyewitness

Barzini, Luigu, *Peking to Paris: Prince Borghese's Journey Across Two Continents in 1907*, Library Press, New York, 1973.

Cable, Mildred & French, Francesca, *The Gobi Desert*, Hodder & Stoughton, London, 1942.

Geil, William Edgar, *The Great Wall of China*, John Murray, London, 1909.

Lattimore, Owen, *The Desert Road in Turkestan*, Little, Brown & Co. Ltd., Boston, 1929.

Lindesay, William, *Alone on the Great Wall*, Hodder & Stoughton, London, 1989.

Newton Hayes, Luther, *The Great Wall of China*, Kelly & Walsh, Shanghai, 1929.

Nieuhoff, Johan, *History of China*, John Macock, London, 1669.

Ricci, Matteo, *China in the 16th Century: The Journals of Matteo Ricci*, Random House, New York, 1942.

Siren, Osvald, *The Walls and Gates of Peking*, The Bodley Head, London, 1924.

Staunton, George, *An Authentic Account of an Embassy from the King of Great Britain to the Emperor of China*, Nicol, London, 1797.

Stein, Marc Aurel, *Ruins of Desert Cathay, Volumes I & II*, Macmillan, London, 1912.

Stein, Marc Aurel, *Serindia*, Clarendon Press, Oxford, 1921.

Stein, Marc Aurel, *Innermost Asia*, Clarendon Press, Oxford, 1928.

Thomson, John, *Illustrations of China and Its People*, Samson Low, London, 1873

Walker, Annabel, *Aurel Stein, Pioneer of the Silk Road*, John Murray, London, 1995.

Wang, Helen, *Sir Aurel Stein in The Times*, Saffron, London, 2002.

Reference Works

Clayton, Peter & Price, Martin, *The Seven Wonders of the Ancient World*, Routledge, London, 1988.

Cronin, Vincent, *The Wise Man from the West*, Harvill, London, 1999.

Franke, Herbert & Twitchett, Denis, *The Cambridge History of China, Volume 6: Alien Regimes and Border States*, Cambridge University Press, Cambridge, 1994.

Franke, Wolfgang, *An Introduction to Sources in Ming History*, University of Malaya Press, Kuala Lumpur, 1968.

Hommel, Rudolf, *China at Work: An Illustrated Record* (etc), MIT Press, Cambridge, MA, 1970.

Huang, Ray, *1587: A Year of No Significance*, Yale University Press, New Haven, 1981.

Hucker, Charles, *A Dictionary of Official Titles in Imperial China*, Stanford University Press, Stanford, 1985.

Kafka, Franz, *The Great Wall of China and Other Short Stories*, Penguin, London, 1991.

Liang Ssu-Ch'eng, *Chinese Architecture: A Pictorial History*, Dover Publications, New York, 2005.

Meynard, Thierry, *Following the Footsteps of the Jesuits in Beijing*, Institute of Jesuit Sources, St Louis, 2006.

Mote, Frederick & Twitchett, Denis, *The Cambridge History of China, Volume 7, The Ming Dynasty, 1368–1644, Part 1*, Cambridge University Press, Cambridge, 1988.

Mungelo, D. E., *The Great Encounter of China and the West, 1500–1800*, Rowman & Littlefield, Lanham, 2005.

Paludin, Ann, *Chronicle of the Chinese Emperors*, Thames & Hudson, London, 1998.

Qian, Sima, *The First Emperor: Selections from the Historical Records*, Oxford University Press, Oxford, 1994.

Rossabi, Morris (ed.), *China Among Equals: The Middle Kingdom and Its Neighbors, 10–14th. Centuries*, University of California Press, Oakland, 1988.

Scarre, Chris, *Past Worlds: The Times Atlas of Archaeology*, Times Books, London, 1988.

Spence, Jonathan, *Emperor of China, Self-Portrait of Kang-Hsi*, Knopf, New York, 1974.

Spence, Jonathan, *The Search for Modern China*, Century Hutchinson, London, 1990.

Sung, Ying-Hsing, *Chinese Technology in the Seventeenth Century*, Dover, New York, 1966.

Temple, Robert, *The Genius of China*, Deutsch, London, 2007.

Tsia, Henry, *Perpetual Happiness: The Ming Emperor Yongle*, University of Washington Press, Seattle, 2001.

Twitchett, Denis and Fairbank, John K. (eds), *The Cambridge History of China, Volume I: The Ch'in and Han Empires*, Cambridge University Press, Cambridge, 1986.

Whitfield, Susan, *Aurel Stein on the Silk Road*, British Museum Press, London, 2004.

Wilkinson, Endymion Porter, *Chinese History: A Manual*, Harvard University Press, Cambridge, MA, 2000.

Unspecified authors, *China's Ancient Technology and Science*, Foreign Language Press, Beijing, 1987.

PHOTO CREDITS

Photo inserts are provided by William Lindesay except where indicated below:

Page 1: James Lindesay

Page 2: top and bottom, Museum of the Great Hunnu Empire, Ulaanbaatar

Page 3: top, James Lindesay

Pages 4–5: spread top, British Library Board OR 5896, spread bottom, Freer Gallery of Art, Smithsonian Institution, Washington D.C., gift of Charles Lang Freer, F 1915.16

Page 6: Museum of the Great Hunnu Empire, Ulaanbaatar

Page 7: James Lindesay

Page 8: National Museum of China

Page 9: Liaoning Provincial Museum

Page 10: top, James Lindesay

Page 11: top, James Lindesay

Page 12: top and bottom, James Lindesay

Acknowledgements

As I write this thank you letter to all those who gifted me with the opportunities, trust, access, help, answers and photographs that made this Great Wall 50 adventure possible, fun and successful, I face a familiar problem, nice though it is: where to begin?

Appropriately, I have in front of me an assisting object, made in 2012. It's a thick wedge of papers, clipped together: a kind of project 'antiquity'. The papers are roughly-cut rectangles, about the size of playing cards. The stack is composed of about thirty-five pieces, and each paper bears a few words, written clearly in thick, black ink.

My youngest son, Tommy, then aged twelve, saw me exasperated as I struggled with a document on my computer screen, cutting and pasting. I was trying to bring some semblance of order and sequence to my draft list of objects. With paper, scissors and pen, he made folds and cuts, and then wrote down the titles of my objects on them. A game began.

The purpose of the game was to make connections. Some pairings related to the objects' materials – for instance, metal, wood, paper or stone. Another approach was based on functions: weapons, maps, messages, books or paintings. Origins worked too: Chinese, nomadic or international. As well as matching pairs to highlight similarities, opposite pairs also worked in an intriguing way, and I ended up launching with one of them: the contrasting ways in which Europeans and Chinese first learned of the Great Wall's existence.

Tommy's system worked well back then for its simplicity; now, the same papers perform a different function. They're like business cards, reminding me of who helped with what object. Some of them, grouped together, show me just how much certain institutions helped.

If I could award a gold medal for accessibility and openness, then without a second thought it is awarded to Mrs Nemekhbayar Nadpurev, owner of the Museum of the Great Hunnu Empire, to whom I am greatly indebted. Just months after the passing of her husband, the founder of the museum, Purevjav Erdenechuluun, whom I had met the year before, she and her staff accorded me every possible help, permitting me to examine bronze ornaments, weapons, armour and ritual articles from the collection. Ultimately, I included six objects from the museum in my final fifty.

Elsewhere in the Mongolian sphere, a number of people offered very special help. Mrs Buuma of the National Museum of Mongolian History assisted me with various objects from the collection, while the curator, Professor Saruulbuyan, was most enlightening as he shared his ideas. Special thanks are also due to Kirk Olson and his wife, Oyuntuya Bayanjargal, for their work in finding various people in Mongolia, in interpreting in the archery workshop of the Batmunkh family, and in organising an outstanding expedition across the Mongols' ancient homeland, the Great Eastern Steppe. I also offer many thanks to Professor Jack Weatherford for guiding me towards a better understanding of nomadic culture and of the history of the Genghis Khan period.

Although this off-Wall book took me away from the ruins, you will have noticed that I have woven into many of the stories various field experiences, encounters and observations from over the years, ever since my first steps on the Wall in 1986. On all my Wall trips I've benefited from the support and friendship of many people. In the early years, my biggest thanks go to those farmers who helped me along the way with food, water and shelter. In the mid-1990s I explored the Wall in the Beijing region with a succession of people who became dear companions. My memories of short adventures with Scott Urban, Tjalling Halbertsma, Yang Xiao, Wang Baoshan and Piao Tiejun are unforgettable and will always be at the heart of my Great Wall experiences: they were the golden years.

Elsewhere in China, I thank Pan Yue from the Shanhaiguan Great Wall Museum; Hou Jingang and Yu Chunrong from the Jiayuguan Great Wall Museum; Li Xiaofeng from Jiayuguan; Li Shengcheng from Anbian; Huang Lijing and Ren Yantao from the Badaling Great Wall Museum; various staff members at the National Museum of China; the Liaoning Provincial Museum, the National Library of China and Peking University Library's Rare Books Collection; and individuals Professor Wei Jian of Renmin University and bowyer Yang Fuxi . A letter of introduction and support for my project from the Beijing Administration for Cultural Heritage helped greatly as I knocked on new doors, and I'm indebted to Mrs Wang Xi and Mrs Li Yixue for their kind assistance.

A number of international institutions and individuals have over the years helped with the Great Wall 50, and I thank the British Library; the Smithsonian's Freer Gallery; the Victoria and Albert Museum; the Bodleian Library, particularly Dr Colin Harris; the Needham Research Institute at Cambridge University, especially Dr Chris Cullen; the Doylestown Historical Society, especially Tim Adamsky, Judge Ed Ludwig and Marilyn Gustafson; the University of Utrecht Library and the National Museum of Korea; and individuals Marcel van den Broecke, Maarten Buitelaar, Leon Guo, Wilt Idema, Freda Murck, Kjell Stenstadvold,

Raynor Shaw, Rodney Shirley, Richard Smith, Tiago Tan, Dick Wang, Hilde De Weerdt and Ying Xue.

I am greatly indebted also to the late Arthur Waley (1889–1966) for his evocative translation of Li Bai's poem 'Fighting South of the Rampart' and to Ian Johnston of Vancouver Island University for granting kind permission to use his translation of Franz Kafka's 'The Great Wall of China'.

The Great Wall 50 has had two stages of production. First, fifty stories were rolled out in *National Geographic* magazine, and then the stories were put into book form. Each aspect is intimately linked to the other. The book could not have happened without the magazine rollout, while the rollout deserved preservation and longevity in book form for various language markets.

In Beijing, Ye Nan, the then editor of the Chinese edition of *National Geographic*, gave me my big chance to make my idea a reality. After I had written a feature story for him on 'The Wall of Genghis Khan', he asked: 'What next?' Given that inch, I boldly attempted to take a mile; he surely expected another journey-story proposal, but I talked of fifty journeys to fifty objects and fifty short stories. But he stuck his neck out and signed me up. Twenty-five months later I'd become one of the longest-standing contributors to any of the magazine's many international editions.

There was more to the magazine editor's decision than trusting in my knowledge and approach. He knew there was a great woman at my side: my wife, Wu Qi. She had already made an impression by editing, rewriting and fact-checking my features on the Genghis Khan Wall. The present project has been a collaboration to such an extent that, for all intents and purposes, Wu Qi is my co-author.

Qi would discuss our joint work piece by piece with Wang Xuenong, emeritus curator of the Shanhaiguan Great Wall Museum. We're greatly indebted to him for his prompt, enthusiastic and sometimes critical responses to our queries over the last two years.

We're also indebted to Evelyn Rao at the magazine, who championed our work in Beijing and in Washington D.C., home of the flagship edition, and to the editors of other international editions.

Getting the words ready was just half the effort: photography was a constant challenge. Thankfully, we managed to meet twenty-five consecutive monthly deadlines with the assistance of photo editor Yang Chang and resident cameraman Chen Xinyu, as well as my eldest son, James Lindesay. Thanks also to Wang Jin and Thomas Mueller for their contributions.

At about a quarter of the way into the project, I mentioned what I was doing to Jo Lusby of Penguin Books in Beijing. Her reaction was promising: 'Now, that is the kind of book we could get behind. Have you read *A History of the World in 100 Objects*?'

Of course, all of us interested in history and museums couldn't fail to be impressed and inspired by Neil MacGregor's refreshingly skilful telling of world history through objects chosen from the British Museum. That milestone project, rolled out on BBC Radio and put to print by Penguin, marked a turning point in the popularisation of history. All history authors following in his wake have had new heights in the art of communication to which they should aspire, and for this we must thank Neil MacGregor, the British Museum, the BBC and Penguin.

After I submitted ten or so of my stories, Mike Tsang, Penguin's managing editor, liked them and signed me up. Once the final instalments of the series were printed in the magazine, I set about transforming the fifty stories into this book, working with Penguin's new acquisitions editor, Imogen Liu in Beijing, and my text editor, Julian Welch, based in Melbourne. The concept of this project was always to make the Wall's complexity more accessible, and the work of both Imogen and Julian has certainly done that, turning a manuscript into a book, and twenty-five pairs of stories into one Great Wall narrative. Finally, wrapping it all up, thanks to

Steffan Leyshon-Jones for his innovative jacket design.

There was one job left to do, to design some maps to help readers who are less familiar than me with the Great Wall's geography. The prospect of putting key place names mentioned in the text on a few maps was neither enticing to me as a mapmaker nor, I thought, particularly useful or attractive for my readers. Imogen, knowing that I am a geographer, suggested making the maps more personal by having me hand-draw them. Although I'd produced some sketch maps before, the task of accurately drawing 51 objects was rather daunting, so I asked my niece's husband, Zhao Zhenguang, a graphic artist, to assist. The two maps we've produced work as a visual geographical index for the book's contents.

As I complete this book, and you do too, I hope that you have enjoyed reading this story as much as I enjoyed planning it, and as Qi and I did writing and researching it. The journey was made possible by the enthusiasm of many people, close and distant, near and far, who've all come together to make a story from fifty parts.

INDEX

INDEX